Museums and Memory

CULTURAL SITINGS

A series edited by Elazar Barkan

CULTURAL SITINGS presents focused discussions of major contemporary and historical cultural issues by prominent and promising scholars, with a special emphasis on multidisciplinary and transnational perspectives. By bridging historical and theoretical concerns, CULTURAL SITINGS develops and examines narratives that probe the spectrum of experiences that continuously reconfigure contemporary cultures. By rethinking chronology, agency, and especially the siting of historical transformation, the books in this series go beyond disciplinary boundaries and notions of what is marginal and what is central to knowledge. By juxtaposing the analytical, the historical, and the visual, the series provides a venue for the development of cultural studies and for the rewriting of the canon.

Museums
and
Memory

EDITED BY

Susan A. Crane

STANFORD
UNIVERSITY
PRESS

Stanford,
California

Stanford University Press
Stanford, California
© 2000 by the Board of Trustees of the
Leland Stanford Junior University

Printed in the United States of America
CIP data appear at the end of the book

Contents

List of Contributors   ix

1. Introduction: Of Museums and Memory   1
   SUSAN A. CRANE

PART I. Thinking Through the Museum

2. Archi(ve)textures of Museology   17
   WOLFGANG ERNST

3. A Museum and Its Memory: The Art of Recovering History   35
   MICHAEL FEHR

4. Curious Cabinets and Imaginary Museums   60
   SUSAN A. CRANE

5. Geoffrey Sonnabend's "Obliscence: Theories of Forgetting
   and the Problem of Matter"   81
   AN ENCAPSULATION COURTESY OF THE MUSEUM
   OF JURASSIC TECHNOLOGY

PART II. Memories in the Museum

6. History and Anti-History: Photography Exhibitions and
   Japanese National Identity   93
   JULIA ADENEY THOMAS

7. Realizing Memory, Transforming History:
   Euro / American / Indians   115
   DIANA DRAKE WILSON

8. Global Culture, Modern Heritage: Re-membering the
   Chinese Imperial Collections   137
   TAMARA HAMLISH

Contents

PART III. Collectors and Institutions

9. The Modern Muses: Renaissance Collecting and the Cult
   of Remembrance   161
   PAULA FINDLEN

10. The Quarrel of the Ancients and Moderns in the
    German Museums   179
    SUZANNE MARCHAND

11. The Museum's Discourse on Art: The Formation of
    Curatorial Art History in Turn-of-the-Century Berlin   200
    ALEXIS JOACHIMIDES

Notes   221
Index   253

Contributors

SUSAN A. CRANE is Assistant Professor of Modern European History at the University of Arizona. Her recent publications include "Writing the Individual back into Collective Memory," *American Historical Review* (December 1997); and "Memory, Distortion, and History in the Museum," *History and Theory* (December 1997). Her book, *Collecting and Historical Consciousness in Early Nineteenth-Century Germany*, is forthcoming in 2000.

WOLFGANG ERNST is a media archaeologist. His publications include *Historismus im Verzug: Museale Antike(n)rezeption im britischen Neoklassizismus (und jenseits)* (1993); and, most recently, co-editor (with Cornelia Vismann) of a book on Ernst H. Kantorowicz: *Geschichtskörper* (1998). His teaching and research experience includes the University of Leipzig; the Institute of Cultural Studies at Essen; the University of Kassel; the German Historical Institute in Rome; the Center of Literary Research in Berlin; the Cologne Academy of Media Arts and the Media Departments of the Bauhaus University, Weimar; and the Ruhr University, Bochum.

MICHAEL FEHR has been Director of the Karl Ernst Osthaus–Museum of the City of Hagen, Germany, since 1987. Prior to that he was an Assistant Professor at the Bergische Universität Wuppertal, and Deputy Director of the Art Museum of the City of Bochum. His dissertation was written on early medieval art. He has published extensively on contemporary art and the theory of museums.

PAULA FINDLEN teaches in the History Department and Program in the History and Philosophy of Science at Stanford University. She is the author of *Possessing Nature: Museums, Collecting, and Scientific Culture in Early Modern Italy* (1994), and other essays on science and culture in early modern Italy. Her contribution to this volume is part of a new book, *A Fragmentary Past: Museums and the Renaissance* (forthcoming).

Contributors

TAMARA HAMLISH is Associate Professor of Anthropology and Chair of the Asian Studies Program at Beloit College. Her research focuses on representations of cultural identity in contemporary Chinese societies with particular emphasis on art, gender, and museums. Her published work has appeared in the journals *Public Culture* and *Museum Anthropology* and in the edited volume *Gender Ironies of Nationalism: Sexing the Nation* (1999).

ALEXIS JOACHIMIDES is an art historian at Ludwig Maximilian Universitat in Munich. He is a co-editor of *Museumsinszenierungen: Zur Geschichte der Institution des Kunstmuseums: Die Berliner Museumsland-schaft 1830–1990* (1995). His publications have appeared in *Kunstchronik*.

SUZANNE MARCHAND is Associate Professor of Modern European Intellectual History at Louisiana State University. Her recent publications include *Down from Olympus: Archaeology and Philhellenism in Germany, 1750–1970* (1996), and articles on the history of archaeology, philology, and classical studies in Germany and Austria.

JULIA ADENEY THOMAS is Assistant Professor of History at the University of Wisconsin, Madison. She is the author of a forthcoming book on modern Japanese political ideology: *Reconfiguring Nature: Japan's Confrontation with Modernity*. Her essay in this volume is part of a book-length project provisionally titled *Still Images, Cataracts of Time: Photography, Temporality, and Nationhood in Japan*.

DIANA DRAKE WILSON is Assistant Research Ethnographer at the University of California, Los Angeles, and has recently authored the discussions of cultural affiliation for UCLA's Native American Grave Protection and Repatriation Act (NAGPRA) Inventory as well as a report for the National Park Service entitled "We Are All Related: Life Experiences of Native American Indian People Living in Communities Surrounding the Santa Monica Mountains National Recreation Area." She holds a three-year fellowship funded by the National Institute of Mental Health for a project entitled "Communication and Experience in Navajo Healing." She also works as a curator at the Museum of Jurassic Technology.

Museums and Memory

1. Introduction

Of Museums and Memory

This collection evolved out of a set of concerns that have hovered around the perimeters of scholarship on the history of museums, without being explicitly addressed: in what ways do museums and memories shape each other? During the 1980s a considerable amount of interest developed in the history of museums, and a new body of research and discussion has yielded a far richer understanding of the social, cultural, and institutional significance of this history than had previously existed. This scholarly interest coincided with an international boom in museum construction and increased visitor attendance. Museums have become increasingly familiar institutions in daily life and in scholarship. At the end of the twentieth century, it is difficult to imagine a literate individual who would be ignorant of museums. It is difficult to imagine a world without museums, when these institutions are so omnipresent and considered so valuable, from small town collection to national gallery, and from school curriculum to tourist itinerary. We begin to consider museums from the vantage point of knowing about them — from personal experience, from the knowledge that exists in our memories.

Although it is an abstract concept, memory has many forms. The mental process of memory takes on corporeal form in the brain, but this physical form is invisible to the naked eye: memory becomes sensible and visible through imaginative recollection and representation, as we seek to hold onto our fleeting sense of its meaning. Memory is not a passive process: it evokes emotions and desires, positively or negatively charged; memory is also driven by a desire to remember or forget. By nature memory is mortal, linked to the brain and the body that bears it, as well as notoriously unreliable and subject to revision; if we would hold onto memory we must find some way to preserve it. Memory is not static, but it can be made to seem so through the creation of forms of representation that attempt to solidify memories' meanings, and it is through this realm of preservation that memories interact with mu-

1

seums. Memory is an act of "thinking of things in their absence," which may well be triggered in response to objects.[1] Memory is both personal and collective; although each individual has memories that belong to her and no one else, other memories are shared, based on common experience, learning, heritage, tradition and more. We participate in so many different kinds of memory-making and remembering—what the philosopher Mary Warnock refers to as "memory experiences"—that in order to discuss museums and memories we need to open up consideration of the interaction among these various types and watch them at play in the museum.

Museums, like memories, "exist" on several levels. We encounter them first as spaces, buildings in the physical landscape of architecture, and then as their spaces of exhibition, shops, and cafés, and in their portable versions, the catalogs. Museums exist in the remembered and lived experiences of untold numbers of many generations of visitors, museum professionals, and readers. In a theoretical sense, museums represent an organizational principle for the content of cultural identity and scientific knowledge. We may speak of a shared "museal consciousness" that understands the significance of collecting, ordering, representing, and preserving information in the way that museums do, a sensibility that has become more common in modernity than ever before. The "exposition" of the museal object, as Mieke Bal suggests, puts on display and embodies the discourse of memorial representation that both affirms and informs: informing the viewer of its significance, the object as display also affirms its significance.[2] Being collected means being valued and remembered institutionally; being displayed means being incorporated into the extra-institutional memory of the museum visitors. "Recollection" is inspired by collections, even though what visitors recollect may be as much informed by what they are prepared to learn or perceive, as by what they had previously known about these objects. What they then learn and perceive, and preserve as memory of that museal experience, becomes mobile and takes the museum beyond its own walls.

To contemplate museums *and* memory is to bring together these multiple and intertwined forms of existence over time. The history of museums is being written with particular attention to the ways in which museums convey specific information about knowledge or traditions, portraying the disciplinary aspect of museums and emphasizing "the signifying processes through which museums endow objects with meaning".[3] Implicit in these discussions is a notion of memory objectified, not belonging to any one individual so much as to audiences, publics, collectives, and nations, and represented via the museum collections. The political and ideological meanings created through the discourse of museal representation have received critical attention from historians. Scholars have traced the transformation of the early modern, private cabinet collections to the modern public museum in terms of the creation of a bourgeois public sphere in Europe, with its reforming and controlling impulses mixed with the goals of education and preservation.[4] Differentiating among the publics within this sphere, scholars have paid careful attention to the aspects of "difference" — race, class, gender, and sexuality — in the formation of collective identities and imperialist and nationalist narratives within museums. In particular, recent works on natural history museums and museums of ethnology have focused on the representational strategies by which Nature, "primitive" peoples, and "exotic" cultures were presented to modern Western audiences as objects for their fascination and consumption — as well as playing a role in the constitution of national identity.[5] A certain timelessness was attributed to "primitive" cultures, as if they modeled an earlier, universal human past, one beyond the memory of advanced societies and yet visible in the evolutionary mirror presented by these peoples. Modern museum displays tended to "freeze time," achieving "a state beyond time" through the permanent display of objects.[6] Preservation in the museum fixes the memory of entire cultures through representative objects by selecting "what 'deserves' to be kept, remembered, treasured, [a]rtifacts and customs are saved out of time."[7] Thus the "fixing" of memory in the museum constitutes an apparent permanence of the re-collected, organized in static time and space. Memory *of* cultures, nature, and nations is set to trigger memory *in* and for multiple, diverse collectives. These memories then become components of identities — even for individuals who would in no other way feel connected to these objects.

The relationships between museum and memory unfold around a peculiar relationship, as intimate and essential as that of a snail and its shell: one houses and protects the other. To pick but one expression of this common-sensical idea, John Locke observed, "this is Memory, which is as it were the Storehouse of our Ideas."[8] Locke renders intangible ideas into goods, cargo to be stored and protected until used. The externalizing of the memory function in museums literalizes Locke's metaphor: the museum stores memories. Like an archive, it holds the material manifestations of cultural and scientific production as records, articulated memories removed from the mental world and literally placed in the physical world. Like an archive, it has its own sense of organization, but that sense is deeply complex. As Wolfgang Ernst argues in this volume, the museum as archive is a resource that has the potential to foster myriad random encounters with the objects of knowledge rather than

3

the singular linear narratives that tend to be formed from it. But the institutional nature of the museum has encouraged the construction of narratives that inhibit random access in favor of orderly, informative meaning-formation. It is worth inquiring whether the memories associated through objects to form meaningful narratives do not in effect prevent other memories from being associated with individual objects, stifling the multiple possible meanings of any single object, perceived subjectively.

The image of the museum as storehouse — repository of memory, location of the collections that form the basis of cultural or national identity, of scientific knowledge and aesthetic value — informs museological studies, which highlight the practice of collecting and the presentation of the collected objects. The image of the storehouse also draws on the medieval and early modern royal treasure troves and curiosity cabinets that prefigured the museum in their assemblages of valuable objects, as discussed in this volume by Paula Findlen and myself. Curiosity cabinets of the early modern period strove for comprehensiveness, striving to encompass "the macrocosm in the microcosm" of a cabinet, so that scholars could learn from firsthand contact with their objects of study. The changing sensibilities of Enlightenment and Romantic thinkers who added historical value to economic, scientific, and aesthetic values in their consideration of objects prompted the construction of museums for preservation of the past.[9] The institutions most obviously connected to a specific form of memory, the historical museum and the heritage museum, have expanded tremendously in the modern era, and scholars have focused on the ways in which the past has been and is interpreted for the present, particularly for national audiences.[10] Yet as Tamara Hamlish notes in the case of the Chinese imperial collections, neither history nor heritage is exclusively national but can also be figured as global as well, in the interests of universalizing one culture's experiences. All museums are storehouses, or containers, of cultural heritage, as Wolfgang Ernst argues in this volume; all storehouses participate in a universal adherence to preservation of memory. To state the peculiar relationship between memory and museum another way, we might paraphrase Philip Fisher: just as each memory acquires reality as a feature of a museum, "so in its turn each museum is a fragment of one ideal museum," an imaginary brain that holds and enables all memory, a globalizing and universalizing principle of preservation.[11]

The museum-memory nexus forms one of the richest sites for inquiry into the production of cultural and personal knowledge. The conventions of cultural studies encourage interdisciplinary inquiry across the boundaries and intersections of established discourses, in order not only to frame their representation and appearance, but to move beyond existing limits and see the objects of study in a new light. Further, the objects of study should themselves become denaturalized, allowed to speak for themselves, if possible, or to indicate a new language that will be appropriate for their new form of representation — including even silences and forgetting, when these are recognized as viable responses. Memory's many aspects offer a range of objects for interdisciplinary study. Remembering as a personal and cultural experience as well as a social process figures into the museum visit, museum design, and theorizing about museums. Collections and individual objects, in their relation to each other and their relations to anyone who encounters them, are used to create meaningful messages about us, them, and the museum, which are not limited to the content of disciplinary knowledge.

In this context, museums need to be discussed across the existing disciplinary boundaries that separate art museums from natural history museums, or local history museums from national galleries. The authors in this collection are scholars from a variety of disciplines, including anthropologists, art historians, museum professionals, and historians, as well as representing a range of geographical, chronological, and aesthetic specializations. In the course of collecting these essays, it became clear that memory was operating thematically among them in quite diverse and provocative ways. Consequently, their organization in this volume follows a loose grouping according to some suggestive themes: experimental ways of theorizing and designing contemporary museums with an explicit interest in history and memory; discussions of personal encounters with historical exhibits; and emphasis on the professional stakes that are put in play by collectors and curators in directing the institutional presentation of memory.

The modes of collecting, organizing, and displaying that characterize the museum have been translated into the very way that publics think about themselves and about their cultures. Museums provide us with objects that are being preserved, saved as memory triggers and archival resources, not only for entire cultures, but at the same time for each individual in that culture. By deliberately conflating the categories of knowledge production and knowledge reception with the category of memory, we can begin to think *through* the museum, beyond institutional histories of any singular type, and imagine ways to study how the museum "medium" becomes a metaphor, as Wolfgang Ernst argues below, for the ways in which collective memory operates. Collective memory has developed into an important theoretical construct in recent years, after emerging from social scientific inquiries into mass psychology and crowd mentalities earlier in this century.[12] The most influential theorist of collective memory was the French sociologist, Maurice Halbwachs.[13] Writing between the wars, Halbwachs postulated that all individual memories rely on the "frameworks of collective memory" for their articulation. Although individuals hold personal memories, their remembrance and expression depends on the changing contexts of the multiple communities and times in which individuals live. By emphasizing the contextuality of even the most personal, intimate memories, Halbwachs built on Freudian and Jungian psychology and added a mode of analysis for group identity formations such as nations and cultures.

More recently, the French scholar Pierre Nora has developed the notion that a wide gulf has opened up between collective memory and history, with history supplanting the former in the sensibility of modern societies.[14] Nora argues that "sites of memory," such as museums or monuments, have been created in the late nineteenth and twentieth centuries because collective memory no longer functions in an organic or natural way. Sites of memory thus artificially organize the past, creating meanings that groups then assimilate in order to cope with modernity. Fearing that the secularizing process of modernity was undermining the foundations of memory's older cultural institutions, studies of the "sites of memory" attempt to articulate how new forms for memory foster collective identity. Nora's notion of the break between history and memory is deeply nostalgic, and yet it raises an important issue: why have history and memory institutions and the way that they organize and preserve the past become so influential? However, this question assumes the dominance of these institutions. We should also ask, where have they not been successful—when have publics rejected them? And despite rejection, how has the museum as medium for understanding ourselves and our collectives persisted?

The widening gap between the histories created in the academy, whether of art, nations, or science, and the memories sustained by publics in the interests of collective memory and identity, while often remarked on and lamented by scholars, is possibly the place where a reconsideration of the role of museums in modern culture must begin. For if museums have been understood to be "controlled" by professionals as educational institutions designed to serve cultural, social, or ideological functions, the uses and experiences of museums by individuals over time continue to demonstrate how the museal experience shifts between expectation and experience—back and forth from an intention to receive, to an actual reception; from experience to memory in the minds of museum makers and museum visitors.[15] Tracing the shifting terms of museal discourse from a dialectic between production and reception, museum makers and museum visitors, to a more complicated interaction among scholars, museum professionals, and publics who share museal consciousness, we can begin to understand some of the recent controversies that have erupted over museums and their meanings, such as the proposed exhibit of the *Enola Gay* at the Smithsonian Institution in 1994, which foundered on public opposition to a perceived "revision" of the history of the end of World War II.[16]

The museum is not the only site, but perhaps a particularly evocative one, where subjectivities and objectivities collide. This collision is not destructive. Like the reactions triggered in a particle accelerator, a series of collisions between the personal and the public, the individual and the institutional, the subjective and the objective, create new, highly energized relationships between museums and memory. Individual memories and academic intentions interact in the production of personal expectations and collective representations, in an ongoing, reciprocal mediation. The viability of these collisions is constantly being tested in museum exhibits, and nowhere more productively than in what might be termed "pathetic" exhibitions — "pathetic" not because they are badly conceived but rather, according to Ralph Rugoff, because they are deliberately attempting to reshape real or imagined museum orthodoxies.[17] When museum professionals challenge audiences' expectations by producing "pathetic" exhibits, the response may well be anger. In this volume, Michael Fehr documents the provoked responses to his deliberately provocative recasting of the Karl Ernst Osthaus–Museum in Hagen, Germany. As director of the museum since 1987, he has collected the work of contemporary German artists who take historical consciousness as their explicit concern. Fehr tells a story about the museum's inception at the turn of the twentieth century, when its founder pursued an interest in modernist art but felt alienated from the local, industrial populace who did not share his passion. The collection was dissipated after his death, the bulk of it going to a museum in nearby Essen. Fehr's attempts to reincarnate the earlier museum's vision of promoting contemporary art stirred controversy among publics who remembered the earlier collection as either problematic in its modernism or a haven for that same modernism. Either way, Fehr's museum satisfied no one and indeed angered many for its insistence on historical consciousness, with its artists taking on taboos about the German past. Fehr then staged exhibits that forced the public to confront what the museum had been, for instance by literally denuding the museum and rehanging what remained of the original collection only as visitors walked in and were asked to select works from the storage basement. In this way, the memories held by the public were recovered for the museum, by the museum, while others were voiced in opposition.

Fehr's Hagen experiment succeeded in stimulating the museal discourse's inherent tendency toward conflict and debate, which does not undermine the institution so much as reshape it. He created a "counter-museum," like the "counter-memorials" described by James Young, which deliberately highlight their memorial functions and force viewers to participate in their construction.[18] An actively fostered confrontation between expectation and experience, objectivities and subjectivities, adds new dimensions to museal discourse. The objectivities constructed by disciplines obviously have an impact on the education and therefore expectations of the museum-going public, or on the readers of books about museums. But the subjectivities constructed culturally and socially in different collectives also must have an impact on what publics will be willing to receive, or reject. Witness the curious case of another counter-museum, the Museum of Jurassic Technology in Los Angeles. This museum has for several years put on display an uncanny relationship to the history of museums.[19] The very name of the museum provokes confusion: since there was no technology to speak of in the Jurassic period, what is on display here? Founded by David Wilson and a group of associates in 1989, the museum houses an eclectic assortment of objects representing natural history, astronomy, medicine, and museums. Skillfully created exhibits are mounted with careful attention to current museum practices, although none of Wilson's group is a professional museum curator or designer. Visitors continue to be baffled by the complex relationships between artifact and artifice on exhibit. While I have suggested in my essay below that Wilson's museum is more like a modern curiosity cabinet than anything else, the museum successfully defies any single categorization or strict interpretation. Fans and critics of the museum alike have grasped at Borgesian metaphors in an attempt to explain the strange lure and repulsion that the museum exerts on its visitors: it is an unending labyrinth, an extended joke, permanent performance art, a real treasure trove. My depiction of one visitor's trip through the Jurassic represents an interested observer's response to the Sonnabend Hall at the Museum of Jurassic Technology. This exhibit is dedicated to an elaboration of Geoffrey Sonnabend's theory of "obliscence," which holds that humans are born with a complete and total capacity for knowledge, which they forget in the course of their lifetimes. In the pamphlet reprinted here courtesy of the Museum of Jurassic Technology, we glimpse how memory discussed within the institution of memory, the museum, can reshape itself and museal discourse simultaneously. The museum pamphlet suggests where the collision of subjectivity and objectivity and the production of counter-museums can lead: to the creation of a nonhistorical exhibit of the historical, which is itself a commentary on the nature of memory, museum representation, and the desire for authenticity.

Diana Drake Wilson's discussions with Native American visitors at the Southwest Museum in Los Angeles also suggest how reception and rejection may redirect museal discourse. These visitors saw what she and other visitors were likely to miss: the incongruity of placing handmade or spiritually significant artifacts next to manufactured ones, and even more the inappropriateness, for one culture, of placing these objects on exhibit at all. Museums around the world are struggling over issues of repatriation and the sacrilege inherent in displays of sacred objects and human remains, responding to specific demands for objects to be removed from view and from museum holdings. The limits thus imposed on museum collections imply a limit on the scope of museal discourse — but they do so without fundamentally challenging the existence of museums, and indeed many of the same Native American tribes that deplore the ownership and display of their heritage in other museums have established separate museums and participate in museal discourse in ways more appropriate to their own desires for collective memory.

Museums deliberately forge memories in physical form to prevent the natural erosion of memory, both personal and collective: this is the task of preservation, of creating a new form for knowledge whose purely mental existence is well known to be ephemeral, or as Rudy Koshar defines it, "the spectrum of interventions in the physical integrity of movable or immovable objects considered to have historical value."[20] But preservation also occurs in the minds of the visitors who remember the objects, the collectors, the museums — and these same minds may also contest the meanings of the objects, histories, and memories provided by the museums. Prior memories and their meanings may resist the museal collection. We are often too quick to dismiss this aspect of preservation, assuming that mental memory is ephemeral and unreliable, or that individuals should not be trusted with interpreting the collections independently — for not knowing enough, for lacking expertise or knowledge. But any individual mind is in fact the single largest realm of re-collection, one that museums address and one that helps conserve what museums have preserved. Museums, like individual minds, constantly select and discard from the limitless realm of material memory, protecting against loss. *Lack* of memory, ironically, may be regarded by curators as less of a problem than *loss* of material memory. "Lost" implies what is desired but missing; "lack" connotes what is absent and unwanted despite its existence, as Julia Adeney Thomas notices in the photography museums of Tokyo. The lack of images from or about the Second World War in these photography exhibits demonstrates not so much a Japan unwilling to "come to terms with the past" as it does a Japan with an edited past, not a memory lost but a memory evaded. As a historian of Japan, Thomas is sensitive to the "contours of absence" in the exhibits, staged in the summer of 1995 when commemoration of the war was at its peak. She presents the debate between curators who insist on the personal and historical context of photographs and those who maintain that photographs are "only" photographs, not documents. The staging of the exhibits demonstrates opposing notions of photography, history, and memory simultaneously. The lack of memory of World War II in these Japanese photography museums testifies to the conflicting desires that separate Japanese museum makers and their publics from other observers, such as Thomas, whose historical instincts are thwarted there. The war is not forgotten; it is everywhere lacking.

As Paula Findlen, Suzanne Marchand, and Alexis Joachimides each show, the idiosyncratic role of determined men of vision in the creation of museums is essential to modern museal discourse. The personal memories and desires of collectors and connoisseurs are bequeathed to visitors' memories, almost as if the minds of these individuals were reinscribed in their museums and communicated to visitor audiences. A desire for fame, Findlen demonstrates, fosters a collection that embodies the reputation of its owner. Findlen traces the relationship between personally passionate collecting and patronage back to the early modern precursor of the museum, the Renaissance *studiolo* or cabinet of the humanist collector-scholar. She demonstrates how the fame of a collector became a token of exchange among early museum builders, so much so that portraits of famous collectors became highly valuable components of the collections. While Kryzstof Pomian has argued that early modern collections were developed as signs of social status, Findlen pursues the evidence of personal passions as motivators in the establishment of collections and the selection of their contents.[21] The memory of the owner is thus part of what is communicated to the audience — they interact not only with the contents of the collection, but with the collector himself via the collection. These memories belong to everyone and no one in particular; the collector can only hope to stimulate his memory and preserve it eternally in the minds of others. The externalizing of the mental into the physical not only shifts the personal to the collective, but also works to prevent memory's evil twin, forgetting, from pursuing its usual course. The hope of fame, of being remembered as renowned (individually or collectively), is one expression of a desire that may be made manifest in a museum collection.

Suzanne Marchand and Alexis Joachimides approach late-nineteenth-century debates over fame from, as it were, opposite sides of the River Spree in Berlin. The fame desired in this case was international prominence in art and ethnological collecting, to be represented in world-class German museums. Marchand and Joachimides urge attention to the institutional and cultural politics of imperial Germany, where ties between academia and museums were particularly strong, as well as the personal conflicts among key players as forums in which universalizing claims to authority and superiority were made through museums. How to achieve this world-class status was a debate on a level with the "quarrel of the ancients and moderns." Marchand suggests that the seventeeth-century dispute between the advocates of the superiority of antiquity (particularly ancient Greece) and the advocates of the brilliance of new wisdom (particularly natural science) was still unfinished in the nineteenth century, especially with regard to the plastic arts. She argues that the nineteenth century struggled between text-based and object-based claims to knowledge, with humanism and philology championing the superiority of the written document over the newcomer disciplines of object assessment, such as ethnology, art history, and archaeology. This disciplinary battle was waged institutionally through the universities and museums and affected the money and space made available for new kinds of ethnographic collecting. With the kaiser himself conducting digs on Corfu, the moderns seemed to have gotten the upper hand. Marchand argues that museums in fact contributed to the demise of humanist scholarship through the success of the new sciences. The memories transmitted through Berlin's internationally influential cultural institutions thus came to reflect a contested heritage of old and new sciences, a battleground where "those whose interests and ideologies had been institutionalized, and those who demanded recognition for their own projects of 'reform'" fought for dominance in cultural politics.

As ethnologists and archaeologists fought for funds and recognition, art historians and museum professionals on Berlin's Museums Island fought for control of interpretation and purchasing power. Joachimides discusses an 1891 debate that highlighted the tensions between the amateur-connoisseur museum professionals and the art-historically trained holders of university chairs, as they argued over the development of the major Berlin art museums. The publicly waged war of words between museum director and connoisseur Wilhelm von Bode and Berlin University art historian Herman Grimm pitted passion against science and inspiration against discipline. The winners not only controlled museum collecting and dispensation of state funding, but also played a vital role in the art market. Both Marchand and Joachimides emphasize the extent to which elite discursive battles over meaning and interpretation shaped the collective experiences available to the museums' publics.

What any individual expects from a museum may or may not correlate with the desires or intentions of curators, but there appears to be significant desire for museums on all sides. If the zeitgeist is the spirit of an age, ours is the age of the "cite-geist" or an age of citation, of desire to be able to refer to what is known or considered to be important and valuable information, whether stored in databanks, archives, or museums. To put it another way, the "cite-geist" is museal consciousness. To each era its own forms of memory: the recent and explosive evolution of the Internet, like a museum, like any of the prosthetic cultural devices created to supplement mental memory functions, offers an externalized, technologized memory that replicates certain brain memory activites without supplanting them. The Internet has revolutionized access to knowledge, the ability to refer to it, and where it can be found, and replicates without fulfilling the intention to find meaning in a way that parallels the museum of modernity. As Ernst suggests, the archival aspect of data-based information may provide clues to a newly emerging form for collective memory and museal consciousness. It may be helpful, then, to redefine museal discourse in terms appropriate to the "cite-geist." A "museum" may be any real or imaginary site where the conflict or interaction or simulation of or between personal and collective memory occurs. Museums are more than cultural institutions and showplaces of accumulated objects: they are the sites of interaction between personal and collective identities, between memory and history, between information and knowledge production.

We go to museums to learn about ourselves, to witness what has been identified as significant art or history or science, and to come away with a stronger sense of ourselves as implicated in a vast web of tradition and knowledge. At the end of the twentieth century, the average museum-goer may well ask, "Who decided which objects I may view here? Who has established this master narrative of meaning with which I am being presented?" But I think it is far more likely that the individual museum-goer continues to go seeking to be impressed by the objects and meanings that s/he either expected to find, or is expecting to be initiated into. The sheer size, antiquity, scale, or scope of the exhibits may sufficiently impress viewers as significant, and we need to consider what kinds of memories inspire and form around these impressions. At the end of the twentieth century, museums are very familiar public spaces. We have learned to expect that the contents of museums will educate us, stimulate reflection, give us an excuse to contemplate "the finer things," allow us to have "been there, done that" as tourists, and allow us to go shopping as well as have a nice cup of coffee. I think it is fair to say that far from trivializing the modern museum experience, these elements of the museum visit have by their very familiarity come to constitute a cherished or at least tolerated memory in many people's minds. Academics and the public alike have become accustomed to thinking of museums as institutions with educational and socializing purposes, accustomed also to the idea that museums are appropriate places to present the contents of certain kinds of disciplinary knowledge. These familiar attitudes condition our expectations for museums and distance us (as academics and as members of publics) from active consideration of how museums represent us to ourselves. One of the goals of this volume is to address that very familiarity — not so much to undermine it, as to see it through a different slant of light.

PART I

Thinking Through the Museum

2. Archi(ve)textures of Museology

According to the UNESCO committe on museums (ICOM), "museology" deals with the technology of museums. But museology is more than the academic self-reflection of the institutionalized museum; as a discipline it might rather be defined as a specific branch of media studies concerned with culture as (literally) "collective" memory.[1] By mapping memory museographically, that is, by collecting, inventorying, storing, processing, and transferring data, the museum has become part of an epistemological grid that turns museology into a field of research extending far beyond the limits of museum walls.

What follows is a series of loosely chronologically linked or methodologically related files that are referenced according to aspects of the changing historical status of museology and museal objects. These files manifest two forms of parallel processing discussed here as ways in which meaning is produced through the medium of the museum: archaeology and archiving. While these files can be read randomly or in sequence, they are meant to represent information that can serve as a starting point for challenging the contextual effect of material presented narratively (whether in museums or in essays).

Curiosity Cabinets

Museology should not be restricted to studies of material culture. The genealogy of museological thinking, from the Renaissance *studiolo*, the metaphorical space of the *artes memoriae*, or Cassiano dal Pozzo's "paper museum" (*Museum chartaceum*) to the literary *musaea* reveals a range of both cognitive and material conceptions of the museum.

"Mediating between public and private space, between the humanistic notion of collecting as a textual strategy and the social demands for prestige and display fulfilled by the collection, the *musaeum* was an epistemological structure that encompassed a variety of ideas, images, and institutions."[2] Conceived as a space of contemplation, the "museum" could be virtually without objects (like the Renaissance *studiolo*), a cognitive field of ideas, words and artifacts that narrowed to a fixed meaning only in its institutional inscription and crystallization.[3] For a long time, in fact, the *museum* was not a place but a text, occupying a position in the discursive field somewhere between *bibliotheca, thesaurus, studio, galleria*, and *theatrum*. Museology was a practice located between cognitive contemplation, philological collation, and a concrete object-oriented collecting activity. Museology in this sense refers more to the disposition of things, the structural relationship that governs their placement, than to the positivity of collections as such. *Museum Britannicum*, for example, could be the name of a book, an encyclopedia of knowledge, rather than referring to the British Museum on Great Russell Street in London.

The museum should no longer be subjected to the paradigm of historical narrative, displaying instead its proper, archaeological, discontinuous, and modular mode of assembling words and objects. The task of the postmodern museum is to teach the user how to cope with information. This recalls the very origins of the museum as inventory of the world[4] in combination with the notion of a universal library, a text-related space where semiotic inventorying operations made the world readable. The current aesthetics of computer-aided visual display of information has led to a renaissance of studies on the cabinet of curiosities, reflecting an awareness of discrete, nonidealistic processing of data.

To paraphrase Shakespeare, all museums are a stage, and all the artifacts merely players; they have their entrances and their exits, and one artifact in its time plays many parts.[5] Steven Mullaney correlates the Elizabethan theater with the contemporary curiosity cabinet: "Early modern collection is not merely an idle assembly of strange and outlandish things. Collection was a ritual process, a rehearsal of cultures that comes into clearest view on the Elizabethan stage."[6]

Around and Beyond 1800:
The Emergence of the Modern Museum

Let us for a moment turn to sociological systems theory and follow Niklas Luhmann's differentiation between medium and form. The specialization and compartmentalization of arts and sciences in the late eighteenth century necessitated a specific memory appropriate to the fine arts in order to

keep them distinct from other discourses. The results were art history and the modern museum. Art of the past thus lost its exemplary metahistorical role and became a repository against which contemporary art, which needed this kind of internal system memory, could be differentiated.[7] The museum as difference engine distinguishes the new from the old. Whereas Aristotle located memory in the same parts of the soul as imagination and fantasy, the new form of the museum canalized the three traditional rhetorical categories of *memoria, imaginatio,* and *phantasia* separately. The aesthetics of invention became separated from the infrastructure of museum inventories; alphanumerical forms of registering, storing, and processing data decoupled the museum object from its traditional placement in a topographical system of *artes memoriae* (in a manner analogous to the late-eighteenth-century separation between art and technics), leaving the museum collection to be addressed and mobilized by historical narrative, i.e., another medium — imagination.

With the institution of the museum, administration and display of objects split apart, separating the power of knowledge from the task of educating the individual visitor. The museological art of ordering and storing data is based on techniques of sense-making of other, nonmuseal media: texts (catalogs), narratives (history), interpretation (philosophy of culture).

To put it in the words of an early essay on the necessity of museums by Ludwig Catel[8], the zeitgeist around 1800 demanded the introduction of museums. At a time when art production seemed to have frozen, "artificial means to stimulate art" were needed — the art museum as prosthesis of the imagination. To the Greeks art had been "immediate"; in medieval times Christianity served as impulse; "today" the author registers a "severe, cold contemplation of the past"[9] — an archaeological gaze indeed. Instead of "theoretical argumentation" about art, Catel requires "contemplation of existing art," which means art in museums. Greek art took place in temples; today museums serve as substitute temples. To display art "as system" required a new institution. Since it was the task of the state to "represent public opinion on art," supplementary art academies were needed. The task of the museum is "rational and historical"; in order to present art in such a way, proper buildings were necessary.[10] Two realms of art were to face each other: the academic (history, auxiliary sciences, poetry, philology, physics, mathematics) and what Catel calls the "technological-educational" branch of the arts. Especially the plastic arts demanded a "historically ordered display," supplemented by plaster casts of antique objects and a numismatic collection.[11] The art of architecture was to be expressed by the museum building itself,

assisted by models, machines, and exemplary fragments. The museum was thus to serve both as work of art and as monument of history. Mind and reason want to order what contemplation perceives individually, Catel (in fact an architect) declares; to that end, "no thread is more reliable and more observable than the thread of history," leading to the vision of the museum as a patriotic "Valhalla." [12]

Only the narrative of art history was able to transform a museal reservoir (in fact a synchronous spatial experience) mentally into a temporally perceived sequence — contrary to the style of re-collecting in the imaginary museum of Aby Warburg's *Mnemosyne Atlas* project, where figurative representations on ancient reliefs were juxtaposed without any historical commentary and confronted with contemporary photographs of analogous gestures of pathos. [13]

Hegel illustrated his idea of world history by the metaphor of the "gallery of paintings"; the evolution of the historical paradigm in the presentation of art in museums replaced the kind of disorderly memory cultivated by the tradition of the curiosity cabinet: autopoetic classification and order replaced the profusion of objects in coexistence with the emergence of the modern (surveillance) society. [14] Such rational configuration gave a value to the individual object that was previously unconceivable; what had been considered worthless in aesthetic terms before gained value by (narrative) insertion into the internal coherence of history. It is the act of placement that decides on the object's status as rubbish or valuable. The "historical" value of objects is normally acquired only after a period of having been rubbish [15] as expressed in Michael Thompson's *Rubbish Theory* (1979). Nowadays museums commission works of art immediately, circumventing the roundabout route via the private collector; museums acquire objects in the present before they enter the circle of valorization.

The category of the universal interrelation of things (*nexus rerum universalis*), borrowed from Enlightenment thinking, became temporalized in nineteenth-century museology; the effect of historical progress in fact was an effect of such museal staging and framing. By providing the material traces of the past with historical significance, those objects were to be deciphered transcendentally. Thompson's rubbish theory has had its historical momentum: the secularization of religious places and the dissolving of aristocratic property in France after 1789 and elsewhere during the Napeolonic Wars displaced countless works of art and brought them into circulation among collectors. Often a sense of loss and deprivation led to a growing consciousness of national cultural heritage. In Berlin, for example, this led to the provision

of a permanent location for objects after their triumphant return in 1815, in the so-called "Old Museum" designed by Karl Friedrich Schinkel. The process of reorganization of displaced objects was already charged with museal historicism. This movement to public collections of objects that had not been accessible in public so far led to a national discourse about art. Historical narrative was a means to master the arbitrariness of collections in a meaningful way; this of course required the supplementation of visual perception by textual catalogs. Beyond the pure inventory of numbers and titles the catalog provided in addition critical examination and objective interpretation.[16] This mechanism of re-collection, described by Frances Yates as "the art of memory," corresponded with the order of the museum. Whereas Hegel made this correspondence an element of philosophy of history in his *Phenomenology of Spirit* by considering the process of digestive remembrance to be the interiorization of the past (*Er-Innerung*), Walter Benjamin broke away from that assumption, associating involuntary memory with a contrary exteriorization of the self that explodes the confines of its private interiority. "The 'disorder' of this anarchic *Bildraum* (which, if spatial, is anything but homogeneous) dislocates the orderly 'gallery of images' designed by Hegel, where the *Weltgeist* passes in review the procession of its spiritual monuments which successively relieve one another after their respective turns of duty." [17]

The (public) museum space of historically internalized cultural re-collection is epistemologically separated from its (hidden) storage space. It is worth noting the resonance created by the difference between *Gedächtnis* and *Erinnerung* in German semantics. *Erinnerung* is linked to organic, personal, internalized memory, which in Hegelian thought is different from mechanical, externally preserved, archival memory (*Gedächtnis*).[18]

Two forms of processing the past took shape in the late eighteenth century: the architectural and institutional container of the (art-)historical museum was created, serving as a grid for memory; and the implementation of historical imagination, based on the literary medium of narrative, led to an "in/formation" of the imaginary. At the same time, the nature of archaeological fragments and the discreteness of archival data challenged these efforts to represent the past in a secular but still coherent form. Anton Raphael Mengs's allegorical painting of the Museo Pio-Clementino in Rome (1772) on the ceiling of the *Camera dei Papiri* (Figure 1) not only links the Vatican Library with the Vatican Museum, but can be interpreted as a link between two epistemologically antagonistic discourses (history and archaeology) and between two distinct epochs (neoclassicism and the baroque).[19] The transmission of knowledge of the past and the status of the museum

FIGURE 1. Anton Raphael Mengs's allegorical painting of the Museo Pio-Clementino in Rome (1772) on the ceiling of the *Camera dei Papiri*. Courtesy of the Vatican Library (Biblioteca Apostolica Vaticana).

object's "mnemic energy" (Aby Warburg) between monument and document are being addressed here. The realm of information (represented by archival documents and archaeological inscriptions) confronts the icons of history (Clio, the statue of Cleopatra/Ariadne) through the (new) medium museum. An ideological confrontation charges this clash: whereas the symbols of history (as signs of the Roman Church) represent the possibility of an identity or identification with antiquity, claiming continuity of power, the archival and archaeological fragments (belonging to allegory) designate primarily a distance in relation to their own origin, and, renouncing nostalgia and the desire to coincide, establish a museal void of temporal difference.[20]

The status of the museum objects depicted in the painting is both material and semiophoric, depending on their internal or external relation to the subject—the allegory of the *Museum Clementinum*. Two regimes conflict here: registering and description on the one hand and historiographical narrative on the other. On the borderline between history and archaeology, it is not clear what Clio is doing in the museum: is she writing in a book or entering items in a register? Her attention is diverted by Janus, who points to the realm of the aesthetic (represented by the Cleopatra/Ariadne in the museum), whereas in fact what is brought to her is data. Instead of being a history of art, her book might be an inventory, appropriately placed in this painting on the shoulders of Chronos.

Both the aesthetic order of history and the technical storage of memory are present; in fact the inscription figuring in the painting is from the *Galleria Lapidaria* installed by Pope Clement XIV close to the famous sculpture court of the Belvedere. Both regimes coexisted in a museum space, which did not yet try to hide its internal discursive tensions. The inscription itself significantly commemorates a Roman imperial archivist, sealing his grave monument. The inscription reads "H.M.H.N.S." (*Hoc Monumentum Haeredes Non Sequitur*: "this monument does not go to the heirs"); its function in the painting, inscribed on an artifact destined itself to be incorporated into the museum, is symbolic, pointing to the Church's duty as legitimate heir to Rome to protect its monuments from desecration and alienation. "As in ancient precedent, the acronym signifies that the heir may neither sell the ancestral plot nor allow it to fall into disrepair, but is required to maintain and honor the site, preserving it for transmission intact to all later descendants."[21] The act of incorporating the archaeological fragment into the museums means metonymically making it part of a heritage called "history," in contrast to the prevailing sense of disconnectedness from the past that is the concern of memory/storage. Thus the museum object is irreducibly caught

23

between information (archaeology) and document (history), a rupture that is doubled by the separation of the modern museum into a didactic display space and a hidden storage and data-processing space.

Whereas historiography (whose medium is the narrative text) tends to achieve immaterial information, archaeology (whose medium is the museum) takes the material support of information seriously, as is seen in a pamphlet published by the Germanisches Nationalmuseum in Nuremberg in 1872 on the occasion of its reorganization under August Essenwein. Not all arts were to be equally represented there. Poetry, the spiritual essence of the arts, was considered to lack corporeality and thus could not become the object of museal collecting and display; poetic monuments were recorded in books and kept in libraries. Music belonged to the realm of the spiritual intellect as well, but — in contrast to poetry — had left the instruments by which it was performed — which were indeed the subject of museum collection.[22]

The Eclipse of Museality: Holocaustal Collecting

The museum medium transforms itself from a destination point for commemorative objects into an intermediary space. A bizarre example of this development has been the destiny of the Jewish Museum in Prague, which was set up under the National Socialist occupation as a storehouse for displaced cult objects. Ironically, in the postwar era the museum retained the function of a repository of an almost extinct ethnic group. The weekly museum report of December 14–20, 1944, announced the processing of incoming objects by the museum staff in an administrative and art-historical way[23] — a fatal perversion of museal transubstantiation, translating previously religious semiophors into pure cultural historical materiality. In an economy of recycling, every piece of rubbish is conceivable as a potential object and vice versa; in the case of the Prague museum, though, the circle of cultural dis/appropriation short-circuited symbolic exchange and death.[24] Objects arriving from closed synagogues in Bohemia and Moravia transubstantiated into museum objects without a time of transition in between — a fatal interlacing of inventory data and death lists. There was a mortal real-time relation between the inventory numbers of dead objects arriving at the musem and the list of living people (their possessors) facing deportation to concentration camps. While the storerooms of the museum abounded with objects, Theresienstadt was emptied in 1943, with the victims being transported to Auschwitz.[25]

The administration of the genocide was a combination of precisely calculated physical violence and psychological steering;[26] the cybernetics of the

National Socialist program of the "final solution of the Jewish question" from mobile death squads up to death camps was performed by a constant feedback of control, as described by Raul Hilberg, in the very language of its administration. Corresponding to the administration of death, a different archival feedback—the opening of the Moscow Central Archives as a result of perestroika—has made it possible for historians to research the technical aspects of the Auschwitz crematoria.[27] At the end stood the closed, self-referential system of death camps. When in the summer of 1944, SS Colonel Otto Moll in Auschwitz saw himself confronted with an exponentially growing number of corpses, actually exceeding the capacities of the crematoria, he had corpses burned in long pits; the human grease produced by this burning was collected in buckets and used to fuel the fire itself in order to accelerate the combustion.[28] In the concentration camps the normally supplementary process of musealization was performed in real time, when the dead bodies were searched for hidden valuables, gold teeth, and women's hair. What the liberating Allied armies were confronted with when entering these camps was heaps of such objects and storerooms. When Auschwitz was turned into a commemorative museum in the postwar era, the essence of the museum had already been inscribed.

Museum and Memory

The historicist attitude at the end of the nineteenth century not only provided us with big architectural projects of places for the storage of history, storing and channeling valuable material and rubbish, but also provided us with grand theorems and thought systems. Memory was being located at the interface between cognitive metaphors and infrastructural agencies of object transmission: the museum, the cemetery, the warehouse.

As depot (for filing and registering), the museum implies not history but rather memory—the preservation of objects as memory triggers and archival resources.[29] Today, the idea of providing the final preservation of artifacts, the traditional goal of the museum, is displaced by a practice of intermediary storage, minimizing temporal duration. The electronic inventory systems of commercial companies reduces their storage time virtually to zero by aiming at real-time access to commodities in the supply-demand relationship, just as electronic random access to computer files turns memory into the omnipresence of data. The museum is no longer the terminal for parcel post from history, art, and culture; instead the institution becomes a flow-through and transformer station. Its demand now is mobilizing, unfreezing the accumulation of objects and images in its repositories, making them accessible to the public by displaying the stacks or recycling them into the exhibition area. This is the equivalent of the evanescence of the past in electronic memory. The points of light on the screen that flash past are reminiscent of Walter Benjamin's comment in his essay "Theses on the Philosophy of History"[30] that the past can be recorded only as an image that simply flashes through one's mind at the moment of its discernibility, never to be seen again. The architecturally supported memory of museums is liquefying in an age that permanently transforms objects into images. Mnemosyne might have been the mother of the muses; the museum, however, is no longer concerned with memory in temporal terms, but has transformed itself from a final, virtually eternal storage place of cultural heritage into a container, a kind of interim storehouse — compare the language of nuclear disposal technology.

In the most recent addition to the Vatican Museums, the Museo Gregoriano Profano in Rome, the display of antiquities challenges art-historical continuity by replicating archaeology. Modular elements in the display consist of amorphous iron tubes, support statues, reliefs, and inscriptions that contrast with the structure that supports them (Figure 2). The techniques of display in the exhibition halls and the storerooms no longer differ; an interchangeable metal framework with antique inscriptions fixed systematically to it makes the museum memory transparent. Pure register, archive, index, the museum becomes a data bank, taking apart the hermeneutic distinction between memory and waste.

The Museo Gregoriano Profano has responded museologically to the plea for a modular processing of past documents by means of a flexible, archive-like presentation of artifacts that no longer separates storage techniques from didactic display techniques. Thus memory becomes inseparable from its representation. Why not undo the separation between analytic data storage and processing and narrative presentation altogether by writing the archive transitively, making the data banks speak, conceiving of history archaeologically, replacing audible narrative by silent computing?

The synchronic standard operations of machine memory based on reversible time differ radically from the individual human memory based on ideas of irreversible time; in computing, archaeological data have nothing to do with remembrance but refer to an ultimate presence. Data are generally stored in files that are not temporally but topologically defined, as organized collections of data in space.

In an analogous sense, the museum as memory-producing machine is a permanent challenge to any positive philosophy of history, replacing histori-

FIGURE 2. Modular elements of display at the Museo Gregoriano Profano in Rome. Courtesy of the Vatican Museums (Monumenti Musei e Gallerie Pontificie).

cal semantics and semiotics by cybernetic operations. Thus there is no re-membrance sui generis — no memory, only addresses, activating data banks that taxonomic classification declares to be storage spaces. Temporal localization becomes a spatial metaphor — "the configuration of a space-as-information-model within a historical context"[31] — not of ontological but of strategic importance, for the purpose of specifying memories. It would be wrong to confuse memory, which operates always in the present, with retrieval of past (but stored) data. Memory is nothing but an actual cross-checking of the state of a given system such as the museum. Time (in respect to memory) is nothing but a construct for checking redundancies,[32] just as the adoption of alphabetical cataloging of books replaced the classical topographical, *artes memoriae*–based classification in libraries after 1800.

Didactic museum display, on the other hand, tends to dissimulate its basis in nondiscursive storage spaces, diverting attention from the administrative logistics of matter storage and its hermeneutic implications. The function of such forms of memory is catechontic — a stowing away, suspension of death.

Maybe the task of the museum today is to reflect on the contemporary loss of substance in objects; a contributor to this dematerialization, however, is the museum itself. The materiality of objects is an obstacle to semiotic sublimation, to the attempt at preservation by immaterialization in writing, photography, and other forms of reproduction (the double sense of sublation). Authority is being conferred upon monumental compositions by material signifiers (bones, letters, stones), a device well known to museologists: the integration of affectively charged objects, such as the inclusion of real funerary objects into the exhibition context or the establishment of museums in buildings that themselves have monumental age value — like the installation of the Germanisches Nationalmuseum in a former convent.[33]

Memory of Waste

Perceived as a sign, any object is subject to acts of registration, of inscription and contextualization. David Crowther differentiates between two groups of artifact attributes: intrinsic (material, decoration) and relative (context, history, function). In this area a defect of semiotic theories comes into play: their neglect of the very materiality of the carriers of signs. As soon as artifacts have fallen out of economic or technical use, their status as waste is what prevents them from being preserved; this nonsemiotic latency is destroyed by the very act of re-membering them for hermeneutic attention, by addressing (that is, reactivating) them as cultural memory. For material objects, their archaeological excavation implies a change of state both conceptual and physical.[34]

While many historical European industrial zones are currently being transformed into open-air museums of the industrial age, these same areas are suffering severely from another kind of very concrete heritage, the burden of waste disposal and soil contamination of the last two hundred years — a kind of memory difficult to cope with in aesthetic ways. Museums of industrial heritage in fact figure as a distraction of attention from the actual industrial legacy, the contaminated soil as a chemical store.

The true tragic archive is the soil, the industrial fallow land. Thomas A. Sebeok posed the question of storage as semiotic challenge: how can a nuclear depot be marked for a future reader who might no longer be acquainted with the alphanumerical code?[35] Andrei Tarkovsky's film *Stalker* shows such a sublime "zone"; in the film *The Museum Visitor* (1989), directed by his student Lopushansky, this zone becomes a museum situated off a waste-covered coast and — inaccessible as it is — it proves the magical solution to the great questions of garbage disposal.

Maybe the true memory of waste is absence, voids, silence. What the Soviet troops left in eastern Germany after 1990 were the open, empty hangars of military jets. Former places of compulsory remembrance — sacred zones, monuments, memorials — are being replaced by the emptiness of previously secret zones — wasteland as voided voids.[36] As long as there is still memory, this absence is a sign of presence. But the historian is always too late: the moment that the formerly secret archives and other forbidden zones become accessible, the secrets of power he seeks to analyze have already receded elsewhere. How to anticipate the archive?

Only a negative shadow indicates what was once the presence of a monumental state emblem of the German Democratic Republic at its parliament building in Berlin near the Alexanderplatz. Never has a state been musealized as quickly as the GDR. What happens when the objects and images of a state get discarded, like those of the German Democratic Republic in 1989–90? There was no time for its material relics to die and become rubbish: they became history immediately. Even the GDR's Central Museum for German History was replaced by a West German substitute in the Unter den Linden Arsenal.[37] What remains is the living memory of the former owners, inhabitants, and administrators of GDR material culture — a true memory of wasted lives?

Virtual Museology

When time is only a function of calculation, the positive idea of history is replaced by technologies of memory. That is why digital archiving — as opposed to mere information retrieval — has consequences for the museum, undoing the alliance with history or historicism that has existed since 1800. Museum objects at that time were subject to the historical-geographical system in which all items were analogous; only on this basis could the history of artistic and commercial techniques and products be studied properly as part of a narrative called "nation." Today, the chronological order in which objects and testimonies used to be stored will be replaced by an order of co-presence, in which they will be linked by means of digital combination, undoing the "aesthetic absolutism of chrono-linear musealization."[38] At the same time, objects will not be subject to the homogeneous medium of printing any more but can be preserved as multimedia monuments under digital conditions; the sequential ordering of historical objects and manuscripts that was the concern of nineteenth-century historians, philologists, and museologists will be replaced by the co-presence of all manuscripts in the digital museum.[39] The binary logic of computing, though, is more than ever a strict filter through which all information is sifted.

One of the most impressive metaphors of the curiosity cabinet was coined by Johann Daniel Major in his comparison of Adam's brain to a tablet that had been erased at the time of the expulsion from Paradise and had been waiting ever since to be reinscribed.[40] This metaphor has been made a reality by Alan M. Turing's 1936 essay on "Computerable Numbers," in which he uses the image of a tape containing a sequence of initially empty squares in which new numbers are constantly entered — the central metaphor of computer programming.[41]

Beginning *medias in res*, the virtual museum visitor navigates on the monitor through the Internet where (s)he faces a kind of profusion of data that might deter traditional archivists, librarians, and museum directors.[42] The digital wonderland signals the return of a *temps perdu* in which thinking with one's eyes (the impulse of *curiositas*) was not yet despised in favor of cognitive operations. Curiosity cabinets in the media age, stuffed with texts, images, icons, programs, and miracles of the world, are waiting to be explored (but not necessarily explained).[43]

Is the classic museum object a point of resistance or a *quantité négligeable*? The "electronic museum," the museal ISDN-socket, and the computer terminal only realize in technical form what was once the concern of Renaissance thought: linkage to a network of outposts that existed at that time in the form of a Europe-wide exchange of letters between humanists, providing permanent communication feedback. The sender's monitoring and adaptation of messages by observation of their effects on the recipients became a key element of antiquarian communication about artifacts.

Today, the Centre Georges Pompidou in Paris unites changing exhibition spaces, the cultural forum, a museum of contemporary art, and an information library — thus actually realizing Paul Otlet's 1934 call for the (re-) convergence of museum, archive, and library in an all-embracing documentation science.[44] Precisely by denying the idea of the *dépôt*, the storage space, the Centre as medium transforms data rendered in different media into information, performing a data-processing cycle. This corresponds to the tendency in commercial distribution networks that strives to minimize data storage time — a function of consumer behavior in late capitalism. Likewise, the accelerating consumption of culture strives to liquidate storage spaces (the basic concept of the anti-monument); hence the ongoing replacement in France of the academic discipline "museology" by "cultural mediation." Only by its radicalization in terms of information can the utopia of the museum be carried further.

Perhaps part of the museum idea will be detached from its connection with architectural spaces and be transferred to the monitor sceen. This is exactly what the electronic Piero Project does for art history:

To celebrate Piero della Francesca's quincentenary, his Arezzo fresco cycle in its architectural setting has been digitized and mapped. . . . Starting with graphic representations of three-dimensional space on the screen of a computer workstation, digitized images are mapped into their proper positions. Using a kind of three-dimensional mouse, called a space ball, the viewer's line of sight moves through the space on the screen freely. . . . Perspective adjustments accompany the movement at a natural rate, called "real-time," and make it possible to view the scanned images from any angle and in their spatial context.[45]

Museal spaces have never been more present than in the age of digital *artes memoriae*, which restore to memory its technical meaning.

Museum, Media, and the Archaeological Gaze

All kinds of indications lead us to think that the museum is about to become a *medium* in the proper sense. "When we ask if the museum is becoming a medium, we find ourselves confronted with two extreme conceptions: on the one hand, the techno-scientific definition of the media and, on the other hand, the traditional conception of the museum as depository of a collection."[46]

Media archaeology traces the channels between storage (archive), transmission (medium) and processing of data (computer).[47] As opposed to kinesthetic media such as film, the museum remains a "cold" medium, asking for the active participation of the beholder's imagination.[48] In terms of information theory as developed for example by Claude Shannon, a given apparatus or institution requires more than just storage capacity in order to be called a medium — it requires, in fact, what H. G. Wells sought in *World Brain* when he called for a world encyclopedia: a "mental clearing house for the mind" that would be "a depot where knowledge and ideas are received, sorted, summarized, digested, clarified and compared" — that is, computed.[49]

As opposed to figurative, narrative (hi)story-telling, modular processing of past data concentrates on archaeological modes of museal representation.[50] To replace narrative museology by nondiscursive display of objects from the past would mean writing the depository. What is true for archaeology as a discipline ("Now archaeologists are having to make judgments on the work of their predecessors as they are excavating in the field *and in archives*")[51] is true for museum memory as well. The question is precisely whether the archival texts and archaeological evidence can be represented in the form of a narrative frame (story, storyboard) or whether they must be dismembered into a modular cluster of monumental units of textual and archaeological data. The spatial order of the museum-as-archive (in its generalized sense) is opposed to the linguistic effect of the (metaphorical) temporal deep dimensions rendered by historiography.

The data-gathering aesthetics of archaeology turn "historical" evidence into a calculable collection of data, to be searched for positive details and precise information. Perhaps, indeed, the computer can re-member the ancient past better than any human historical imagination. In the exhibition *Pharaonendämmerung* ("Dawn of the Pharaohs"), held in Paris and Berlin in 1991, an Egyptian temple was reconstructed by digitizing the scattered elements of its ruins. Alphanumeric data processing might lead to nondiscursive forms of dealing with the archival archaeologies of the past.

The current, or postmodern, implosion of the mnemonic museum frame has consequences for the form of representation of the past. Instead of being governed by the apparently seamless logic of a continuous, discursive literary text, driven by rhetorical devices and dramatic emplotment, modular museology is governed by the nondiscursive logistics of vector fields, graphically expressed by means of inventory marks (the directing codes and operators): networking rather than narrating the evidence.

Archaeology, by emphasizing material culture, represents a provocation to event-centered history, challenging didactic or pedagogic museum display. An archaeological aesthetics acknowledges the semiotic difference and discontinuity between the (re)presented materiality of the object on the one hand and documents on the other.

The problem of all historical exhibitions is the pretension to re-presenting a past that is by definition absent, notwithstanding the authenticity of the original exhibits. Archaeological artifacts are subject to a semiosis that turns them into objects that are meant to be decipherable as historic documents. They are a database that has undergone a change of state when entering into the domain of the discipline: "From *in situ* and unknown, to removed and researched, before it has any impact on knowledge, the evidence has largely lost its original integrity. Its meaning rests only in the information attached to it in the form of associated records." [52] Complex historical configurations can hardly be constructed by museum display without the assistance of supplementary media in addition to the authentic object, such as video documentation and film. [53]

The most effective medium for cutting down historical complexity, however, is narrative; only by means of such supplementation by a rival, textual medium (as part of the documentation area) is the proper museal exhibition free to concentrate on the presentation of material artifacts and their expressive value, creating the illusion for the visitor of entering a direct dialogue with the objects of the past — not hermeneutically controlled (as in historical narratives) but along the lines of the open logic of signifiers. Thus the archaeological and the historical dimensions of the museum are decoupled: since the effect of continuity, of coherence, in reading the past can be achieved only on a level beyond the concrete disconnectedness of discrete artifacts (whether textual documents or visual objects), it requires narrative to transform monumental objects into documentary information. This is the challenge faced by the museum as proper medium, a fact that had emerged from the discussion over the future arrangement of the former Soviet Museum of German Capitulation in Berlin-Karlshorst, where original objects, by themselves, cannot tell the whole story of the war and of German-Russian relations. "In order to achieve this, the museum is dependent on a third form of presentation, that is, historical documentation. . . . In order to enlighten one needs to inform." [54]

The director of the German Historical Museum in Berlin, Christoph Stölzl, draws a genuinely museological rather than ideological consequence from former socialist modes of display, and asks us to visualize the fragmentariness of the past just as it has been transmitted to us, in ways oblique and difficult to interpret. The museum as medium should resist the temptation of becoming a media theater in a kind of mimicry of cinema where the MGM fanfare resounds, the lion roars, and the history of the Middle Ages starts to get told. It should always be clear that the museum visitor is in a kind of archive, in a collection of materialities, not to be confused with the narratives symbolically or imaginarily (in the form of accompanying labels or of discourse, respectively) wrapped around them. Museographical dramaturgy is about the art of displaying missing links and about creating a sense of distance; only when space is left can the imagination of the viewer step in, and objects communicate with one another. Figurative staging of objects is unavoidable, but it should always be clear that no one-to-one representation of a moment of the past is being attempted. Even though it is perfectly obvious in the Munich Glypothek which part of the Greek frieze of the temple of Aegina is a marble original from the fifth century B.C. and which is neoclassical restoration in plaster by Thorvaldsen, "something like an archaeological narrative could be achieved" by marking interpretations and auxiliary constructions discretely.[55]

The museum is indeed based on fragmented, dismembered, isolated, defigured, and disjoined objects. The gap between the isolated presence of museum objects and their previous contextuality should not be blurred completely by interpolating narrative texts in the mode of the discourse of history. The gulf separating the two components of museal memory—visual evidence and literary explanation (reminiscent of an aesthetic dissonance that humanism desperately tried to reconcile)[56]—will not be overcome by subjecting both to narrative emplotments. Instead, the gulf will be bridged in digital space where the difference between word and image no longer counts technically at all—if not on the terminal, that postmuseal screen memory.

3. A Museum and Its Memory

The Art of Recovering History

In his book *The Clothing of Clio*, Stephen Bann developed the idea of an "ironic museum": one that would support alternative readings or versions of the exhibited objects — for example, by presenting them as goods stolen in the course of imperialistic war as well as objects important for the cultural discourse that was a result of their displacement.[1] More generally, Bann defined the ironic museum as a museum able to work within two different rhetorical tropes, metonymy and synecdoche — the technique of dispersal and isolation as well as the technique of integration or combination of different things into a whole — so as to render transparent the intrinsic principles that guide viewers' perceptions within the museal display.

Looking back, I find that the idea of an ironic museum, which I first encountered about fifteen years ago, was the key I had been looking for. In the course of my research, I had come to the conclusion that the basic operation of museums has almost nothing to do with science, but rather more or less exclusively to do with rhetorical forms of argumentation.[2] This research concluded a decade of practical work at art museums in the 1970s, during which time I sought to improve the social position of museums by, for example, bringing city planning or the cultural situation of foreign workers into the context of contemporary art. However — perhaps because I had some success with these and related programs — a bourgeois opposition was triggered at the same time that, as it were, finally managed to put me out of business. Thus forced to rethink my engagement, I came to the conclusion that if — as Herbert Marcuse wrote in "On the Affirmative Character of Culture"[3] — the museum is indeed the site into which bourgeois society projects its dreams and utopian projects, it would be a good strategy to thematize these in a specific way, that is to take art and its institution, the museum, seriously and recycle their achievements back into social life. In other words, when I had the chance to get back into business again twelve years ago, I no longer viewed my task as that of changing the museum from outside but in working out of its own *epistēmē*, which I felt would provide more critical perspectives on the mental state of our society than I could see at that moment.

This is the first time I have tried to expose the concept of my work as an attempt to construct an ironic museum. What I will explain in the following is not a secret, since everything I will talk about already exists, but I have not previously formatted my conception into a text and related it to a context shared by a larger audience — one, in particular, beyond the town of Hagen, Germany, which funds the Karl Ernst Osthaus–Museum. But when I put together this text reflecting my efforts along the lines of an ironic museum, I realized that — despite the fact that I am still engaged in this effort — I would be talking about history. For some time, I have felt that yet another paradigm has arisen and is beginning to define my work — at least as far as it seems to able to contextualize even the idea of an ironic museum. But let me begin at the beginning.

As an introduction to the background of my work, I would like to present a story — more exactly, a fairy tale — that captures better than any history the dynamic of the psychohistorical context within which I have developed my text. This fairy tale is entitled:[4]

The Young Man and the Small, Dirty Town
A FICTION BASED ON SOME TRUE EVENTS

Once upon a time there was a young man who was born into a family that had achieved great affluence in a short time through its business activities. But the young man did not want to become a businessman or an entrepreneur. He was more interested in politics and the finer things of life. So he traveled around, studied various subjects in big cities, became involved in several political associations, and indulged in expressing radical thoughts. However, his family did not agree with this lifestyle, and his father in particular was very concerned about what would become of his son.

Then something unexpected happened. The young man's grandparents died suddenly, one shortly after the other, and to the surprise and annoyance of the whole family, left him the lion's share of their enormous fortune. But the grandparents had known exactly what they were doing. For when the young man claimed his inheritance, he declared that he did not intend to keep most of this unearned income but to use it for the benefit of the community at large.

The young man lived in a town that had been particularly ravaged by industrialization and had become very ugly and dirty as a result. The town was also reputed to have no tradition or culture and its inhabitants to be interested only in survival. And that was true. For the town was relatively young and inhabited almost exclusively by workers and factory owners, that is to say, people who for one reason or another had neither the money nor the time to spend reflecting on their lives.

The young man was very conscious of this, and it hurt him. For he loved his hometown and he reacted to prejudice against it as if the criticism were aimed at him personally. So to the astonishment of his friends and family, he decided to stay in this small, dirty, and cultureless town despite his great wealth, which would have allowed him a comfortable life anywhere in the world, and to do everything in his power, as he put it himself, "to interest our art-forsaken industrial region in modern art."

However, he had only a vague notion of how to go about this. On the advice of some friends, he decided first to establish a museum in his town, following the example of aristocratic traditions. But he was not sure what kind of museum he ought to found either, so he began to collect all sorts of different items: natural history and ethnography, arts and crafts, and fine art. He hoped that the museum building, which he commissioned from the architect who had built his father's villa and which was to be located in a prominent position in the town, would unite the collections.

When the shell of the museum building was completed two years later, the young man realized that this project was not much different from what he had been trying to change. Disappointed and perplexed, he discontinued the construction work and sought new inspiration.

Then came another unexpected event in the young man's life. He discovered a report in an art magazine about an unusual foreign artist and architect whose work he greatly liked. As he himself later wrote, he recognized "at a glance that this was the path for the future, the path that led to beauty via reason." That very same day, he sent a telegram announcing his intention to visit the artist.

The young man and the much older artist immediately hit it off and agreed on a mutually beneficial form of collaboration. The commission to develop the museum gave the artist the long-awaited opportunity to implement his ideas on a grand scale, and he accepted the fact that this was to take place only in a dirty little town. The young man, on the other hand, saw the artist's involvement as the opportunity finally to achieve his desire to overcome the ugliness of everyday life and make people happy.

For the interior of the museum, the artist developed a new design concept that was regarded by his contemporaries as truly revolutionary. However, the museum gained importance not only because of its unusual interior design but also because the young man, under the influence of the experienced artist, altered the thematic concept of his museum, turned his attention to contemporary art, and rapidly built up a collection that contained important works by artists who later became world-renowned.

The dirty little town thus received the world's first museum for contemporary art. It was a splendid museum that within just a few years became famous and a place of pilgrimage for artists and art enthusiasts. But the townspeople understood none of this. They saw it as an intrusion and reacted increasingly aggressively to what they regarded as impertinent behavior. For the young man, soon realizing that he could not achieve his objective with the museum alone, had not restricted himself to the museum but begun to involve himself in all kinds of campaigns in the town's daily life.

What he called his "art mission" was now aimed at making "beauty once again the dominating power in life": in short, the reorganization of social life through art. So the young man did everything he could to attract excellent artists to the town, to obtain commissions for them, to establish an artists' colony, workshops, and a teaching institute. And people came from far and wide to see what had suddenly become of the dirty little town. And they praised and supported the young man. And he became famous and had a lot of friends.

However, the people who came to see what the young man had done or organized also saw that the town had remained small, dirty, and cultureless; that the young man — despite all his good deeds — was not accepted by the inhabitants of the town but was regarded as a crackpot and good-for-nothing and was even scorned.

But the young man did not give up. Instead he tried now to change the town itself. He bought an entire hill on the edge of the town and invited the most celebrated architects of his day to build a garden city, an artists' colony, and a large school devoted to the integration of all arts. For he was now convinced that he would be able to realize his utopia, his *Gesamtkunstwerk Gesellschaft*, built as an integrated work of art, only if the living conditions of the people were improved.

Yet the young man made only slow progress with this project since he needed the approval of the people of the town to achieve it, and virtually all of them were mistrustful and did not want to follow the young man. Consequently, only a small part of what was planned was actually built. Other broad initiatives that the young man had launched increasingly did not make as much progress as he had hoped.

And yet another unexpected event happened. A major war broke out. Nobody was interested in art and the aesthetic improvement of life any longer. But the young man, who was now no longer quite so young, lost a large part of his possessions due to the war, and he had to economize and even sell some of the items from his museum to which he had become very attached. Finally, his wife — tired of his exclusive interest in art — left him and ran off with another young man to seek the simple country life.

Then the young man fell ill and died. After the young man's death, a dispute flared up about what to do with his estate. The young man had decreed that the museum should be handed over to the town. But the town was willing neither to pay the purchase price demanded by the heirs nor to guarantee that the museum would be preserved in the same state as it was received. The town felt that it was automatically entitled to the museum and everything its "son" had created.

However, in a nearby big city people had recognized the importance of the museum and were prepared to fulfill all the conditions. Thus the administrator of the estate, who took the young man's wishes seriously and believed in his ideas, sold the entire museum to the big city. And as a result the dirty little town was once again just a dirty little town. And from now on, it also had the reputation of being a town where the people understood nothing about culture and were too stupid to give such an important matter the treatment it deserved.

Most people in the dirty little town did not really care about the whole business. Some were angry about the sale of the museum since they believed that they had been cheated out of what was rightfully theirs and theirs alone. But others were sad about the loss and regarded the whole affair as an additional blemish on the town. And many of them abandoned all hope of the town's ever becoming more beautiful and more interesting and left as soon as they could.

But because the town was still young and not very much had happened there yet, the story of the young man's failure became the town's main talking point. People discovered that in other cases, too, the town had not been able to preserve valuable things, and so the case of the young man became symbolic of the fact that nobody could achieve anything in this town. All those who wanted to achieve something, especially the young people, constantly had the example of the young man before their eyes, and so they left as soon as they could. Others who came to the town stayed only for a short time. When they heard the story of the young man, which was repeatedly recounted by those who wanted to make something of their lives, they realized that it would be difficult for them to achieve anything in this town and preferred to try elsewhere. Those who did not manage to leave the town in time were regarded as losers. So the small, dirty, and cultureless town not only remained a dirty, small, cultureless town; it also gained the reputation of being a losers' town. And anyone who came from this town or lived there was treated with malicious condescension by people living in other places. Those who had remained in the town reacted defiantly and defended their hometown against outsiders or people who wanted to change things. They insisted on being right and accepted into their community only people who agreed with them or fawned on them. As a result, many people came to the town who had failed elsewhere and thus added to its reputation of being a town of losers.

But even those who had stayed in the town eventually had to admit that the young man had been very important for the town and that it had been a mistake to reject all his ideas and not to keep his museum. For this museum was now making the big city that had bought it world-famous, whereas people just made fun of the dirty little town. And the young man was now more and more frequently referred to as the town's first son.

And because the pressure grew, it was decided many years later to start again from scratch and to found a municipal art museum. It was dedicated primarily to a painter who had originally been brought to the town by the young man himself and who had stayed there. A short time later, others came who did not agree with this painter's work and plundered the museum. But at the same time, they renamed it after the young man. So he finally got his museum in the dirty little town, although his name was misused for something he had not intended.

Then came a second war. And almost everything that had remained was burned and lost forever. After the second war, the museum was re-established in the young man's name. Now people tried to reconstruct the old collection, but this was virtually impossible since the old collection had been sold and comparable works of art had meanwhile become so expensive that the little town could not pay the prices. Nevertheless, the museum did gain a certain reputation. But the more people attempted to cover up what had happened, the more insistent became the questions about its history. Everything that happened in the museum was measured against what had once been, and the more time elapsed, the more dazzling the lost history appeared and the less possible it became to meet the resulting expectations.

So the young man, the town's first son, unintentionally and surreptitiously became the town's enemy. And sooner or later, this contradiction defeated everyone who worked at the museum.

I came across this story some four years ago; it is, I believe, quite a plausible explanation of what happened in Hagen in consequence of the initiatives of Karl Ernst Osthaus between 1900 and 1921, and what continues to influence life in the town. This text is obviously a narrative, rather than an objectifying, approach to what Hans Sedlmayer would call the "endothymic ground" of the Karl Ernst Osthaus–Museum.[5] How far, if at all, this story carries any truth and could be verified by scientific research, I can hardly say — and actually it is not important, since the story functions in many ways as an explicative model of the specific cultural circumstances Hagen offers to those who live within its boundaries.

It was a long time before I came across this text, or speaking in psychoanalytical terms, this script, and was able to recognize my own position in it. Although I did have some notion of the history of the Museum Folkwang, its sale to the city of Essen, and the history of the Karl Ernst Osthaus–Museum, and I did have a general conception of how to cope with it, I was thoroughly unprepared to deal with a situation that was and remains essentially marked by the fact that, as Ernst Bloch has put it: "what will be especially remembered will be what has not been carried out."[6]

Thus, with my first two exhibitions, I lumbered quite naively right into the scarcely tilled field of Hagen collective memory. I was elected director of the Karl Ernst Osthaus–Museum and established in this capacity almost overnight. Having lost its small museum staff due to quarrels and illness, the city of Hagen was in desperate need of someone to carry out the organization of scheduled events. Thus, I took over without any time or opportunity to prepare for the job, nor to do planning, nor to get familiar with the collections and the history of the museum, but was obliged to carry out the projects my predecessors had left in a half-finished state. Having done this work

FIGURE 1. Exhibition: *Silence*, 1988. Main Gallery, Karl Ernst Osthaus–Museum. Courtesy of the Karl Ernst Osthaus–Museum.

I felt that it would be necessary to set a formal caesura, that is, to create some kind of a demonstrative break, making clear that with my election a new era had begun.

The envisioned opening event not only had to cope with two difficulties —the facts that the museum was extremely short of money and that I had actually no time to prepare an elaborate debut—but, at the same time, had to demonstrate to the public, and especially to the art community, that I would run a completely different program — one that would overcome the extremely negative reputation the museum had acquired over the years.

The no-budget exhibition that launched my new directorship was entitled *Silence* and as such was an attempt to transpose John Cage's piece *4 minutes 33 seconds* into the field of fine arts: literally, to exhibit "nothing" (Figure 1). I planned it at first to be an event with Cage himself, and negotiated with him to come. Unfortunately, the opera project he was preparing at that time in Frankfurt fell victim to fire, an accident that made him flee Germany and that led to the breakdown of our contact as well.

So I stayed without any backup in something like an artist mode when I opened *Silence*. The exhibition exposed the whole museum, which I had cleared out completely (including the bookshop) in a single afternoon, so that anything having the character of an image was eliminated. To ensure this I even took away some of the lights illuminating parts of the architecture, and finally removed the sculptures from the famous "Minne" fountain in the main hall.

As one can imagine, this three-day exhibition elicited some vivid reactions, especially from people who did not know about it and who wandered naively into the house, and from the local media where some critics suggested that I should be fired right away. The one really striking experience I had during the event that, in retrospect, proved to be the most important was that at the opening of the exhibition the public not only behaved as usual and walked through the empty spaces just *as if* something were on display, but also began to recollect the previous placement of the collection and to discuss the works of art I had taken away. Moreover, the architecture of the building, stripped bare, came into view and became the main topic of conversation. In the end everyone focused on one architectural feature, an elaborate art nouveau–style wooden railing that I had not been able to demount or cover. And this is how I learned from some of the older visitors that this railing, which I had believed to be a relic of the old museum, was in fact a replica manufactured in the early 1970s when the building had been extended and renovated.

Thus *Silence* proved that John Cage's concept *4 minutes 33 seconds*, which up till then I had taken as a more or less formal idea, can operate even outside of a musical setting and, depending on the context within which it is performed, can evoke quite different "noises" or texts — the memory of the museum literally crept out of its walls or was projected onto them by the participants in the event.

But this exhibition thematizing the empty museum touched a sore spot in the community in a very direct and unanticipated way. Some visitors, especially the older ones, comprehended the act of taking away the works of art as a repetition of historical events: the museum's loss of its collection, once in its entirety, in the early 1920s, and again in great part, after the museum had been refounded in the early 1930s, in greater parts in the time of the Third Reich and World War II. With this experience it became obvious to me that an important part of the memory of a museum can be assumed to reside in the minds of the community.

This memory became even more visible at the opening of the exhibition that followed *Silence*. This show I entitled *Revision*, and it started within the empty museum on a Tuesday morning at the customary opening hours (Figure 2). I had set up my office and placed the inventory book of the museum

FIGURE 2. Exhibition: *Revision*, 1988. Hall, Karl Ernst Osthaus–Museum. Courtesy of the Karl Ernst Osthaus–Museum.

in the main hall and opened the exhibition by asking my (at that time one and only) technician to go down to the storeroom and fetch any piece of art he chose. He came back with the painting *Pine Forest* (1908) by Christian Rohlfs, a painting that together with about four hundred other works by this painter had been confiscated from the museum's collection in 1937 but had survived the *Bildersturm* (when the Nazis purged German art collections of so-called degenerate art) and been repurchased by museum sponsors in the early 1980s—the only work of art left from its former collection. This painting I put on an easel and presented to the small audience that had gathered for the opening. I then checked it in the inventory, marked it "O.K.," and hung it on the wall at a place determined by drawing an imaginary line across all the walls of the museum, and by the inventory number (Figure 3).

Working this way in public for four hours a day over a period of three weeks, we hung all the works from the collection that we could display without reframing, number by number: about one thousand items, a scant third of the collection, so as to portray the collecting history of the museum from its refoundation in 1945 to the day of the exhibition.

No question, *Revision* was certainly a very brutal exhibition; perhaps it would be better termed a performance, which in general gave precedence to

FIGURE 3. Exhibition: *Revision*, 1988. Gallery space, Karl Ernst Osthaus–Museum. Courtesy of the Karl Ernst Osthaus–Museum.

panels and the better works and made the more informal and minor works look very bad. However, the exhibition was very instructive. One could read from the walls the diverse interests of the directors, their predilections, their hits and flops, relate them to recent art history, and get an idea of their struggle to cope with the increasing prices of artworks that, for example, prevented the very good but small collection of Expressionist art from the early 1960s from being extended.

Once again, the most interesting aspect of this event was the reaction of the audience. While we mounted the show most people did not show any interest in our process—waiting instead, as I was told later, until we were finished—and therefore missed the exhibition, choosing not to believe my announcement that after the final hanging we would remove it all in one night and again simply exhibit an empty space. But we did, and this caused some turbulence. On the other hand, even those people who did come while we worked out our performance, or who attended the *finissage*, would primarily search for the well-known works of art and tended to overlook the rest. This made two things quite clear. First, the standing reproach that museums hide their "true treasures" in storage, and show only what their directors like, is usually uttered only by a special group of the museum's clients, people who, varying a term from Theodor Adorno, I would like to define as "resentment visitors";[7] this reproach simply marks a general fear that something of importance could have been forgotten or improperly valued. Second, the memory of the audience is not a reliable source but tends, like any individual memory, to keep only what has somehow been confirmed elsewhere or anchored in a wider context.

Against this very human tendency to deal with things of little actuality, to overlook and finally forget them, *Revision* pointed out the function and possible meaning of an artificial memory, in this case the inventory book. This made visible two important facts: first, that a museum in spite of its pretension to objectify past phenomena in fact develops itself necessarily into a truly individual place; and second, that the content of a museum, taken only as a stored text, has no meaning at all if it is not related to a context shared by a community.

At this point another aspect of the Janus-like character of past in the present is already visible, the fundamental dialectics of remembering and forgetting—which are after all two sides of the same coin: (human) identity. Memory and amnesia have to be related, and have to work together; otherwise, separated from each other and fixed absolutely, they both lead by different paths to chaos and death. *Silence*, as Cage defined it—freedom from anyone's intentions—or as a completely empty space, is a utopian idea or a space in which any being, and surely human beings, cannot survive. To be lived in, it has to be furnished, at least with memories; on the other hand, the inability to forget, as for example described by Jorge Luis Borges in his story about Ireneo Funes, the man who could not forget anything, leads to death as well. So any place defined only by memories or relics, like many museums, will cause death by suffocation. Therefore, only by remembering *and* forgetting, by reflecting the past within the present, and by measuring the present against the past, are life and a future possible.

Two further exhibitions turned out to be of great importance in this regard. The first, entitled *Vom Trümmerfeld ins Wirtschaftswunderland* (freely translated: "Rising from the Rubble"), took place in 1988 and was curated, or rather made, by Enno Neumann, an art historian. This exhibition knew no boundaries: it mixed whatever remained as a relic from the time between 1945 and 1955 into a gigantic installation, not shying away from relating recent experiences to historic knowledge, constructing something like a vast combined painting exposing the main topoi of German postwar iconography. As we moved and fixed about four truckloads of rubbish to install this show, the usual modes of handling objects within a museum for contemporary art came somehow to a definite end, and we developed a certain freedom with respect to our collection that I continue to apply to exhibition installations as much as possible.

The second event took place in 1990 and was the result of a collaboration with the Museum für Gestaltung in Zürich. Our show was entitled *Imitations — The Museum as the Location of the As-If*. It displayed all kinds of imitations and fakes, from pure copies to simulations, reconstructions, reproductions, dummies, and clonings, incorporating all media and a wide range of objects and goods from everyday life as well as from science and art. The specialty of the version in our museum was that I extended the exhibition from our white-cube exhibition space into the permanent collection, intending to put this itself, that is to say, "true values," into a form of subjunctive. I tried to do this for example by labeling "fake" all parts of the architecture that, like the wooden railing already mentioned, had been somehow redone. In addition, I changed certain data on labels of works of art; instead of an original painting I hung a copy of it in the same place; and I even declared two major works from the collection to be copies by relabeling them. The audience responded to the exhibition with great pleasure, touched and questioned absolutely everything inside the building, but actually lost all orientation — in fact they seemed to believe everything the exhibit told them.

These striking experiences led me to believe that there is a chance to re-define the museum as a specific space that goes beyond presenting art and artifacts in a more or less neutral manner, but projects the concepts exhibited onto the exhibition space itself — in other words: by being infected by the exhibits and no longer run as a "White Clinic" (Ralph Rugoff). Thus these exhibitions encouraged me to believe that even an established and public institution dedicated to modern and contemporary art could hold a specific reality, a reality telling its own truth — a truth that I hoped to find by considering and applying reconstruction and fiction as serious methods so as to achieve a balance within the dialectic of total freedom conceived by *Silence*, on the one hand, and on the other, the prison of a relentless memory represented by the conventional concept of museums.

I found some important support for my museum conception while collaborating with the Museum of Jurassic Technology in Los Angeles, which opened up a branch within our space in 1994. One basis for our collaboration was the exhibit based on Geoffrey Sonnabend's theory of memory. This theory departs from all previous memory research with the premise that memory is an illusion. Sonnabend argues that forgetting, rather than remembering, is the inevitable outcome of all experience. From this perspective, "We, amnesiacs all, condemned to live in an eternally fleeting present, have created the most elaborate of human constructions, memory, to buffer ourselves against the intolerable knowledge of the irreversible passage of time and the irretrievability of its moments and events."[8] Sonnabend's theory does not attempt to deny that the experience of memory exists: the theory is predicated on the idea that what we experience as memories are in fact confabulations, artificial constructions of our own design built around sterile particles of retained experience that we attempt to make live again by infusions of imaginations.

In this notion of memory lies an interesting parallel to Hans Vaihinger's book entitled *The Philosophy of the As-If* (1911), an important source for systems theorists such as Paul Watzlawik. Vaihinger argued that, since thinking serves only an organic function, it performs fiction as a specific mode of logical argumentation that utilizes helping terms or helping constructions to reach its goal. "Just as the *Meleagrina margaritifera*," he wrote,

when a grain of sand happens to get caught in her glossy coat, will cover it with mother of pearl she produces herself, transforming the inconspicuous grain into a dazzling pearl, so — but in an even more refined manner — the psyche, when stimulated, utilizing the logical function transforms sensations into glittering thought-pearls: figments in which a logician might pursue even the secret paths of the acquiring, organism-serving character of the logical function.[9]

In Vaihinger's framework lies a striking explanation for the fundamentally fictional character of memories, comparable to the Sonnabendian notion that short-term or immediate memory is an illusion as well. Thus, "there is only experience and its decay,"[10] suggesting that what we typically call short-term memory is in fact our experiencing the decay of an experience. Consequently the Sonnabend theory describes this process of decay as true memory, which is in actuality our only real connection to the past, as near or as distant as it may be. Yet this assessment of the structure of memory can be compared to theories of perception that, opposing the common division of perception into "recognizing" and "seeing" seeing, hold that the experience and the true structure of perception, like the experience of decay, create a balanced notion of diverse or even contradictory phenomena and in this sense lead to the experience of bold equivalencies.[11]

However far one chooses to follow Sonnabend's theories and their possible parallels in philosophy and art history, there is no question about the fact that what is described as "obliscence" does not necessarily have to be understood as a form of decay but can be experienced as an "overwriting" (*Überschreiben*) of the past as well.

FIGURE 4. The Main Gallery of the Museum Folkwang, about 1905. Courtesy of the Karl Ernst Osthaus–Museum.

This at least was an experience that Hagen provided for me in an exemplary manner. Having questioned the architecture of the museum, one day I could no longer suppress the urge to scratch the walls of the sacred halls with my key, and in doing so, activated the memory of the building almost unintentionally. What I found under five layers of white paint was a straw-yellow tone that upon professional examination proved to be the original hue the whole building had been given in 1902. It was only a question of weeks until we had repainted the building in that yellow color with our own hands and in consequence achieved a very unfamiliar setting for a museum of contemporary art.

In retrospect I see that this experience was something like a turning point in my relationship to the history of this building as well as to the museum in general. This alternative, not-White-Cube-white color restored the golden gleam of the building and seemed to demand a reconstruction of the old interior designed by Henry van de Velde and destroyed in the twenties when the museum served as an office building. In 1992, ninety years after the opening of the Museum Folkwang, the original building was renewed. With funds raised by the citizens and companies of Hagen, it was possible to restore important parts of the van de Velde interior (Figures 4 and 5).

The interior refurbishment not only served to reconstruct an important art nouveau work, but also highlighted the idea that had distinguished the

49

FIGURE 5. The Main Gallery of the Karl Ernst Osthaus–Museum, 1997. Photo: Achim Kukulies. Courtesy of the Karl Ernst Osthaus–Museum.

Museum Folkwang from other museums since its inception. This idea was based on the perception of the museum building as an organism, as a sophisticated whole whose individual parts—functioning like organs—complement and interact with one another in a specific way. Obviously such a museum imposed—and continues to impose—special conditions for the presentation of fine art. As an organic structure, this museum building is not bound by the fundamental principle governing "normal" museums, namely, to present exhibits in a neutral and academically legitimate manner. It calls rather for "responsive or reflective hanging" or, to put it another way, for the development of a *Gemeinschaftskunstwerk*, a "teamwork-artwork."

In consequence, the Karl Ernst Osthaus–Museum now had two different spheres at its disposal that, along with the idea of a discontinuous history of art, we began to thematize as two different environments for the presentation of art and artifacts. This could be realized only through an intense collaboration with different artists who agreed with our intention not to just hang or drop things within the space but to create customized forms of display. We developed three basic criteria for each artistic solution: first, guarantee the possibility of an autonomous perception of the specific pieces; second, mount them and balance them in dynamic ensembles offering as many different positions as possible; and third, create in this way a structure independent from the historical character of the building. We wished to keep open the possibility of exhibiting works contemporary to the time of the building's construction, that is, artworks of the late nineteenth century and of classical modernism.

Several artists have contributed to the realization of this concept to date. Allan Wexler's *Crate House* was purchased in 1992 (Figure 6).[12] It is a white cube roughly two meters square, containing four movable racks furnished like aircraft cockpits, with all the items a two-person household needs. From spoon and refrigerator to TV set and a complete bedroom, the *Crate House* creates an autonomous living unit, done in an elaborate do-it-yourself technique. And this is why I placed it right in the middle of the art nouveau Fountain Hall: as a White Cube, it thematizes the current design of art spaces in a historically avant-garde setting and turns the idea of the White Cube, understood as a space excluding life, upside down. Finally, it represents the state of the art of our time as a do-it-yourself piece against the extremely elaborate craftsmanship of the museum's interior furnishings.

herman de vries's *natural relations* is a major collection of about two thousand mind-altering plants and herbs, brought together in the 1980s from all over the world and organized in a custom-made cupboard from the artist's memory.[13] This piece represents a lifelong effort to relate the human body to nature via plants. I placed it in the basement of the building, where we believe Karl Ernst Osthaus had his (now lost) collection of natural history objects on display. This piece was purchased in 1990, and for the past two years it has been accompanied by a herbarium constructed in the classic manner, which holds all the plants from de vries's collections that grow in the vicinity of Hagen. Thus anchored in the local environment, *natural relations* finds

FIGURE 6. Allan Wexler, *Crate House*, 1991. Permanent installation, Karl Ernst Osthaus–Museum. Photo: Achim Kukulies. Courtesy of the Karl Ernst Osthaus–Museum.

its counterpart in Michael Badura's *Eingeweckter Welt* ("Canned World"), done first in 1967 and as such, at least as far as I know, one of the first artworks dealing with ecological questions. This piece, a rack with about two hundred jars containing cocktails concocted from all sorts of materials one can find in house and garden, custom-reconstructed for a small room in the building, caused a major scandal in Hagen when we purchased it in 1992, because it houses several life-forms, slowly changes its appearance over time, and for many, especially elderly people, just looks disgusting. Established in our collection as a work of art that reflects our relation to the natural environment, it became something of a test case, dividing our audience in two groups, one of which — the older and more conservative — we eventually lost, since they would not accept this piece's being in proximity to what they believed to be beautiful works of art.

On the other hand, Johan van Geluwe's *Curator's Cabinet*, which was set up in 1991 as a major contribution to the exhibition *Open Box — An Exhibition to Extend the Idea of a Museum* and has since then been permanently installed, never encountered much objection though it occupies a very prominent position within the collection of the Karl Ernst Osthaus–Museum (Figure 7).[14] Located on the upper level of the old part of the build-

FIGURE 7. Johan van Geluwe, *Curator's Cabinet*, 1991. Installation at the Karl Ernst Osthaus–Museum. Photo: Achim Kukulies. Courtesy of the Karl Ernst Osthaus–Museum.

ing, the *Curator's Cabinet* functions as the focus and turning point of a tour through selected examples of modern as well as contemporary art. This exhibit introduces reflection on the nature of museums and their claims and can also be read as an ironic comment on the presentation and historical importance of the world's first museum for contemporary art in its historical context—while simultaneously superelevating it as well. Its imperial setup not only discloses a normally hidden museum agenda, the global claim of museal institutions and their agents, but at the same time reduces museal processes to their relations to really powerful systems within our world—not much more than playing in a sandbox, a theater with borrowed properties, a symbolic action that legitimizes itself too often only by its forms, a commanding architecture and rites derived from it, instead of by that which it is to serve.

I would like close by focusing on another major work within our collection, in some ways a counter-piece to the *Curator's Cabinet*: Sigrid Sigurdsson's space entitled *Vor der Stille* ("In the Face of Silence") (Figure 8). This project is a work in progress begun in 1988, parts of which we purchased in 1993.[15]

FIGURE 8. Sigrid Sigurdsson, *Vor der Stille*, 1988 (in progress). Permanent installation, Karl Ernst Osthaus–Museum. Photo: Milton Friedberg. Courtesy of the Karl Ernst Osthaus–Museum.

"Broadening the eventful here and now": [16] Ernst Bloch's expression can be regarded as the guiding principle behind Sigrid Sigurdsson's construction. [17] Beginning with her own biography, she collects all kinds of material and documents — letters, photos, postcards, newspaper cuttings, forms, plans, maps, diagrams, and other records of this century — and arranges them, often annotated with sketches or texts, in very different ways in books and showcases. After a five-year compilation phase (1989–94), *In the Face of Silence* is now a room defined by its room height, subdivided into 380 compartments, a *lieu de mémoire* currently housing about 730 books, objects resembling books that have been created by the artist, and showcases containing, at a rough estimate, about thirty thousand documents, drawings, and other objects. All of these items are to be used by visitors: they can be taken out of the compartments, placed on specially provided tables, examined or read there, and afterward replaced into any of the free compartments. Furthermore, *In the Face of Silence* includes a visitors' book that lies together with writing material on one of the tables, ready to receive spontaneous comments by visitors/users. This book, which was initially empty, thus represents both the present and the history of *In the Face of Silence* in the Karl Ernst Osthaus–Museum or in other places where the work has been shown; users' comments are directly incorporated into *In the Face of Silence* since the volumes written by visitors (currently about three thousand pages) are stored on the shelves and can be read like all the other books. In addition, the visitors' book is also the gateway through which major contributions by visitors, sometimes many pages of them, reach the artist for processing.

In the Face of Silence thus gives the impression of a mixture of archive, library, and cabinet of relics, but this construction has no fixed arrangement apart from the fact that the shelves are divided up into compartments. Its use by visitors consists in a constantly changing sequence of books, book objects, and showcases on the tables and the shelves. *In the Face of Silence* thus appears to be less an archive than the functional equivalent of a (collective) memory, particularly if one looks at the details or, in other words, if one begins to read the books and compare their contents. But in Sigurdsson's work one can recognize not only the construction of an equivalent to memory and its workings; it is rather the reflection of and artistic reaction to the evolution of *lieux de mémoire*, i.e., of places of memory, which take the place of a *milieu de mémoire*, a vital and living memory.[18]

It should be noted that *In the Face of Silence* is a constructed *lieu de mémoire*, an artificially created place of memory, and remains recognizable as such; the work is not a relic of a destroyed tradition, not a memorial to an event or a person, not any kind of monument intended to serve a regulated memory insofar as it attempts to fix a very specific view of the past,[19] but a construction in which remnants of the process of historification, the rubbish of historiography — namely, what it has not been able to take into account or perceive for whatever reason — are collected and arranged.

However, it is not arranged according to the customary taxonomies or criteria of historiography but according to aspects and with methods that are developed out of the material itself. Therefore, contrary to normal archiving and academic processing, it is not the identical or comparable features of the collected material that emerge, but rather its own intrinsic value and its own inherent characteristics, i.e., what makes it special and not comparable with something else. The result is that these remnants produce a surplus of meaning that — not covered or restrained by historiography — reaches the user of *In the Face of Silence* directly and activates his own powers of recollection.

The works I have presented so far are dependent on the (art) museum only for practical reasons but not for their conception. Furthermore, they share a nonlinear concept of time and do not integrate into a typical art-historical chronology, because they are still being processed, are developing their own history, or have been repeated intentionally. Therefore, I believe, these works

FIGURE 9. Salon de Fleurus, *Moderne Kunst aus dem Museum Folkwang*, 1984. Permanent exhibit, Karl Ernst Osthaus–Museum. Courtesy of the Karl Ernst Osthaus–Museum.

can have an effect on the museum, an institution that takes chronological development in particular as a guiding principle. This principle can subjugate the past as well as the future and even permits a conception of current developments as historical processes, thus making them judicable according to historical points of view. Though this concept of time has been roundly criticized, and from different positions, the museum still functions as one of its best-guarded fortresses, and in consequence of its inability to take up a different concept of time, crammed as it is with art and artifacts, it must some day collapse. To leave this spiral of everlasting progress, and to break with the business founded upon it, is, I believe, the common ground shared by the artists who have contributed to our collection—and that is certainly true regarding the last installation that I want to mention. It is a piece reflecting the history of the museum in Hagen and entitled *Moderne Kunst aus dem Museum Folkwang* ("Modern Art from the Museum Folkwang"), a title that deliberately mimics the title of the first catalog of the former collection, published in 1912 (Figure 9).

The collection consists of twenty-six paintings done in oil on wood in different formats, which show views of the interior and some major works of the collection of the Museum Folkwang as it existed in Hagen between 1902 and 1921, obviously created from contemporary photographs. We received this collection from The Salon de Fleurus, a Soho-based nonprofit art space dedicated to research on the historical sites of modern art. The collection was accompanied by a note:

The paintings appeared first in the late eighties at Debris, an Antique Shop located on W. Broadway and Grand St., New York, and were acquired by The Salon de Fleurus in 1992. As the owner of this shop remembered, the paintings came into his father's possession in the mid-fifties as part of the leftovers of the estate of Ernst Fuhrmann. Although the origin of the paintings is not certain (no date or signature) it is presumed that they in fact have been in possession of Ernst Fuhrmann (1880–1956), who, as author and publisher, was in 1919 engaged by Karl Ernst Osthaus, the owner and director of the Museum Folkwang, to establish and run the Folkwang-Verlag (Folkwang-Publishing-House) Hagen. Soon an intimate of Osthaus', he also was placed in charge of the Museum Folkwang, and even was nominated to execute the founder's last will when Osthaus fell sick from a severe disease that was to cause his premature death in 1921. In the Thirties, Fuhrmann was prosecuted by the National Socialists for his activities as publisher, and, forced to emigrate, finally settled in New York in 1938, where he died in 1956. It is most likely that Fuhrmann, in remembrance of his time in Hagen, had these paintings created by an anonymous painter, furnishing him with photographs of the Museum and its collection.[20]

This a probable story, a story that gives a plausible explanation of the provenance of the paintings, and, furthermore, a nice story to append to and conclude the fairy tale presented above. All the details it reports are indeed true — except for the fact that the artists who run the Salon de Fleurus five years ago accepted the commission to create these images for our building.

This commission was a consequence of the art concept realized at the Salon de Fleurus: to reflect through specially installed paintings some important events and places in art history, such as the Amory Show or the Salon de Fleurus run by Gertrude Stein and her brother in Paris. On principle, the authors working at and with the Salon remain anonymous, taking a position somewhat similar to medieval copyists, who achieved significance primarily as transmitters of the works they handled. But in contrast to medieval artists — and in a way that proves them to be our contemporaries — the authors of the Salon de Fleurus do not simply hand down works designated by authority; they work rather with a critical view to art history, its authorities and institutions, artists as well as art dealers — in their very own *ductus* or characteristic style. For example, they continue the work of certain artists who have been long buried and extend it into our time; transpose that of others, who might still be among us, to a time past; reconstruct places and events of art history, including the history of their effects upon history; or, by painting and installation, link people who, in terms of chronology, would never have had a

FIGURE 10. Salon de Fleurus, *Moderne Kunst aus dem Museum Folkwang*, detail (Main Gallery, Museum Folkwang, about 1905), oil on wood, 1984. Courtesy of the Karl Ernst Osthaus–Museum.

chance to meet. In other words, the task of the artists of the Salon de Fleurus is to set a definite end to thinking in chronological terms. When the story of Karl Ernst Osthaus and the effects of his initiatives was heard at the Salon de Fleurus, they jumped at the chance to visualize the trauma that the loss of the Museum Folkwang had caused to the soul of the city of Hagen (Figure 10). Clearly, traumata such as this are very typical examples of phenomena that cannot be obliterated but are sustained, over time, and can be resolved only so far as they are accepted and integrated as a part of life by those who suffer from them.

However, an attempt to somehow treat the soul of the people in Hagen by including the collection "Modern Art from the Museum Folkwang" in our permanent collection, was only one aspect of this move. More important, in my understanding, is that so far as this piece takes the desire for the lost works of art seriously, but does not serve it in a nostalgic or even revisionistic sense, a chance is thus created to turn this desire into a reflection on what Osthaus's efforts to change life through art represent. If today this fundamental concept endures only in the insight that the ideology of everlasting progress and growth — naturally promoted by Osthaus as well — is indeed the important obstacle that impedes the integration of art and life, then any effort to deconstruct this ideology and its base makes sense and is legitimate. The method provided by the Salon de Fleurus to initiate such a process is that of a recontextualization of texts or an aggregation of a text and its context through painting — through images that, as far as they reflect the context within which they are on display, make exactly this context readable as a text itself. Thus there unfolds something similar to a Möbius strip, on which, short-circuiting chronology, the past and the future as well as remembrance and decay, the old and the new stroll along,[21] defining the space within which it is spread out as identical with itself, and thus providing an opportunity to come into very close contact with an autopoetic system, and at the same time, to reflect its constitution.

The idea of an autopoetic or self-reproducing system is a concept that includes and contextualizes the idea of an ironic museum. While museums are historical entities that generally have a highly complex structure, this structure does not usually become its subject matter since this would impede its functionalization for different purposes. To put it another way, wherever possible — including in art museums — the contingency and heterogeneity of collections is suppressed and an attempt is made to present the material in academically legitimized taxonomies. This normally seems to be the only way to assert the value and importance of the material: by using it, stripping it of all coincidences and personal references, as evidence of more or less abstract canons and presenting it as an anchor for certain sections of the "great narrative." But this means that most museums are in fact representation machines that point via the material stored inside them to something outside themselves; that is, they function like pictures through which one looks, almost as if through a window, into an illusory room, into history, the history of art or some of its fields. These are mostly laid out as perspectival constructions that draw the viewer inside them and thus not only do not conceive him as a historical subject but also tend to uproot him, in a similar way to the media.

Against this accustomed design and use of museums, I hold that it is nevertheless possible to design museums differently, namely, as spaces that present the fiction we require to find our bearings in the world, as fiction, and as rooms that comprehend the viewer as a historical subject and emancipate him vis-à-vis history. In other words, I believe that it is possible to conceptualize museums as second-order systems, within which visitors can become observers of the rise and decay of orders — to conceptualize the museum as a space whose inner organization matches what it organizes and thereby enables us to shift to a new, structural perception.

SUSAN A. CRANE

4. Curious Cabinets and Imaginary Museums

Imitations

The universe (which others call the Library) is composed of an indefinite and perhaps infinite number of hexagonal galleries, with vast air shafts between, surrounded
by very low railings. . . . First: the Library exists *ab aeterno*. This truth, whose immediate corollary is the future eternity of the world, cannot be placed in doubt by
any reasonable mind. Man, the imperfect librarian, may be the product of chance or
of malevolent demiurgi; the universe, with its elegant endowment of shelves, of enig-
matical volumes, of inexhaustible stairways for the traveler and latrines for the seated
librarians, can only be the work of a god.

—Jorge Luis Borges, "The Library of Babel"

The Museum of Jurassic Technology opened in Los Angeles in 1989, the brainchild
of a visionary collector, David Wilson. A special effects expert in the film industry and
a life-long habitue of natural history museums, Wilson's ambition was to found a museum of his own. His fine collection now includes the Cameroonian stink ant, a rare
specimen of the prong-horned antelope, and the only known recording of the De-
prong Mori, a rare South American white bat capable of flying through solid walls.
Following in a time-honored tradition of private collectors who have brought their
collections to a wider public, Wilson brought the collection to its current home on
Venice Blvd. in West Los Angeles. Utilizing his effects expertise to invigorate modern museum technologies, Wilson has incorporated holograms into the exhibits, as
well as olfactory simulations (one exhibit tests Proust's principle of memory stimulus
via the aroma of a madeleine), audio/video displays and the newly requisite museum
fixture, the context-establishing video presentation at the entrance. In this presentation, the museum acknowledges its debts to forerunners, from ancient to modern
times, and stresses the continuing pedagogical purpose of public natural history museums. Until now, Jurassic technology has been relegated to the realm of museological criticism and study, although it was prefigured in discussions of early modern
curiosity cabinets or *Wunderkammern*. And like the museum innovaters of the nineteenth century, who began to coordinate the efforts of individual collectors, Wilson's
personal quest has evolved into a collective effort on the part of a group of museum

reformers. Jurassic technology thus finds its own representative space through the collective vision of these collectors, and the public is treated to a visit in heretofore unexplored regions of the natural world.

—Susan A. Crane, "Imitations, Intimations"

The Museum of Jurassic Technology traces its origins to [the] period when many of the important collections of today were beginning to take form. Many exhibits which we today have come to know as part of the Museum, in fact, were formerly part of other less well known collections and were only subsequently consolidated into the single collection which we have come to know as the Museum of Jurassic Technology. "Cyclopean Twilight," for example, was originally part of the Devonian collection, as was the exhibit reconstructing Dennis Gabor's early holographic experiments. Other exhibits which were later included in the Juarassic collection were once part of the less well known Eocene collection. These include the exhibit documenting the now extinct European Mole as well as "Possession, Delusion, Paranoia, Schizophrenia and Reason" (demonstrating the relative ultraviolet absorption rates of the ashen remains of these states). These exhibits from the various collections were, over the years, consolidated into the Museum of Jurassic Technology and, thus configured, received great public acclaim as well as much discussion in scholastic circles.

—*The Museum of Jurassic Technology and You*

Intimations of Curiosity: A Museum Visit

I don't enjoy visiting museums anymore, or at least not the way I did before I began to study them. Too close a proximity to the subject has produced a familiarity akin to contempt. Tradition gets in my face. When I go to a museum, I am aware of a production of knowledge more blatant than Foucault's panopticon could survey. The expectation of having a particular cultural experience prevents all but the random joy of discovering something new — and it is difficult to experience something as "new" when the literature of museum history and practice so thoroughly conditions my visits. Expertise can enrich one's delights; expertise can also blunt any claims one may wish to make to the uniqueness of a personal encounter with any exhibit. Hasn't someone else already described it, had your experience, placed you within the phenomenology of museum visits? Aren't we all collectors of museum visits, our own and those of catalog writers, postcard producers and postcard senders, teachers and students, scholars and critics? Familiar as we are with museums, and familiar as those who study museums are with exhibits, visitors, and museology, where and how can we allow ourselves to have that unsettling experience of the truly new, feel the tickling sensation of curiosity aroused?

The Museum of Jurassic Technology confounded me, and intimated that there might be room for a new pleasure in the museum. Being confounded is intimidating: as a scholar, I felt the bounds of my professional knowledge were being tested; as a museum-goer, I felt vastly uncertain whether following all the usual cues (reading the text accompanying the exhibits, following the organization of exhibits, paying attention to what was lit) would result in the usual satisfaction (or stupor). Instead, I became more and more uncertain, lost in a Borgesian labyrinth. Which parts were "real" and which parts only seemed so due to my ignorance? I could believe that there was research about bats that had eluded my knowledge, but when I came to the "Sonnabend/Delani Halls," it seemed to me that the gaps between my knowledge and the information I was confronting should not have been so great, and I began to have disturbing, fascinating intimations of mendacity. It is an exhibit about memory, or rather about forgetting.

The exhibit opens with the story of Geoffrey Sonnabend, "neurophysiologist and memory researcher," whose life is, oddly enough, represented by a scale model of a running waterfall: Iguazu Falls as it was first spanned by a suspension bridge. This was purportedly the work of his father, Walter. Walter had fortuitously encountered a Chicago candy-manufacturing millionaire sometime in the late nineteenth century, when such millionaires were making themselves in the Midwest. The millionaire wanted bridges in Chicago rebuilt after the great fire of 1871; fate brings the Sonnabends to Chicago, although hereafter it is unclear what Chicago has to do with the Sonnabends. This much information is garnered in the first Sonnabend Hall, through audiophones and representative photographs.

Then, a break in the narrative occurs as I move into the next room, a dark space in which a glass case is lit, offering the accoutrements of an opera performance, including fine gloves and recital programs. A museum attendant manually starts the audio portion of the Delani Hall ("we're still installing this exhibit," she apologized). Madelina Delani, I learn (still sorting through my memory for references) was a soprano who specialized in German lieder, selling out concert halls in the 1920s. She suffered from a rare disorder that retards short-term memory (wouldn't that present a problem for a singer?). Her life was tragically ended in a car accident in South America (not in Iguazu Falls, but close enough). Still puzzling the meaning of Delani's memory loss and South American demise, I move to the next hall, which marks a return to Sonnabend. Photographs continue across the wall, and in front of them is a desk, on which repose scientific-looking apparatuses, although none of them seem to belong to any one scientific discipline (what would a neurophysiologist want with botanical prints and a generic beaker?). The audio narrative resumes: Sonnabend, it turns out, was in South America with his mother, recovering from illness, when he chanced to hear Delani's last concert. That night, whether inspired by her singing or by the sheer synchronicity of fantastic events, Sonnabend sleeplessly roamed the town, formulating what was to become his famous theory of "obliscence," or a theory of memory as the decay of experience. This theory is outlined in an audio/video presentation on the opposite wall, complete with schematic geometrical diagrams taken from Sonnabend's famous book. Memory is seen as a cone, and planes of experience cross it at different angles, the most interesting of which is the "perverse" (as opposed to the "obverse") angle, by which déjà vu and similar sensations can be explained (see pp. 83–90). This delights me, and, temporarily cured of doubts by curiosity, I am eager to find Sonnabend's book and read about his theory of memory.

On the way out of the museum, I stop to chat with the museum attendant and her companion, who is David Wilson. I tell him that the Sonnabend/Delani halls baffle me, that I still have questions about them that I cannot formulate. I tell him the exhibit reminded me of Borges's writing, where I am never sure which elements are fictional, since I recognize some but not all of the references. He is interested in my work on museums, asks for references about an early modern collector, and gives me a press kit containing what has been written about the museum in the media.[1] I am wary: desirous of being savvy, wanting to have my hard-won expertise intact, and yet professionally sceptical of that expertise and willing to be surprised. Wilson responds with earnest sincerity, and gives me the précis-pamphlet of Sonnabend's "huge three-volume work," which the museum staff has conveniently compiled for sale in the museum-requisite gift shop. I tell him I want to read Sonnabend, and I leave with the intention of finding the book in the UCLA library. He neither encourages nor discourages me, but smiles with enormous ingenuousness and good will.

The library catalog does not list the author or the title. Nor does the National Union Catalog list any such publication, although according to the museum publication, the book was published by Northwestern University Press in 1946. All the intimations in the museum, all the hints that suspension of belief is a requisite for the functioning of Jurassic technology, all my parenthetical questions—none of this had quite prepared me for the disappointment I now felt. I could smile at my own complicity in the museum's veracity-confirming/conforming function, whereby the "natural" in natural history implies commonplace acceptance of the representation of the physical world in museums. As Samuel Johnson wrote regarding the appearance of the apocryphal Ossian manuscripts, "had it really been an ancient work, a true specimen [of] how men thought at the time, it would have been a curiosity of the first rate. As a modern production, it is nothing."[2] I wanted Sonnabend to be real. I was intensely disappointed to find that Sonnabend did not exist: I would have preferred to feel that Wilson had let me in on a discovery, that I had become privy to knowledge about an obscure theorist. Instead I was embarrassed. I had been duped.

I did discover, in my obsessive search for verification, the term "oblivis-cence." According to the *Oxford English Dictionary*, the word has obsolete roots in fifteenth-century French usage and means "the fact of forgetting or state of having forgotten." There is also a book by memory researcher Phillip Boswood Ballard entitled *Obliviscence and Reminiscence* (1913). Did someone just make an extended typographical error at the Museum of Jurassic Technology? Is this sheer coincidence, sly humor, or a case of mistaken identity? I approached Wilson with the xeroxed evidence bravely in hand on my next visit to the museum. He was surprised, puzzled, delighted. I gave him the copy for future reference, and forbore to ask the question that was pounding in my brain, a plea to be let in on the secret. But I didn't really want to know. Had I been in Oz with Dorothy, I would never have let Toto pull the curtain from the little man operating the machine.

The pleasure of that particular museum visit, the first trip through Sonnabend, remained. Now that I have (almost) dispelled the last of the doubts remnant from my unsuccessful suspension of disbelief, it occurs to me that Wilson has successfully created a modern curiosity cabinet. To turn Johnson on his head: the value of curiosities is the opposite of that of antiquities. Rather than being "nothing," the modern curiosity is what curiosities have always been: a mixture of the natural and the artifactual (in the old sense of the word, meaning "man-made"), the historical and the ahistorical. Wilson has in effect made a curiosity of the very notion of museums, much as the inscription of the Lord's Prayer on the head of a pin was a curiosity based on the notion of infinity. A museum exhibit could thus be seen as a curiosity: a combination of the real and the artifactual, historical information and the ahistorical permanence of timelessly valued artifacts. Recent historical recreations of art exhibits, such as the Nazi *Degenerate Art* exhibit of 1937 at the Los Angeles County Art Museum and *Stationen der Moderne* at the Martin Gropius Bau in Berlin, have reproduced historic exhibits as events for modern viewers. These are attempts to restage the original exhibitions whose ephemerality is then recorded in catalogs that are collected in libraries, whereas Wilson creates exhibits in order to collect them. Curiosity cabinets have declined since the nineteenth century, except those preserved as such or those translations of the concept that have appeared as freak shows, wax museums, and Ripley's or Guinness's amusement parlors. The current fascination in the art world with deconstructing the museal space and its exhibition techniques opened the mode of artistic production of museums to aficionados of the curious such as David Wilson.[3] Asking whether Jurassic technology is fact or fiction is beside the point. In the presence of museums, whether actual or represented, we still ask about veracity; to visit a curiosity cabinet, one must be prepared to be confounded.

The scale of Wilson's museum also matches that of a curiosity cabinet. It consists of only three rooms, each subdivided into darkly grounded but highlighted display spaces that provide a sense of intimacy and focus. One subdivision, so small that I missed it the first time around, is a "library," whose books range wildly over the spectrum of scientific knowledge and museum practice. Early modern cabinets often featured library spaces as private study rooms for their owners, retreats into the world of knowledge that complemented the collection. The Museum of Jurassic Technology's location is also not in keeping with that of a public museum, residing as it does in an obscure storefront on a wide, busy boulevard with nothing around it to attract that particular public which interests itself in art or the Jurassic; nor does this site refer in any way to an "original" context for its objects, as a local historical museum would (Figure 1). This museum does not match either the private collection kept at home or the institutional siting of a public collection. Word of mouth thus becomes the operative form of publicity — another aspect more characteristic of the cabinet than the museum. Cabinets were known by reputation and the occasional catalog published at auction; museums regularly produce catalogs and guidebooks and are listed among educational institutions. Cabinets were intensely personal and private by nature, even when their contents reflected participation in a universal discourse of science and natural history. Cabinet admission was regulated by the owner; museums are open to the public.

Wilson's curious museum is, paradoxically, an "imaginary" one. It exists, it is a real place, but it is "made up" — a natural historical museum of what might have existed, or a museum of museum exhibits that should have existed. The objects contained in this cabinet are wonderful curiosities that happen to be inventions about history and about museums. The best curiosities were always examples of fine craftsmanship, or of cases in which Nature seemed to have surpassed the skills of humans; Wilson's creations are no ex-

FIGURE 1. Museum of Jurassic Technology. Courtesy of David Wilson.

ception. But when a curiosity purports to be representing "historical" events or objects, an uncomfortable bending or blending of categories ensues. Even those who are willing to conceive of history as a production, as a perpetually changing and interested construction of what the past means to the present, even these individuals would be uncomfortable with the idea that history can be entirely made up, produced as a curiosity for a quasi museum. To make this historical conception "safe," the Museum of Jurassic Technology has to be relegated to the realm of art, specifically "performance art." But Wilson's cabinet participates in an imaginary that is not simply that which is made up. When theorists speak of an "imaginary," they are seeking a term that incorporates the realms of the said and the done, the possible and the inarticulate, all that lies within the boundaries of imagination but possibly beyond discursive frameworks. In another sense, "imaginary" museums often precede actual ones, in draft conceptualizations or philosophical speculations. What is the difference between a curiosity cabinet and a museum? Does it really matter? Perhaps the more interesting question is, what does it take to make an object or a museum historical? What gives an object or exhibit its claim to veracity, and is it possible for an object to be both a curiosity and a historical object? Indeed it is, but to understand this strange combination, I would like to look back at earlier curiosity cabinets, to imagine a context in which what are now considered historical objects had other identities, one of which was as a "curiosity"; a context in which their historical value was not only not recognized, but *unnecessary*; a context that was perhaps supplanted by the modern creation of a museum space of collection, display, and representation, and the written history of the museum. The status of the curiosity and the curiosity cabinet is as much determined by its figuration in historical accounts of the evolution of museums as it is by the collector's personal interests. For a modern curiosity cabinet to make historical claims, whether about memory or natural historians, as Wilson's does, the history of curiosity cabinets provides a very fertile ground for intimations of curiosity.

Curiosity Killed the Cabinet?

The phenomenon of the curiosity cabinet in Europe dates at least from the Renaissance.[4] While elaborately decorated, portable *Schränke*, or cabinets, might house a special collection of valuables, the curiosity cabinet was a larger, immobile entity characterized by an interest in displaying a wide variety of natural and man-made objects in one place — the plenitude of the world represented in the microcosm of a single room or space. This small space was also often called a "museum." The Italian humanist scholar Paolo Giovio is credited with reviving the use of the word with his "Museum Jovianum," a collection of historical portraits and busts begun in 1520.[5] The formation of a cabinet also indicated an affinity for quiet reflection or study, for "museum" initially meant "a temple of the Muses." Zedler's *Universal-Lexikon* (1732) defines "museum" as a building in which intellectuals live communally and study, a meaning that he felt was losing currency in favor of the museum as a private study space.[6] Roger Chartier identified this usage in the context of eighteenth-century French libraries: "as a place of study, it also became an intimate retreat, the best place for communion with oneself, and a storehouse for beloved objects."[7] In German, the cabinet/museum had another cousin, the *Kunst-* or *Schatzkammer* where art, jewels, and other royal or Church valuables were housed and where study was less the intention than establishment of the owner's wealth. The early modern terminological proliferation continues: in English usage, the word defining the collection was determined by the included objects — a "gallery" contained paintings or sculpture rather than "curiosities," which would be found in a "closet" or "repository."[8] What they all have in common is the designation of a private space for the display and enjoyment of valued objects.

"Private" should be understood here as "personal." Cabinets were the results of individual efforts, expressions of the tastes and interests of a single collector. The amount of learning that had to precede the devotion to cabinet collecting was not prescribed; learned amateurs could compete with scholars in the creation of cabinets. The very word "curiosity" indicates a human passion or desire to know, and the cabinet was intended to open the mind to the wonders of the world equally as much as it was intended to further study; however, it was generally assumed that most people would not be able to appreciate both facets. Zedler, who had already cross-referenced *Curiosität* to *Neugierigkeit* (inquisitiveness) in his dictionary, separated the general quality of curiosity from what he called *gelehrte Curiosität*, or intellectual curiosity:

In common curiosity, one delights in those things which concern the external senses, memory, and ingenuity, as when one always enjoys seeing something, listening to pleasant anecdotes, or wanting to read clever and funny writings. . . . intellectual curiosity is when one takes a delight in clever inventions. . . . But not to ignore the curiosity which belongs in cabinets: here again it is the intellectual curiosity . . . that awakens reflection; reflection in turn produces discerned truths, and these show a previously unknown and diverse usefulness of the things.[9]

This definition stresses the pleasure derived from the satisfaction of curiosity, but common curiosity is limited to responsiveness whereas intellectual curiosity involves study. "The curiosity which belongs in cabinets" could refer either to the attitude of the individual in the cabinet, or the object itself; either way, this curiosity "proper" to its cabinet domain is a characteristic of the intellectual who has brought it — the object or the emotion — with him.

Krzystof Pomian has traced the early modern meanings of the French words *curieux* and *curiosité* and shown that a particular individual could be defined by them. The French Academy, in its 1694 dictionary, gave the following definition of *curieux*: "someone who takes pleasure in collecting rare and curious objects or who is very knowledgeable about them; an enthusiast's cabinet; he [who] mixes daily with those who have an inquiring mind." *Curiosité* similarly means the objects of the *curieux* interest: "It also signifies a rare and curious thing; 'his museum was full of curiosities.'"[10] The object and the collector were defined in terms of each other. The value judgment placed on this identity, however, was laden with moral strictures against the common aspects of curiosity: indecent curiosity, wanting to know too much, and its potentially sacrilegious effects were all to be avoided.[11] To this negative potential we might add another: that of dilettantism. Pomian cites an antiquarian's text from 1739:

This word *Curieux* is very ambiguous indeed and its meaning should be determined once and for all. In effect, if this term applies to any man who builds up a collection of Medals, the man of Letters becomes confused with that ordinary mortal, the simple man of taste, who only seeks and values in Medals the beauties of ancient engraving. The true scholar is no longer differentiated in any way from him who merely seeks to appear to be and whose wealth permits him to satisfy his vanity, since both collect Medals, even though to very different ends. Their Collections are therefore entirely dissimilar, and the studious man who toils uniquely for his proper instruction will assemble objects with care, objects which will be neglected by him who seeks to flatter his self-esteem or his taste, rather than to form his mind and perfect his knowledge.[12]

During the course of the eighteenth century, the "merely curious" collector began to be disparaged in opposition to the "connoisseur." The distinction rested primarily on the amount of skill given to the study as well as the depth of the desire to learn, as opposed to the desire to be reflected in the glory of the possessions. The stigma attached to "dilettante" derives from this early modern association of "curiosity" with acquisitiveness and desire to improve social status.[13]

These negative attributes pertain primarily to curiosity as the motivation behind the emotional impulses of the collector, and this valuation only really began to take hold toward the end of the eighteenth century. The rare and wonderous nature — or rarity and value — of the curious object remained its most attractive quality. "Curiosity" was a broad category, including natural-historical as well as man-made objects, antique as well as contemporary objects, art as well as objects lacking any aesthetic value. Paula Findlen has shown how the curious objects that were designated "sports of nature" had a role to play in the development of early modern science. These objects included both verifiable and speculative entities such as the giant, the unicorn, the monkfish, or, still weirder and more wonderful, zoophytes such as the Scythian Lamb, a creature that "consisted of the body of a lamb rooted to the ground by a stem, [which] reportedly survived by eating the grass around it."[14] While the Scythian Lamb may not have appeared in any curiosity cabinets, giants' thighbones and unicorn horns certainly did.

Scientific thought and collectors' curiosity melded in such objects as "fossil men," one of which was displayed in a cabinet as an example of "the story of a monk who, having stolen a chalice and denied it upon oath, was turned to stone."[15] Such a story may strike us as fanciful, and it certainly seemed so to David Murray, author of a 1904 history of museums that is still cited frequently. Murray scornfully used this story as an example of typically mistaken mid-seventeenth-century attitudes toward science and its representation. But Murray's remarks reflect the changed attitudes toward museums and their purposes that resulted from nineteenth-century developments in museum practices and Darwinian scientific thought. The criticism is misdirected. If early modern curiosity cabinets included objects such as fossil men, giants' thighbones, mermaid tails, and unicorn horns, we must consider the possibility that these were not expressions of irrationality, antiscientific or mystical in their conception, but rather were consistent with the scientific imaginary of the time, structured within a concept of Nature's inexhaustible plenitude. Even more strikingly, modern depictions of the curiosity cabinet continue to repeat the stories told about the objects without actually acknowledging that the objects' interest derived as much from the stories as from themselves or their appearance — precisely because, I think it is fair to say, the stories still engage us even though our scientific framework is much changed, just as they do in the Museum of Jurassic Technology.

Correcting the designation of an elephant bone that was misidentified in the seventeenth-century Ashmolean collection as that of a giant, Murray also complains, "There were many similar cheats. The object of showing such things was that they were expected and that the museum should not seem to be incomplete by their not being there."[16] Rather than discrediting the Ashmolean Museum, the "mistake" raises another question: what determined the desirability of these "cheats" and why were they "expected"? Possibly the criteria for authenticity have changed; as Walter Benjamin noted, "the concept of authenticity always transcends mere genuineness."[17] For the earlier, "fantastic" objects, it appears to have been sufficient that a folkloric or superstitious story attested to the object's potential existence. Though this fact was not always indicated by labels or signs, many of the objects in a curiosity cabinet were essentially accompanied by stories. These objects were not "cheats," then, except when the story criteria are regarded as inauthentic.

The story would be related by a guide. Random access to a cabinet's contents was unheard of; cabinet visits took place in the presence of the owner or a designated guide, until late-eighteenth-century experiments with the first public museum days.[18] In essence, modern histories of these cabinets reproduce the guided visit, by listing the stories along with the object. The following stories are culled from a recent example of this historiography, by Arthur MacGregor:

The collection of Duke Albrecht V of Bavaria (1528–79): "Another personal obsession manifested itself in series of plaster casts of deformed limbs and paintings of dwarfs, human deformities, bearded women and convicted criminals, the latter complemented by an inventory enumerating their crimes — one such person was said to have been wholly or partially responsible for the murder of 745 people." [19]

The famous cabinet at the University of Leiden, known for its medical specimens, founded in 1590: "In addition to various animals, ranging from a ferret to a horse, the rearticulated skeletons of a number of notorious criminals could be seen. These included the remains of a sheep-stealer from Haarlem and of a woman strangled for theft; more impressively, one could see 'The Sceleton of an Asse upon which sit's a Woman that Killed her Daughter' and also 'The Sceleton of a man, sitting upon an ox executed for Stealing of Cattle.'" [20]

The collection of Bernard Palissy (1510–90), Huguenot potter and philosopher: "His large shell-collection contained foreign as well as local varieties, and fossils were also richly represented. One of Palissy's particular interests was petrification, the basis of which he discussed [in his philosophy]: no doubt his interest was fuelled by the tales he records of whole companies of men and animals and even entire villages turned to stone." [21]

In the Bodleian Library at Oxford, the following highlights were recorded by visitors: "'a piece of the salt pillar' (which may have been intended for Lot's wife), and a coat attributed to Joseph 'which he wore when he was sold to the Egyptians.'" [22]

The Tradescant natural history collection in London, c. 1683: "More widely appreciated (and collected) were the 'Barnacles,' of which the Tradescants had four sorts. Barnacle geese attracted the curiosity of collectors on account of the tradition, enshrined in their name, that they sprang from barnacle shells adhering to driftwood and trees rather than from eggs." [23]

Finally, the Tradescant collection included "the remora, a sucking fish (*Echeneis remora*) anciently believed to have the power to bring ships to a halt by attaching itself to the keel." [24]

I have given these details at length because they amply illustrate two important, and distinct, points. First, the desirability of the curious object lay in its relation to a known or acceptable story; why otherwise would it have mattered which human skeleton or deformity one was viewing? And why else that fish, or that oxbone, unless it had a tale to tell? And even where the objects did not refer to a particular tale — say, the samples of geological materials or a butterfly collection — they could be said to refer to another narrative, the one constructed taxonomically around their distinction into species and categories by type. This was a narrative of scientific knowledge, and a story that would be just as well known (to the scientists) as the fantastic tales were to the larger cabinet-visiting public. Second, historiography of the cabinets, and therefore of museums, repeats the story for the very same reason, even though we supposedly no longer believe in the mythic or fantastic origins of the objects: because the desire for the story remains, even if the desire for the object has subsided.[25]

The continuity of the appeal of stories sheds interesting light on other kinds of collections as well, such as antiquarian ones, which also might be assumed to have been developed according to scientific, scholarly standards of authentication. The object of an antiquarian's interest will be a relic of verifiable antiquity — as determined by comparison and reference to reliable sources of authenticity, earlier reports or documents. The collector of curiosities is thrilled by the plenitude of Nature; the antiquarian is thrilled by the continuity that can be found even in exoticism, through comparision and identification. The one works to aggregate/incorporate by including everything; the other will only seek, and therefore only find, what "fits" the historical idea of antiquity that is the foundation of his interest: the history is the story to be told.[26]

One such case of the new relation between curiosities or "cheats" and historical authenticity was the publication of the Ossian poems in England in 1760. James Macpherson's invented Ossian manuscripts, presumably fragments of ancient Celtic poetry, which he claimed to have found in a trunk in a remote and desolate church and which he insisted were unavailable for verification, neatly fit contemporary expectations for the discovery of historical documents. His copious footnotes and formal referencing methods added credence to the fictional manuscripts.[27] The initial success of the Ossian manuscripts, and their resilience in the face of scepticism, indicates how well Macpherson mimicked historiographical standards. Authenticity, as noted above, is a concept that encodes its own standards of verification. In this case, the authenticity of historical documents was shown to be as easily made up as were the fantastical stories associated with some natural historical objects. Curiosities could be a kind of historical object—if not to say, an object of Jurassic Technology.

Olaus Worm's cabinet in Copenhagen, or "Ole Worm's Museum Wormianum" as it is known, has been famous ever since the publication of its catalog in 1655, with its well-known and much-reproduced frontispiece illustrating the single-room museum in all its polymorphous plenitude (Figure 2). Since then, Worm's collection—or rather, its catalog—has (pre)figured in every history of the museum, part of a triad of significant early modern writings and collections: the others are C. F. Neickel's *Museographia* of 1727 and the Tradescant collection in Oxford.[28] These three examples are cited as sources for the advent of the modern museum because they can be used to illustrate a crucial distinction between personal and collective collecting. For those who argued that early modern museums were a chaotic jumble of natural and artificial, exotic and mythic curiosities, these three collections (and, by implication, their collectors) are seen to have recognized the necessity of ordered intentionality, the organization of museums into instructional venues for the transmission of knowledge. In other words, they are seen as participating in an ongoing collective effort to establish a scientific narrative of knowledge. Although they are early modern museums, their founders are credited with "realizing" that standardized order was necessary and that principles as well as passions should guide collecting. In the process, their collected "curiosities" took on the status of scientific objects, and whatever resisted incorporation, the true "curiosities," were indulgently categorized as cases of mistaken identity. This historical revision of the role of the collector and the typology of the collection appears to have begun in the nineteenth century.[29]

The first modern German history of museums of which I am aware was written by Gustav Klemm, librarian to the king of Saxony and director of the royal porcelain collection, in 1837. Klemm's *Towards a History of Scientific and Art Collections in Germany* rehabilitates earlier libraries, cabinets, museums, and archives as precursors of the modern historical museum. Worm's and Neickel's collections are discussed at length as examples of collections in which "the historical viewpoint dominated"[30]—even though "historical" in this case referred to "natural historical," an entirely different organizing principle, as Michel Foucault demonstrated in *The Order of Things*.[31] Klemm then provided a detailed listing of significant contemporary collections of all

FIGURE 2. Ole Worm's cabinet of curiosities, 1655. Courtesy of The Getty Trust.

types, with a separate category for "collections of history and ethnography." A perpetually present desire to collect was reinterpreted by Klemm as a progressive history of collecting for the representation of history — sometimes misguided, sometimes misrepresented, but always recognizable as a trend toward the current era's historical interests.[32]

This interpretation prevails even though, as Klemm also notes, "Certainly collections were formed whose beginnings clearly reflected the character of their times, when particular value was placed on the unusual, rare and remarkable, and when it was enough to bring the materials together in order to judge first of all according to their scope, to be able to sort and order according to their differences."[33] Such collections — Klemm cites that of August I, forerunner of the Dresden royal collection of art and antiquities — are characterized as "jumbles," well intentioned but limited by the sixteenth-century scientific worldview. Klemm contrasts early-eighteenth-century cabinets — "conglomerates of the fruits of bad taste, which offer food for conversation but at best only rarely can provide instruction" —with the museums of his time, in which the attempt was being made "to create organic wholes, to vouchsafe as complete as possible an overview of the subject . . . before it takes into consideration the superfluous or the mere curiosity." [34] This overview, the organic form, was History. In crediting selected earlier collections with "a historical viewpoint," he subtly and successfully translates any earlier evidence of interest in narrative organization into a prehistory of the modern historical museum. Natural history continues to benefit from collection of specimens, Klemm argued, but historical museums need to be developed so that their collections offer instruction to the viewer, through a visible historical narrative.

What happens to the "mere curiosity" under this new collecting rubric? Curiosity is no longer sufficient grounds, nor a satisfactory object, for museum collecting; plenitude is no longer representative of a worldview but of disorder; and persistent interest in curiosities now relegates the collector to the status of dilettante. "No mere attribute of age or empty curiosity value" would give an object a place in the Berlin royal antiquities collection under the direction of E. H. Toelken in 1835. [35] The new museums wanted to represent history through selected historical objects, whose historical value was not determined by sheer age or uniqueness. If curiosities are "empty," lacking historical value, they do not qualify as monuments (*Denkmäler*) of German history. The German word for remembering, *Erinnerung*, literally means "filling-in" (*er-innern*), and a *Denkmal*, as opposed to a curiosity, is an object that best effects this memory process. The difference between a curiosity and a *Denkmal* is crucial to understanding the changes in historical collecting that began at the end of the eighteenth century.

Collections of antiquities would seem to be the most obviously "historical" collections of the early modern period, if we agree that natural history collections were operating under a different epistemological framework and intention. The objects of Greek, Roman, and Egyptian antiquity that were being traded and collected as European explorers extended the range of the collectors' market were ascertainably "old" —and even if they were not, even if they were "cheats" of some kind, their appeal lay in a connection with old stories, myths and legends. What, then, would prompt a curator such as Toelken to dismiss "mere age and empty curiosity value" for the Berlin collection? It was a concern not for "mere" authenticity, but rather for the nature of the collection as a whole. Curiosities belonged in a cabinet, where their unique stories retained them each a place; historical objects, however, derived their significance as much from their original site, or their collection site, as they did from an individual story. In this sense, the historical object participated in a narrative uniting location and experience, whereas the curiosity represented a transferable story.

To understand Toelken's position, we can look to earlier descriptions of antiquarian collections and see how historical value was attributed. One of the best-known collections of the later eighteenth century in Cologne belonged to the Baron Johann von Hüpsch (1730–1805), who collected antiquities as well as natural-historical objects and what would now be considered ethnographical objects (costumes, weapons, handicrafts). The antiquities came from all over the world and were not intended to represent local history. The personal nature of the collector's enterprise becomes clear when we look at Hüpsch's frustrated attempts to sell the collection as a single unit. As was often the case, potential buyers desired only certain objects from the collection — which also supports the argument that collector idiosyncrasy was a determining factor in collecting. Another hindrance was the lack of a catalog or inventory. Hüpsch did not catalog his own collection because, as Gudrun Calov explains, "the overall sensibility of his cabinet could not be understood through a 'systematic' presentation, because for him from the very beginning it was a matter of an overall conceptualization, not of the individual curious objects."[36] French authorities interested in the collection (during the Napoleonic occupation of the Rhineland) offered to buy it intact if the disorder of the collection could be recompensed by a catalog. Hüpsch, despite financial straits and a desire to preserve his collection, refused.

The collector was able to maintain whatever sense of order he desired so long as the collection remained in his cabinet, but once the collector tried to market it, the collection had to offer something besides the fascination it held for its creator. What for him was representative of plenitude became to observers a sign of disorder. Later visitors to the cabinets who had an interest in purchase, including the illustrious Johann Wolfgang von Goethe (who was himself a passionate collector) complained of the disorder that characterized some of the best collections of antiquities. After 1813, Goethe undertook to visit and describe the major collections of art and antiquities in the Rhine and Main regions and was also asked by the Prussian government to make recommendations regarding the purchase of some of these collections for Berlin. Goethe's reaction to the collection of Ferdinand Franz Wallraf, professor of botany and rector of the university at Bonn, is typical of this new criticism:

He [Wallraf] belongs to that sort of people who from a boundless desire to possess things, are born without any methodical sensibility or love of order. . . . The chaotic condition in which the priceless objects of nature, art, and antiquity lie is unthinkable: they lie, stand, and hang all over and under each other. He guards these treasures like a dragon but without at all sensing that day by day something exquisite and worthy is losing its value through dust and dry rot, and through being shoved and rubbed and stuffed together.[37]

A contemporary lithograph depicts Wallraf amid his objects very much like a dragon in his lair: his foot resting royally upon a book, objects piled about him, the knights in their armor almost alive to his interests (note that one has his hand resting possessively on what appears to be a medieval relief) (Figure 3). This depiction of the collection stresses its chaotic nature as well as the formidable presence of its owner, the one responsible for the disorder, as Wallraf is the central element in the illustration.[38] The critique of disorder can be seen as a development from the descriptions of early modern cabinets in which the proximity of different kinds of objects made for an impression of plenitude. Goethe was impressed by the sheer amount of interesting objects but did not see in Wallraf's protectiveness the kind of protection — preservation — that historical collectors desired.

In contrast, Goethe visited another famous Rhineland collection in 1815, that of Franz Pick (1750–1819), which impressed him more favorably. Early in his career, Pick had served as house chaplain and secretary to Count Franz-Wilhelm von Oettingen-Baldern, who possessed an art and curiosity cabinet "in the style of the sixteenth century."[39] Pick's interest in collecting was developed along with this collection, and he became friends with Wallraf. By the time of his death, Pick's own collection included "about 250 paintings, 7,500 engravings, 200 wood carvings (including 35 by Dürer), hundreds of manuscripts, valuable books including those printed before 1500 (incunabula), medieval stained glass, Roman stone monuments, antique coins, ivories and antiquities from several centuries" — most of them local artifacts.[40] Clearly this was no curiosity cabinet, nor yet was it a *Schatzkammer* of the royalty; it was a collection in which the historically sensitive observer could find much food for the soul. Goethe found that Pick's collection stimulated the historical sensation:

This bright and clever man has conscientiously collected each and every antique thing that came into his hands, which would be enough of a service, but he has served an even greater purpose in that he has earnestly and wittily, sensitively and cleverly brought order to a chaos of ruins, enlivened them and made them useful and enjoyable. . . . one looks through the collection with ever changing interests, which each time necessarily take a historical direction.[41]

FIGURE 3. F. F. Wallraf sits amid his collection like a dragon in his lair. Pen and ink drawing by Nicolas Salm, c. 1820. Courtesy of the Rheinisches Bildarchiv Köln.

The collection might still appear a "chaos of ruins" to modern observers, since the objects were not necessarily ordered by period or type. The effect the collection had on Goethe seems to have been intensified by its location in Pick's own house. Goethe wrote in a recommendation to Berlin that "to move Pick's collection from its place would be to destroy it; while in contrast one must move Wallraf's collection if one is to make anything of it."[42]

The most salient feature of the historical object, as it was being brought into consciousness in the early nineteenth century, was its ability to inspire its beholder. This intense revelation of historical sensation occurred initially in the place where the object was "found": in German, the expression *an Ort und Stelle* was used to signify the appropriate locale and instance of the experience. Pick's house functioned as *Ort* for Goethe because many of the objects were locally significant. August Schlegel, after visiting the collection in 1819, concurred: "[Pick] has assembled many things which, left alone, would have been exposed to the danger of ruination; and these things are of particular local [*örtlich*] importance for Bonn, since they were found locally and thus refine memories of the near or distant past and provide historical enlightenment, and put before our eyes examples of the artistic abilities and taste of different eras."[43] Locally found objects were significant because of their origins: both because the initial encounter with them was conditioned by that environment and because increasingly the value of a historical object as opposed to a curiosity was being determined according to its site—both the original site of the find and the secondary site of its display. Curiosities could be traded, bought, and brought from around the world, and even antiquities necessarily came from abroad, but historical objects had to have a local resonance, according to the new sensibility.

Curiosity did not "kill the cabinet," although both cabinet and curiosity became marginalized where they were not incorporated into modern museum narrative strategies. I am deliberately highlighting the genealogical relationships between curiosities and historical objects in museums, rather than following the obvious lineage between curiosity cabinets and museums of natural history, in order to demonstrate that curiosities were redefined in several ways after 1800. Curiosities continued to play a role in historical museums even if they were no longer being assembled by antiquarians or other collectors. In an 1844 guide to the royal art collection at Berlin, its director, Leopold von Ledebur, described some curiosities that were deliberately included in the section devoted to "the history of the fatherland." Among them, "as witnesses to superstition: two pieces preserved as amazing curiosities from the close of the seventeenth century": a belt that supposedly had turned a prince's valet into a werewolf, and a horseshoe that had been thrown at a milkmaid by the devil and turned her into a horse.[44] Curiosities appeared in the museum, but they were "witnesses" to the past, curious objects turned into historical artifacts. Their presence in the designated "historical" section marked them as objects with not only their own stories to tell, but a narrative of seventeenth-century history to fill in, to *er-innern*, as historical objects. What can be "re-membered" participates in the always already constituted context of the "historical."

An object that was a curiosity yesterday and is a historical object today does not necessarily face a secure future. There is nothing to guarantee the persistence of the historical object's identity, except the museum, and habit. As Michael Fehr writes, "This 'thingifying' of our memory function does not guarantee that we will be able to remember, nor does it account for the reason for the fear of forgetting: the fact that the past does not owe any kind of duty to our present."[45] The modern history of museums is a history of imaginaries that became realities and of realities that became naturalized. Museums present objects but demand response to ideas, or, in the case of curiosity cabinets, to stories. It is not so ironical, then, to find a curiosity cabinet in Los Angeles today. The Museum of Jurassic Technology can simultaneously exist as art installation, curiosity cabinet, museum of museums, fact, and fiction—a cabinet, moreover, that uses its collection of museum exhibits as witnesses to museums past, artifacts of the evolving narrative of the history of museums. We can write the history of museums in many ways; the Museum of Jurassic Technology is one of them.

The Museum Of Jurassic Technology

GEOFFREY SONNABEND

———

OBLISCENCE: THEORIES OF FORGETTING
and
THE PROBLEM OF MATTER

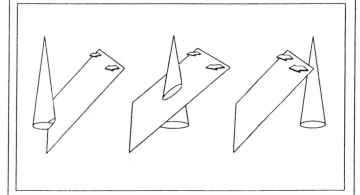

An Encapsulation
by
Valentine Worth

SUPPLEMENT TO ABSTRACTS NOTES AND QUERIES
VOL. IV, NO. 3
Guide Leaflet No. 7

First Edition, abridged

the Museum of Jurassic Technology

The Museum of Jurassic Technology is an educational institution dedicated to the advancement of knowledge and the public appreciation of the Lower Jurassic and is in cordial cooperation with all similar institutions throughout the world. The Museum authorities are dependent upon private subscriptions and the dues from members for procuring needed additions to the collections and for carrying on research into *life in the Jurassic.*

The Museum is open to the public for a modest donation. Admittance is free to Museum Members.

The Membership fees are:

Senior / Student $25
Active ..... $ 35
Contributor $100

Donor $500
Benefactor $1000
Founder's Circle $5000

All money received from membership is used for increasing the collections.

———————

GEOFFREY SONNABEND'S

Obliscence: Theories of Forgetting

and the Problem of Matter

AN ENCAPSULATION

BY

VALENTINE WORTH

WITH

DIAGRAMATIC ILLUSTRATIONS

BY

SONA DORA

Funded in part by the InterArts Program
of the National Endowment for the Arts

SOCIETY FOR THE DIFFUSION OF
USEFUL INFORMATION—WEST COVINA
1991

Society For the Diffusion of Useful Information Press
9091 Divide Place West Covina, California OX2 6DP

Billings Bogata Bhopal Beirut
Bowling Green Buenos Aires Campton
Dayton Dar es Salaam Düsseldorf
Fort Wayne Indianapolis Lincoln
Mal en Beg Mal en Mor
Nannin Pretoria Teheran
Socorro Terra Haute Ulster

Published in the United States by
The Society for the Diffusion of Useful Information
© The Museum of Jurassic Technology, Los Angeles 1991
Published in cooperation with the Visitors to the Museum
by the Delegates of the Press
British Library Cataloguing-in-Publication Data
I Geoffrey Sonnabend: Obliscence: Theories of Forgetting
and the Problem of Matter, An Encapsulation
II. Drake, Diana.
III. Simons, Sarah.
IV. Rossi, M. Francis.
V. Wilson, David.
069'.06937'75 AP 101.0794
ISBN 0-17-735925-3
Library of Congress Cataloging-in-Publication Data
Main entry under title:
I Geoffrey Sonnabend: Obliscence: Theories of Forgetting
and the Problem of Matter, An Encapsulation
Includes bibliographies and index.
1. Museum of Jurassic Technology. 2. Simons, Sarah 1952 –
3. Rossi, M. Francis 1967– 4. Drake, Diana 1947–
5. Wilson, David 1946–
II. Museum of Jurassic Technology
AP 101.0794 093'.06937'7 88-73931
ISBN 0-17-731315-7
Set in Xerox Ventura Publisher.
Printed in the United States of America

84

Obliscence: Theories of Forgetting and the Problem of Matter

— AN ENCAPSULATION —

In April, 1991, The Museum of Jurassic Technology in Los Angeles, California opened the Delani/Sonnabend Halls – a series of exhibits detailing the lives and works of two extraordinary individuals: Madalena Delani, a singer of art songs and operatic material and Geoffrey Sonnabend, a memory researcher and neurophysiologist. The exhibits also document the effect that Madalena Delani's work had upon the formation of Geoffrey Sonnabend's theories of forgetting as described in his controversial Obliscence: Theories of Forgetting and the Problem of Matter.

In his three volume work *Obliscence: Theories of Forgetting and the Problem of Matter*, Geoffrey Sonnabend departed from all previous memory research with the premise that memory is an illusion. Forgetting, he believed, not remembering is the inevitable outcome of all experience. From this perspective,

> We, amnesiacs all, condemned to live in an eternally fleeting present, have created the most elaborate of human constructions, memory, to buffer ourselves against the intolerable knowledge of the irreversible passage of time and the irretrieveability of its moments and events.[1]

Sonnabend did not attempt to deny that the experience of memory existed. However, his entire body of work was predicated on the idea that what we experience as memories are in fact confabulations, artificial constructions of our own design built around sterile particles of retained experience which we attempt to make live again by infusions of imagination - much as

---

[1] Geoffrey Sonnabend, *Obliscence: Theories of Forgetting and the Problem of Matter* (Chicago: Northwestern University Press, 1946), pp.16

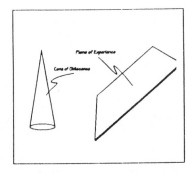

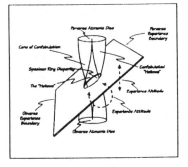

1.1 The basic *Sonnabend Diad* — characteristic cone and plane of experience.

1.2 The complete Sonnabend model of obliscence as realized by the end of Sonnabends reserach.

the blacks and whites of old photographs are enhanced by the addition of colors or tints in attempt to add life to a frozen moment.

Sonnabend believed that long term or *distant* memory was illusion, but similarly he questioned short term or *immediate* memory. On a number of occasions Sonnabend wrote, "there is only experience and its decay"[2] by which he meant to suggest that what we typically call short term memory is, in fact, our experiencing the decay of an experience. Interestingly, however, Sonnabend employed the term true memory, to describe this process of decay which, he held, was, in actuality, not memory at all.

Sonnabend believed that this phenomenon of true memory was our only connection to the past, if only the immediate past, and, as a result, he became obsessed with understanding the mechanisms of true memory by which experience decays. In an effort to illustrate his understanding of this process, Sonnabend, over the next several years, constructed an elaborate Model of Obliscence (or model of forgetting) which, in its simplest form, can be seen as the intersection of a plane and cone (1.1). It is this model that Sonnabend first came to understand during a sleepless night in September, 1936, at the Iguassu Falls. By the end of his life this model reflected a complex of forms and designations including such terms as the cone of confabulation, the perverse and obverse atmonic discs, spelean ring disparity and the attitude and altitude of experience (1.2).

In its most basic form Sonnabend's model of obliscence consists of two elements: the Cone of Obliscence and the Plane of Experience (sometimes also known as plane experience).

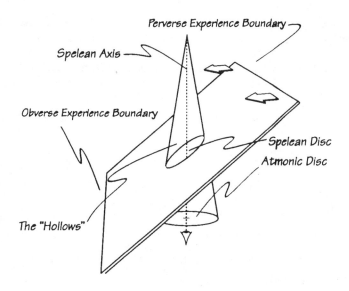

1.3 Geoffrey Sonnabends *Model of Obliscence* detailing the basic elements of cone, plane and discs.

All living things have a Cone of Obliscence by which the being experiences experience. This cone is sometimes also known as the Cone of True Memory (and occasionally the Characteristic Cone.) Sonnabend speaks of this cone as if it were an organ like the pancreas or spleen and like those organs its shape and characteristics are unique to the individual and remain relatively consistent over time. This cone (occasionally referred to as a horn) is composed of two elements - the Atmonic Disc (or base of the cone) which Sonnabend described as "the field of immediate consciousness of an individual" and the *hollows* (or interior of the cone). A third implied element of the Characteristic Cone is the Spelean Axis, an imaginary line which passes through the tip of the cone and the center of the Atmonic Disc. The Spelean Axis can be thought of as the individual's line of sight or perspective, with the eye of the individual firmly held at the intersection of the Spelean Axis and the Atmonic disc.

The second element of the basic Sonabend diad – the Plane of Experience – is far more dynamic. Planes of Experience are always in motion, always (in Class I planes) moving from the Obverse Experience Boundary (or leading edge) to the Perverse Experience Boundary (or trailing edge).

In the course of its migration, the path of a Plane will cause it to intersect the less dynamic Cone of Obliscence. The intersection of the plane and cone creates what Sonabend called the Spelean Ring (or Spelean Disc.) When such an intersection occurs, a three tiered series of events ensues, which (from our perspective) would be described as:

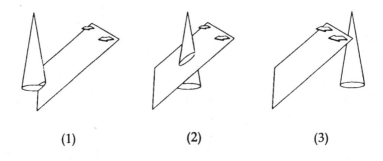

(1)   (2)   (3)

(1) being involved in an experience
(2) remembering an experience
(3) having forgotten an experience.

Under *normal* circumstances, the Obverse (or leading) Experience Boundary is the first element of the plane to cross the Atmonic Disc. This situation creates the condition we describe as being involved in an experience. Once the Obverse Experience Boundary clears the Atmonic disc we say that we remember the experience. And when the Perverse Experience Boundary clears the cone altogether, and we no longer "truly remember" the experience, we say we have forgotten the experience. From our perspective, at the intersection of the spelean axis with the atmonic disc, this series of events is seen as a progressively constricting or diminishing disc - in other words experiences pass and memories fade.

Every Experience Plane has a pitch or attitude as well as an altitude. The pitch of a plane can be thought of as the angle at which it comes into contact with a particular cone. This pitch effects the length of the decay of the experience. Similarly, the altitude of a plane can be can be seen as the elevation of the plane in relation to a particular cone. The altitude of the plane effects the apparent intensity (or brightness) of the experience in question.

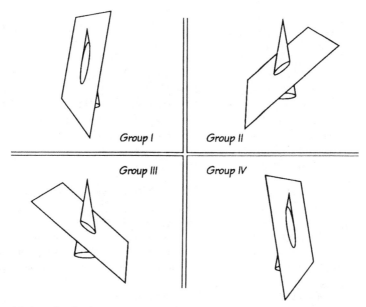

15 *Sonnabend's Groups* - system of classification of planes of experience based upon attitude.

Sonnabend devised a system of classification of experience based on the division of the planes into four groups (1.5), depending on the pitch or attitude of the plane:

> Group 1 – within 7 degrees of arc of vertical
> Group 2 – between 8 degrees and 90 degrees of arc
> Group 3 – between 91 and 173 degrees of arc
> Group 4 – between 174 and 180 degrees of arc.

Beyond 180 degrees a plane reverts back to a Group 1 plane (but changes to Class II which will be discussed later).

Clearly, a Group 1 Experience Plane with a vertical or nearly vertical experience pitch passes through the cone (and, accordingly, from memory) far more rapidly than a Group 2 plane with, for example, a 53 degree experience pitch.

A normal individual under normal circumstances is primarily aware of Group 1 and Group 2 planes with the great predominance being Group 2. According to Sonnabend, however, there is absolutely nothing to indicate that the population of planes is not evenly dispersed among the groups and classes - which is to say that for every Group 2 plane there exists a Group 3 plane and for every

Group 1 plane there exists a Group 4 plane as well. The great majority of volume three of Obliscence, Theories of Forgetting and the Problem of Matter is devoted to the discussion of Group 3 and 4 planes as well as the whole world of Class II, or negative experience pitch planes, in which the Perverse Experience Boundary in fact leads the Obverse.

The Group 3 & 4 planes, in conjunction with the Class II planes, make up, according to Sonnabend a full three quarters of the experience of everyday life. Yet, because of the nature of the construction of these experiences, we are, by and large, unaware of, even, their existence. When we are aware of these experiences they appear to us as fleeting or insubstantial and we ascribe to them such names as premonition, Deja vu and forebodings. It is precisely this area of Sonnabend's work that has, on the one hand, caused such controversy while, on the other, provided a structure and a vocabulary with which to discuss these often difficult experiences. For example, let us consider the case of a Class I, Group 3 plane. In this case, the Obverse Experience Boundary is still the leading edge of the plane, however, its first point of contact with the Characteristic Cone is not the Atmonic Disc, as is the case with *normal* Group 1 and 2 experiences but, the Obverse Experience Boundary, in fact, first contacts the cone's *hollows*, that part of the cone with which we associate the sensation of memory. Accordingly this class of experience has a quality of being pre-remembered or foreshadowed.

This discussion has only been able to outline in the broadest of strokes the extraordinarily detailed and far reaching work of Geoffrey Sonnabend. A more thorough and detailed study of Sonnabend's work offers its student rich rewards as well as many surprises.

PART II

Memories in the Museum

6. History and Anti-History

*Photography Exhibitions
and Japanese National Identity*

As you walk toward the Tokyo Metropolitan Museum of Photography (TMMP), you find yourself surrounded by history. This history isn't real, if "real history" means landmarks created in time past or the preserved sites of long-ago events, but faux history, clean and tidy reminiscence in the service of contemporary commerce. At one end of Ebisu Garden Place, the spacious outdoor mall where this new museum is situated stands a full-scale, approximate reproduction of the Meiji-era[1] Sapporo Beer Company building that used to occupy the site. This "brewery" combines — or its original combined — the solidity of red-brick Victorian architecture with a heavy, elaborate roof line that somehow suggests a Japanese temple. At the other end of the mall, past an open-air atrium with a large mobile dangling precariously over the heads of shoppers, stands a quite convincing French chalet. Here and there, its copper gutters stain the otherwise pristine, muted yellow plaster. In this "chalet" (if you can afford it) you can eat French (or perhaps "French") food. Both "brewery" and "chalet" are part of an "imeiji appu" or "image-up" public relations campaign for the Sapporo company, a rare instance of "retro-chic" in a city where modern architecture seldom traffics in nostalgia.[2]

Although for over four hundred years Tokyo has been the country's de facto political capital, material remnants of the city's past are hard to find. Earthquakes, fires, bombs, constant demolition, and rapid rebuilding have scoured these traces of history from Tokyo's urban landscape. With half a million construction companies to be kept busy nationwide, no premium has been placed on the preservation, renovation, or recreation of architectural "theatres of memory," to use Raphael Samuel's felicitous phrase. Almost every structure goes up quickly, meant to last only a few decades. Rare is the individual building, let alone entire area, devoted to recalling the Tokyo equivalent of, say, an Edwardian shopping street.

FIGURE 1. Ebisu Garden Place. Photo: Alan Thomas.

In these circumstances, Tokyo's many museums assume a particularly important role in relation to the visual images crucial to public memory. Indeed, as the city outside obliterates its built history, museums might be seen to serve as oases, pools of time, nourishing the popular imagination and allowing people, by reference to the past, to locate themselves in the present. Yet, as I will argue, these museums are themselves caught up in the question of the value and the status of the Japan's past, and this is especially true of museums o concerned with modern and contemporary artifacts. While the premodern past is cheerfully embraced for its capacity to represent "Japan" in ancient ceramics, Buddhist statues, or woodblock prints, more recent history is treated gingerly.

Given Tokyo's fraught relationship with the past, it may be fitting that the capital's preeminent museum of photography, which opened its spacious Ebisu building on January 21, 1995, stands between facsimiles of other ages in a postmodern wonderland where time is bent and twisted back upon itself. Already, even before you enter the museum, the value of preservation is questioned throughout the city and the issue of reproduction raised by the very architecture of the museum's immediate surroundings. Inside, this diffidence toward the past is underscored. Indeed, the TMMP's exhibitions during the building's first year can be read as oblique arguments about the appropriate relationship between photography and time, and about Japan's national identity as it relates to modern history.

I had first visited the Tokyo Metropolitan Museum of Photography with no broader purpose in mind than seeing its current offerings. However, the photographic exhibitions at this museum and others raised insistent questions not about the images themselves but about how the images were being contextualized for and presented to the public. It became apparent from conversations with curators and from observing their work that a subtle contest had developed between those, on the one hand, who frame photographic images according to aesthetic and social histories and those, on the other, who see photographs in strictly formal or personal terms. This divide sweeps aside the dichotomy, familiar in Europe and America, between photography as art and photography as document.[3] Instead, in Japan, photography situated historically through narratives of both artistic and social change stand together in tension with exhibitions which insist that history — particularly Japan's history — is irrelevant to understanding photographic images. In the first instance, curators work to contextualize images socially, politically, and aesthetically. In the second, they celebrate the essence of the image outside the vagaries of time.

While this contest — never fully articulated as an open debate — is interesting in itself, the wider importance of the rift between history and anti-history becomes apparent against the background of the troubled year 1995, the year the TMMP opened. That year's troubles included the deepening peril of the Japanese banking system (teetering from bad loans made during the 1980s "bubble economy"), the sharp rise of the yen against other currencies, the deadly Sarin gas attacks on the Tokyo subway system by the bizarre Aum Shinrikyo cult, the political turmoil caused by a weak coalition government, and the Kobe earthquake, which revealed the government's desperately inadequate preparations for this inevitable form of emergency. Added to these woes, and perhaps most potent of them all, the fiftieth anniversary of Japan's defeat in World War II recalled an unexplored past.

For decades after the war, the image of the economic wonder kid of Asia protected Japan from considering its past. Japan knew itself through the medium of its astounding GNP figures. This postwar identity obscured the prewar reality of militarism and empire in the minds of many Japanese, and of Western leaders as well, although other Asian countries tended to forget less easily. The end of the "economic miracle" in conjunction with the fiftieth anniversary of the war's end and accompanying pleas from Japan's neighbors for apology and recompense raised once again the fundamental question of the nature of the Japanese nation. Does Japan need to face the recent past — both good and bad — to know itself, or can Japan's national essence be secured through a form of cultural nationalism that is remote from historical change? [4] Is Japan a nation in the making, or is it a nation whose distinctive characteristics do not change with time? These questions, voiced in many venues, necessarily filter into art museums, since they are essentially questions about the relationship between culture and nation, and culture and time. During the summer of 1995, the problems of Japan's relation to modern history and of photography's relation to time converged in striking fashion.

This article focuses on the Tokyo Metropolitan Museum of Photography through its opening year, tracing the submerged but pointed disagreements over history that marked its various exhibitions. In describing these exhibitions, I will not move sequentially through the year but will analyze two anti-historical exhibitions first (-ism '95: The 1st Tokyo International Photo-Biennale and Objects, Faces, and Anti-Narratives—Rethinking Modernism) [5] and place them in the context of photography shows elsewhere in Tokyo. I then return to the TMMP and efforts of other curators there to create visual histories in the Tokyo/City of Photos and The Founding and Development of Modern Photography in Japan exhibitions. My purpose is to distil and clarify the tension over photography's nature and function against the broader national concerns over Japan's modern identity.

'-ism '95'

During its new building's inaugural year, in a bold and imaginative bid to claim a place for itself in the international world of photography, the Tokyo

Metropolitan Museum of Photography initiated a biennale series, modeled in part on European and American biannual shows. -ism '95: *The 1st Tokyo International Photo-Biennale*, consisted of the work of fourteen artists selected by a five-member international jury. According to the show's catalog, these five jurors spent three intensive (and, undoubtedly, exhausting) days culling six prizewinners and eight other exhibitors from 17,221 images submitted by 2,172 photographers from fifty-seven countries. Concentration must have been at a particular premium during the three-day judging period of "voluntary confinement"[6] from March 20 to March 23, since the outside world was coping with the Sarin poison gas attack on Tokyo's subway. Despite the anxiety sweeping Japan in the wake of this atrocity and their own staggering task, the judges managed to select an interesting range of work by mostly quite young artists from ten different countries. Among the group were three artists from Japan, two from Germany, and two from the United States, one of whom was a native of Poland and the other Japanese-American. As an exercise in self-conscious internationalism, the process appears to have been successful.

There was no reason to expect this biennale to make a cohesive statement, since there were neither extensive criteria for entering the competition nor a stipulated theme. Despite the title -ism '95, implying interest in particular ideological and aesthetic commitments, curatorial commentary takes "ism" to mean personal style rather than the articulation of broad social and artistic theories. In his exhibition notes, Nakamura Hiromi of the museum staff comments: "Since we had not defined a theme for the exhibition, there was only one theme left: the characteristic of individuality and the -ism that the artist espouses. . . . To open the exhibition to all -isms would invite chaos — but in a sense, that summarizes this 1st Tokyo International Photo-Biennale."[7] Three of the judges in their own separate statements also focus on the diversity of individual approaches. To look at the end result of all the judging, however, is not merely to be confronted by a predictable multiplicity of individual styles. Indeed, it seems quite possible to interpret the show as conveying — with startling precision for so much chaos — an exact and particular message. This message is not as evident in what is there as in what is not there, in a troubling and insistent aporia at the center of TMMP's first biennale.

Indeed, viewing this exhibition reminded me of watching Marcel Marceau, the famous French mime, outline the contours of an absent object. With graceful and deliberate movements, Marceau's hands can trace an invisible shape, bringing it to our mind's eye in uncanny concreteness. Just as vividly, although not, it seems, consciously, -ism '95 traced an absence. That absence was the history of Japan.

The only way to be precise about what was so visibly absent from the show is to describe what is present within the fourteen bodies of work that it comprised. Almost all these works are meditations with historical overtones; these artists are in fact conspicuously interested in commenting on history and the problem of how to place the past within the present. Some of these meditations are overt. For instance, Reinhardt Matz makes black-and-white photographs of the sites of former concentration camps in his series, *The Invisible Camps: Fifty Years Later.* The combined beauty and horror of his photography is not macabre aestheticism, but rather a direct attempt to come to grips with the presence of that past — a message underscored by the final picture in the sequence, in which pupils stand crowding around their teacher on the mist-shrouded grounds of what we know to be Dachau only from the wall label.

Japanese-American photographer Osamu James Nakagawa, who writes that his viewpoint is "Eastern in origin and Western by immersion,"[8] also contemplates history overtly. In Nakagawa's digitally altered prints, icons of American history—Vietnam veterans, the KKK, Martin Luther King, and beauty queens — are transposed to the screens of broken-down drive-in movie theaters and wayside billboards.[9] The only hint of his "Eastern" viewpoint in *-ism '95* was a picture of the half-destroyed clock tower at Hiroshima projected onto a giant television screen high above Tokyo pedestrians. In the context of the series, even this image resonates less with Japan's history than with what Nakagawa calls his "critical inspection of Western society."[10]

Other artists in the exhibition play with the shadows of time in less didactic, more imaginary ways. The series *Babylone*, by Frenchman Thierry Urbain, won first prize with its fabricated scenes of ancient Mesopotamian courts and sand-scoured, empty monuments stark against a desert sky. The titles *Sancuaire d'Hammurabi* and *Porte de Sumer* combine with images of imaginary cosmographies and the austere abstraction of the photographs to suggest the grandeur and fragility of historical ambition and, perhaps, a longing to return to a golden age. In a more contemporary vein, Tse Ming Chong of Hong Kong portrays the atmosphere of Hong Kong's Victoria Harbor through thirty-five-millimeter transparencies positioned in strips against the windows in TMMP's foyer. Since each exposure represents a passing day and each strip a week, the twelve sequences resemble a yearly calendar, making visible the sound of the ticking clock of Hong Kong's last years as a British colony. Tse Ming Chong has translated the famous dictum of Roland Barthes — the camera is "a clock for seeing" — almost literally.[11]

In another poignant meditation on contemporary history, Croatian Boris

FIGURE 2. Installation shot of Tse Ming Chong's sequence. Photo: Alan Thomas.

Cvjetanović presents a series of exquisite black-and-white prints of domestic objects and quotidian urban scenes that he entitles *Scenes Without Importance*. Cvjetanović, with an eye for rich textures and playful shadows, evokes a world of quiet value in cities the newspapers tell us are far from quiet. The titles—*Zagreb, Dubrovnik*, and other place names in the former Yugoslavia —punctuate the apparent serenity framed by the black border of each print. Calling these precious scenes "without importance" becomes an ironic political commentary on the world's helplessness before the turmoil in the Balkans. Their seeming lack of historical worth underscores the brutal relentlessness of the history in which they are enmeshed. Along with Matz, Nakagawa, Urbain, and Tse, Cvjetanović uses the camera as a tool for engaging the dialectic between past and present.

Regardless of the images and words of the photographers, the jurors of the competition and Nakamura of the TMMP staff insist upon a depoliticized, dehistoricized reading of the exhibition and of its individual contents. For instance, Nakamura glosses Cvjetanović's title, *Scenes Without Importance*," as meaning "'unimportant to others,' 'unimportant to the photograph,' or both at once." Deaf to any possible irony, Nakamura insists that Cvjetanović's pictures have nothing to say historically or politically but rather are "consistently individualistic. No matter what the subject is, it always bears the shadow of his own mentality."[12] Juror Kim Seung-Kon, a lecturer at Hongik University in South Korea, also strains to deny the social and historical charge of the photographs in this show: "The true significance of international cultural exchanges, one of the important functions of an art museum, is to transcend differences based on regional and ethnic backgrounds, history and religion, gender and generation and to capture a common body of artistic values."[13] The criterion of artistic worth used by himself and, as he tells us, by all the judges, was "the level of emotional involvement expressed in the works."[14] Only Anne Wilkes Tucker, curator at the Museum of Fine Arts in Houston, Texas, hints that artists might claim a broader purview than pure individual expression in her observation (which ought to be unremarkable) that "artists distil the experiences, issues, and products [sic] of their time."[15] With the possible exception of the lone voice from Texas, it would seem that the jurors and the museum staff quite consciously promote an understanding of artistic expression emptied of social, political, and historical overtones.[16]

Despite this curatorial agenda, even those photographers whose work is devoted overtly to private family life place their concerns within national narratives. Second prizewinner Leon Borensztein tackles this issue directly in his exploration of the loneliness of American families. Whatever the jurors may say, Borensztein quite overtly claims the role of social critic for the artist. He writes, "It is my belief that the task of an artist is not to applaud, flatter, or judge, but rather to warn, to question, and to provoke."[17] In carrying out this mission, he contrasts America's promise of boundless opportunities with its boundless frustrations, a tension he sees embodied in the broken families and tense individuals who present themselves unsmilingly before his camera. In a separate body of work, which is also part of the show, he meditates on the chanciness of his own family's personal history as he documents his daughter Sharon's struggle against visual and other congenital disabilities. These loving portraits suggest a commentary on fate that sets the individual within the frame of shared social and political histories.

Another exhibitor, Wolfgang Stahr, might also be interpreted simply as a family portraitist, but he too proposes a close connection between private life and public history. Stahr presents color photographs of a five-member eastern German family crowded into the only two rooms they can heat. In documenting the intimate relationships that evolve as Stahr, a west German from Würzburg, photographs this family from across the former border, his work creates a personal echo of German reunification, which is underscored by the series title, given in three languages: *Hōmu*, *Heimat*, and *Home*.

Despite the show's curatorial stance, then, the artists themselves do not divorce personal expression from public concern. Their work points insistently to our embeddedness not only in our own bodies, emotions, and experiences, but in the national and international narratives of which we are also a part. In making social, political, and mythic histories of other places visible, the photographs I have described also outline, like Marceau's fingertips, the absence at the core of this exhibition — the absence of Japanese history as a resource or a matter of interest.

Since four of the fourteen exhibitors have ties to Japan, this absence is striking. As we have seen, Japanese-American Nakagawa's work focuses on America. Of the three native Japanese artists, none concerns himself or herself with Japan's past, and indeed two of them, Takeshita Koshi and Yamamoto Masao, recall European histories instead. Takeshita's images picture rural France at its most romantic. His trees, cows, fields, old stone buildings, and a decaying wooden door exemplify pastoral prettiness. On the other hand, Yamamoto Masao's nostalgia for Europe's past is of a completely different order, and his installation is a bracing departure from Takeshita's straight black-and-white prints. On a large, old-fashioned wooden desk accompanied by an antique chair, Yamamoto places a small, handsome, prewar leather suitcase. Inside the suitcase is a small but conspicuous label listing the colonies supplied by the English company that manufactured it: India, Kenya, as well as place names such as Ceylon that are no longer in use. The atmosphere recalls Somerset Maugham; the desk, chair, and suitcase are so evocative that you can almost see the fevered British civil servant longing for his gin and bitters under an ineffectual ceiling fan. In keeping with the theme of old memories, 145 artificially yellowed and stained photographs of nondescript objects and unplaceable places are stashed inside the suitcase. Ya-

mamoto invites museum-goers to take them out and finger them. Their order, whether in the suitcase or spread out on the old desk, is as unimportant
as chronology usually is to the play of memory. They can serve as templates
for any recollection we happened to cast upon them, but this *Kū no Hako* or
A Box of Emptiness, as Yamamoto calls the piece, is deliberately framed by
the very particular history of European colonization.[18]

In contrast to works of Takeshita and Yamamoto, redolent with the histories of other places, the third Japanese artist and only woman in the group,
Ampo Fumiko, swims in the present moment. Her bright, fuzzy, miniature
color snapshots (eighteen in all) of Tokyo scenes — "flowers, people, grass,
cars, rivers, trees" — are encased in acrylic board and dangle from the ceiling
in three rows. The visitor walks among the rows, trying to make out the translucent, swaying images against the gallery's lighting. With this technique,
Ampo underscores her view of the photograph as "only a square of light."
The work's title, *Kokū o hakaru* or *Measuring the Void*, seems to refer not
only to a translucent light within the photograph's frame but also to her own
sense of internal emptiness. In her conversational "Artist's Statement" for the
catalog, Ampo begins with the question "Am I alive?" In answer, she tells us
that she uses the act of taking photographs — of standing in front of flowers
and trying to press the shutter, as she puts it — to create a moment when light,
hands, and picture come together. When this happens, she writes, "I have a
faint feeling that maybe I am alive after all." [19]

Ampo's sensibility recalls the involvement with the present of Japanese
novelist Yoshimoto Banana, a woman of about the same age, who also tries
to grasp life through the medium of impressionistic sensation.[20] Paralleling
Yoshimoto's use of casual and deliberately unartful language, Ampo's loosely
composed photographs affect a from-the-hip spontaneity. Like Yoshimoto
Banana, she refuses to cloak her art with pretensions to social and political
commentary.[21] Living in the spacious blankness of a present unstructured by
memory, Ampo claims that she must struggle to realize her own faint existence. Without any history to anchor it, the individual subject appears as indistinct as the "flowers, people, grass, . . ." that Ampo captures on film. Indeed,
Measuring the Void is most provocative as commentary on the historical void
at the exhibit's center.

The TMMP's first biennale provided a brisk introduction to the vexed
question of photography's appropriate role in the construction of historical
awareness. Despite curatorial emphasis on transcending historical specificity,
most of the artists in this show had insisted through their work that the present
is sustained and shaped by the past. Several of them had specifically urged

the view that the personal is also social and political. By and large, this diverse group of photographers had chosen to engage not just an art-historical past but also political and social pasts; yet Japan's history was scrupulously avoided by native and foreigner alike. Why this reticence? One possible explanation, of course, is merely the chance workings of one multinational jury. Although this exhibition was the one that first piqued my curiosity about the uses of photography as history in Japan, it alone was hardly the basis for firm conclusions. Further observation, however, suggested that these judges' reluctance to engage history in this international show was hardly unique or coincidental.

'Objects, Faces, and Anti-Narratives — Rethinking Modernism'

Running concurrently with -ism '95, another major exhibition at the TMMP, Objects, Faces, and Anti-Narratives—Rethinking Modernism, was presented in three parts from April 1995 through January 1996 in the central galleries of the museum. Here it was not only Japanese history that was effaced, but histories of any sort. The anti-narrative effect promised by the show's title was achieved by displaying a great many photographs and arranging them so as to frustrate any chronological or historical sense the viewer might be inclined to impose on them. The first room of the exhibition contained a hodgepodge of photographic and even prephotographic images ranging from Noël-Marie-Paymal Lerebour's 1841 engravings of ancient Syrian sites to NASA moonscapes. Other rooms displayed photographs organized under the rubric of "objects" and then of "faces" as the museum rotated its large permanent collection throughout the exhibition's ten-month run.

This curatorial strategy had the interesting effect of dissociating any individual image from the events it might represent or from any artistic development it might embody. The connections between the prints on the walls were strictly formal, based principally on the shape within the frame. For instance, a sequence in the Objects installment on display from April to August invited the eye to move from the oval form of an egg, to the oval form of a spoon, to the rounded form of an electric fan, and on to pears and apples with their rounded shadows. Vision was lulled by repetition of the circular form. How easily and lightly the eye then glided over Kawada Kikuji's photograph of a soiled Hi no Maru, the Japanese flag associated with militarism, with its round center suggesting the sun. Other circles, too, appeared. Another Kawada image titled A-Bomb Dome — Ceiling and Sky draws the eye up through the oval remains of the tower at Hiroshima that partially withstood the atomic blast. Curated in the context of "objects," the image is taken to be compelling not by what it might convey about nuclear horror but by tendentious formal resemblances to a series of unrelated still lifes.

Although the exhibit's title promises a "rethinking" of modernism, the catalog essay of prominent photographic historian and critic Iizawa Kōhtarō argues merely that a discussion of modernism is "doomed to end in complication and confusion." [22] Beyond pointing to the two formal elements of "cropping" and "repetition" that he takes to be essential to modernism, he shrugs off any attempt to redefine the movement. Nor does curator Kasahara Michiko offer us any revisionary guideposts by which to understand modernism. By choosing a range of works from early-nineteenth-century travel engravings to Sandy Skoglund's contemporary installation photographs, from early Japanese experiments in pictorialism to Morimura Yasamasa's gender-bending self-portraits, she flattens the history of photography into a single undifferentiated epoch. Kasahara tells us that "it does not mean very much whether a particular work is in the modernist or postmodernist style," [23] and it is clear that this principle extends to the show's handling of the pre-modernist, the pictorialist, and indeed all categories except those broadest designations of subject matter, "objects" and "faces." Kasahara thus effaces documentary history, technical evolution, and aesthetic development. The resulting show succeeds in being anti-narrative, leaving us in a continual present from the moment that photographic processes were invented. Altogether, this exhibition was remarkably consistent with -ism '95 in its diffidence, if not hostility, toward using photographs to create social, political, and aesthetic histories.

Photography Exhibitions Outside the TMMP

The curatorial stances of the two photography exhibitions at the TMMP during the summer of 1995 resonated with the resistance to historical recollection found outside the museum. In particular, the question of how to mark the fiftieth anniversary of the end of the war plunged the highest levels of government into turmoil. Arguments among the three parties in Japan's uneasy coalition government over the substance — and even the date — of a memorial ceremony highlighted the lack of consensus in Japan about what was to be remembered and even the value of memory itself. [24] A mild resolution apologizing for wartime aggression had failed in Japan's legislature, the Diet, earlier in the spring. Finally, at an August 15 news conference, Prime

Minister Murayama Tomiichi expressed his "heartfelt apology" for the "tremendous damage and suffering to the people of many countries, particularly to those of Asian nations" caused by Japan.[25] Although this apology had the unanimous agreement of the cabinet, many ministers immediately undercut it by visiting the controversial Yasukuni shrine to pay their respects to the deified Japanese military dead, some of whom were responsible for that same "tremendous damage and suffering." Ambiguity about the content and importance of national commemoration persisted at national and international levels.[26]

In the face of official discomfort with this one aspect of national history, the Tokyo photography world appeared hesitant to insist on history of any kind. Curators hung back, reluctant to court controversy, possibly because taking any politicized stance might have immediate effects on funding: public museums in Japan are ultimately under the control of the conservative Ministry of Education.

The reluctance to historicize was a phenomenon not only at the TMMP that summer, but also at other public museums. One prime example was the first exhibition of the new Department of Photography of the National Museum of Modern Art, Tokyo. Running concurrently with the TMMP shows described above, this exhibition, entitled *Photography and the National Museum of Modern Art, Tokyo, 1953–1995*, flirted with the possibility of an aesthetic history of Japanese photography. In the end, however, Masuda Rei, the museum's first curator of photography, saw his task as defending photography's claim to the status of high art, which he did by hanging selected photographs in isolated splendor rather than as part of a story of changing visual styles, a record of the shifting role of the artist, or any other possible narrative. The exhibition featured the achievements of established photographers Kimura Ihei, Domon Ken, Ei-Kyu, Ueda Shoji, Ishimoto Yasuhiro, Tōmatsu Shōmei, Moriyama Daidō, Ishiuchi Miyako, Sugimoto Hiroshi, Shibata Toshio, and others. Many of these works are beautiful, some playful; most are famous.[27] Under Masuda's careful curatorship, their neat chronological order asserted at best a continuum of creative productivity without suggesting relationships among the photographs or between the photographs and the contexts in which they were made. In this way, with these ninety-four works by twenty-five Japanese photographers, Masuda canonized Great Japanese Photography.

Canonization is, of course, a form of history, but one that suggests there are certain works that transcend time and contain a beauty or truth remote from passing idioms of aesthetics and philosophy, let alone social and political history. Canonization is the form of history that most denies the historicity of any work, because genius, axiomatically, rises above mortal constraints.[28] In his creation of this compendium of talent, Masuda has defended photography against the skeptics, especially in Japan, who claim that the photograph should have no place in the art museums that serve as the treasurehouses of the nation's visual heritage.[29] He has insisted that photography of the past has a brilliance that we should continue to admire in the present. In one sense, then, he has returned photography to history. On the other hand, the history he suggests is of a very rarified kind, hardly belonging to the quotidian world. As Masuda himself makes clear, works of genius defy context; "what we need to do now," he tells us, "is to begin to recognize that there is no inherently correct site for a photograph and that a photograph can be nothing other than a photograph whatever the circumstances."[30] As such, these canonized images present only themselves, forbearing to enter the fray of recollection and contextual interpretation.

Other smaller museums and photography galleries, some of them private, might have been expected to feel a rebellious urge to engage modern Japanese history in that silent summer of 1995, but they too were quiet. The Meguro Museum of Art, run by the local ward office, drew crowds with a display of Domon Ken's photographs of the ancient temples in Nara and Kyoto but declined to exhibit his wartime propaganda work. The private Hara Museum, one of the leading proponents of contemporary Japanese art, offered a show curated by American Robert Nickas called *Pictures of the Real World (in Real Time)* in which Nickas juxtaposed Kawara On's "date paintings" (each consisting literally of a date, say "Dec. 2, 1979," painted on canvas) with well-known American photographs from around the designated time. Other private galleries likewise avoided modern Japanese retrospective themes.[31] If, as Raphael Samuel suggests, pictures "provide us with our stock figures, our subliminal points of reference, our unspoken point of address,"[32] the pictures available to the public in Tokyo photography galleries provided few visual points of reference to Japan's experience of the twentieth century.

The single exception that I came across was in Gallery One's *Tokyo-Tokyo* show of July and August 1995, which hung Gochō Shigeo's gaudy, color *Familiar Street Scenes, 1981* alongside Kuwabara Kineo's atmospheric black-and-white views of the rough-edged street life of *shitamachi*[33] theaters, parks, and shops from the 1930s. Kuwabara's brooding photographs supplied a nostalgic contrast to Gochō's contemporary vibrancy. Placed side by side, the two bodies of work contrasted the forms of sociability and wealth to be found on Tokyo's streets half a century apart.

The historicity of Gallery One's *Tokyo-Tokyo* exhibition seemed at first apolitical, steering clear of the problematic issues of war and colonization. It seemed to have managed this delicate maneuver despite exhibiting photographs from the 1930s, when Japan aggressively extended its hold on Asia, and despite featuring the work of Kuwabara, whose oeuvre includes photographs forthrightly documenting Japanese soldiers in occupied areas.[34] However, a closer look at the titles of Kuwabara's photographs, available on a sheet at the gallery desk rather than with the photographs on the walls, proved that the selection had not avoided war images entirely, as I had first surmised. Although most of Kuwabara's images bore only the name of the Tokyo building they depicted, the title of the largest picture in the show proved an exception. This photograph was greatly enlarged, four times the size of the others in the show, but without the title its atmospheric muted-gray tones and indistinct forms suggest little beyond a generic snowy winter sun touching the horizon and silhouetting a few men standing in the foreground. Its title, however, reads *Kōjimachi-ku, Babasakimon, Ni ni roku jiken tōji, 1936* [At the Time of the February 26 Incident, Babasakimon, Kōjimachi-Ku, 1936]. For those who remember the salient dates of that decade, the reference makes the blood run cold. The February 26 Incident was a violent coup attempt by right-wing army officers to "rescue" the emperor, who was, according to their lights, in the thrall of timid advisers and military leaders unwilling to speed the advance into Asia and too deferential to the few spiritless civilians with whom they shared governmental authority. Kuwabara's rising or setting sun — it is impossible to know which — hints at the aura of uncertainty that hung over Tokyo during those three days before the young officer's superiors moved to quell the mutiny. Only when the lack of broad support for the coup in naval and financial circles became evident did the authorities stymie this murderous attempt to push national policy along an even more aggressive course.

Like a whisper in a hushed space that cuts louder than a shout, the presence of this image made all the absent images in all the other galleries more apparent. Curators at TMMP and elsewhere had avoided representing the war during the fiftieth anniversary of its end and, it appeared, in avoiding the war had avoided representing the modern past in any form. The techniques used were various: a curatorial emphasis on personal expression in *-ism '95*; an insistence on formal content in *Objects, Faces, and Anti-Narratives — Rethinking Modernism*; the canonization of the genius in *Photography and the National Museum of Modern Art, Tokyo, 1953–1995*. Each of these techniques positions the photographic image in such a way that it becomes an element of the present where memory can find no foothold. Like much else in the

FIGURE 3. Kuwabara Kineo, *Kōjimachi-ku, Babasakimon, Ni ni roku jiken tōji*, 1936 [At the time of the February 26 Incident, Babasakimon, Kōjimachi-ku, 1936]. Courtesy of Kuwabara Kineo.

city of Tokyo itself, these photography exhibitions provide no spur to measure the distance between now and then.

The power of Tokyo curators to effectively defuse photography's ability to represent modern history underscores the fact that photography's relationship with the events it records, indeed with time itself, is not inherent in the medium. To some, including contemporary critic John Berger, this connection between photography and history has seemed innate. Berger argues forcefully that photography's world is the public world of events. He insists that the photograph always gestures outside itself because "photography has no language of its own. One learns to read photographs as one learns to read footprints or cardiograms. The language in which photography deals is the language of events. All references are external to itself."[35] What Tokyo's exhibitions demonstrate is closer to the reverse of Berger's proposition: photography cannot gesture outside itself unless the world lets it. That world — the world of curators and of national agendas — can deny photography's historicity and disallow its public gestures. The summer of 1995's exhibitions prove as much. Even Gallery One's subtle reference to wartime politics through the Kuwabara photograph, which dramatically energized the exhibition's broader account of urban change, could be ignored. Indeed, critic Iizawa Kōhtarō in his brief essay on the exhibition failed to mention this image.[36]

The Founding and Development of Modern Photography in Japan

In this atmosphere where curating images as reservoirs of public history was discouraged, a few startling voices of dissent emerged to suggest that the calm surface of Japan's art world is in fact more fraught than it appears. Not all the staff of the Tokyo Metropolitan Museum of Photography felt that photographs were best divorced from history. In fact, both of the two shows with which the museum opened its new facility in January 1995 — before the difficult fiftieth-anniversary summer — suggested a critical role for photography in marking change and providing perspectives on the past. Both of these earlier shows embraced history in its political and social aspects *and* its art-historical aspects.

One of these exhibits, *Tokyo/City of Photos* (January–March 1995), dedicated itself to recent photographs of the capital, but even with this seemingly contemporary mission, an understanding of photography emerged that respected its capacity to grapple with the city's metamorphosis. Photographers such as Hayashi Takanobu and Nagano Shigeichi struggle to gain perspective on the writhing behemoth of Tokyo, as it grows grotesquely during the bubble economy of the 1980s and after. This engagement with Tokyo, a city seen as a "configuration of memories and landscapes" that "dramatically acts out its history of rebirth and development,"[37] has political overtones since these pictures are taken to "cast images of a future Tokyo in high relief."[38] Almost all the show's twelve artists consciously juxtapose past and present. Taken together, their art is neither purely personal, nor presentist, nor formalist, but a critical, affectionate portrait of a great city in the middle of great changes.

The second of these opening shows, *The Founding and Development of Modern Photography in Japan*, also running from January through March, embraced history even more overtly than *Tokyo/City of Photos*. The catalog's foreword tells us point-blank that "this exhibition takes the view that the history of modern photography is part of the history of modern Japan."[39] In other circumstances, this pronouncement would seem prosaic and banal, but given the tension in Japan over the relationship between culture and nation it takes on the gloss of radicalism. Curator Okatsuka Akiko's sophisticated and deliberate commitment to historicizing photography combines a narrative of technical advances with aesthetic, social, and political change. The story she orchestrates moves from early-twentieth-century pictorialism and the emphasis on self-expression to the late 1920s and 1930s when advertising, mass culture, and photojournalism pushed photographers into an awareness of their social roles. She argues that the history of photography is neither a self-contained aesthetic chronicle nor a compendium of Greats; rather, it is related to the larger history of Japan through the emergence of new, modern forms of subjectivity among photographers.

Modernity, for Okatsuka, is a consummate value; for her, it is the development of a conscious individualism that begins with an awareness of the inner self and expands through recognition of the dynamic between subject and object that allows photographers and others to focus upon wider social issues. To support this point, she quotes Ina Nobuo, who in the inaugural issue of the 1930s photomagazine *Kōga* wrote, "Those who hold the camera must never forget they are social beings."[40] While the exhibition remained dedicated to the photographs themselves, it framed them in this historical narrative of burgeoning modern consciousness.

To anchor modern photography in a history beyond aesthetic styles alone, Okatsuka must date modernity. The modern (*kindai*), she argues, consists of those years from "the rise of Taisho Democracy, with its respect for the individual as a human being" to the beginning of the contemporary (*gendai*) period—in other words, from 1922 to 1945. She has not only positioned photography within the history of Japan in general but by extending her range to 1945 has also placed it in relation to the great unspoken darkness of Japanese history—the war. The expressive richness of modern Japanese photography is seen both in contrast to and in continuum with the war, which she calls "a tragedy arising from the strains of modernization" leading to "the collapse of everything that had been built up over the previous decades."[41] Her narrative has the elements of classic tragedy, which, through recounting, provides catharsis.

Okatsuka's deliberate recollection of the war seems to release curatorial creativity. The complexities of modernity, both its light and dark sides, are explored on the walls of the museum in a suggestive national narrative. Each individual image is enriched by its relation to other images because this curatorial context directs our attention not to shapes alone or to sheer excellence, but to the whole complex of style, composition, and content within the frame and to the aesthetic ideals and political experience outside it. Recollection of the war also releases photography's powers of contemporary political commentary. By giving Japan and Japanese photography a past, Okatsuka suggests that artistic creativity can do more than simply affirm the present; it can structure future possibilities. The relations between subject and object, she suggests, are not only formal artistic devices, but political positions as well. The narrative that Okatsuka has created projects a continuing national chronicle open to popular participation.

It is difficult to discuss individual images from *Modern Photography in Japan* since it included in its purview not only 241 photographs but photographic illustrations from books, magazines, and posters as well. Demonstrating an appreciation for photography produced in and for contexts remote from the art world, Okatsuka's exhibition moves fluently between artistic and commercial photography, personal expression and public propaganda, images of aesthetic and journalistic power. The exhibit ends with a series of covers from illustrated magazines such as *Nippon*, *Hōmu Raifu* [Home Life], *Manchuria Graph*, and *Front*. Many are unquestionably propagandistic but most are mild in their heroic and bloodless scenes of smiling seamen far from battle, of industrial might, and of calm civilian life.

Okatsuka herself takes particular pride in nine images, mostly portraits, from the *Wandering Jew* series. These photographs, produced by six members of the amateur Tanpei Shashin Club, depict displaced European Jews living briefly in Kobe on their way elsewhere. Most of these deeply sympathetic black-and-white pictures have been lost from public view since the club's *Twenty-Third Tanpei Exhibition* in May 1941, and it has only been through Okatsuka's careful research and the generosity of the photographers' families that so many have been recovered.[42]

As it happens, Masuda Rei's *Photography and the National Museum of Modern Art, Tokyo, 1953–1995* show also exhibited two of the photographs from this series by the amateur photographer Shiihara Osamu, including the one titled *Nap*, in which an exhausted refugee is curled up fully clothed in suit and fedora. This coincidence permits a direct comparison of the effect of curatorial emphasis on the reading of an image. While Masuda's canon-making agenda emphasizes the beauty and formal power of these photographs, it also deprives the *Wandering Jew* series of its capacity to suggest social and political narratives. The TMMP exhibition, on the other hand, trains our eye to see the series simultaneously as revealing, in Okatsuka's words, "the interiority of the photographer" and "the inner turmoil of the Jews."[43] By exhibiting more pictures from the series, by placing these pictures in the context of other works attempting to come to terms with problems of subjectivity, and by insistently recollecting the world war that forced these Jewish refugees out of Europe, the TMMP's *Modern Photography in Japan* dem-

FIGURE 4. Shiihara Osamu, *Nap*, from the *Wandering Jew* series (1941). Courtesy of Shiihara Tamotsu.

onstrates greater faith in both photographic and curatorial power than does Masuda's proposition that "a photograph can be nothing other than a photograph whatever the circumstances."

Observing the fundamental tension in Tokyo's museums between curators who use photographs to create histories and those who do not prompts two conclusions, one about the role of museum curators and another about the power of national concerns to shape culture.

In his essay "Photography," German film critic Siegfried Kracauer makes perhaps the most cogent case against the notion (which we have seen articulated by John Berger above) that history and time inhere within the photograph itself. As Kracauer argues, although a photograph may seem to be "a representation of time," "time is not part of the photograph."[44] Unmediated, no collection of photographs necessarily produces a meaningful history. Indeed, the raw accumulation of images has the capacity to kill meaningful narrative, as was evident in the exhibition, *Objects, Faces, and Anti-Narratives — Rethinking Modernism*. It is in their handling of images that the power of

photography curators lies. Curators can release images to function historically as points of reference for the viewers' engagement with the past, or they
can highlight the qualities of these images in such a way that the photographs
fail to intersect with any dialectic between past and present. In other words,
photography curators create histories not from necessity but from desire and
from aesthetic, social, and political commitments. If this desire is not present, the photographs themselves will not by themselves emerge as resources
for public recollection.

A second conclusion to draw from Tokyo's 1995 photography exhibitions
is that the globalization of the art world has not yet erased the way concerns
over national identity shape cultural consumption. Photography is internationally ubiquitous, and yet it is made to speak in the voice of the nation and
to resonate with national concerns through museum curatorship, especially
where museums are as closely supervised by government bureaucrats as they
are in Japan. The question of photography's ontological relation with time
cannot be answered abstractly or globally since politics, particularly the politics of national identity, intercedes in this relationship. In a nation as yet un-
decided whether to confront its actions in the 1930s and 1940s, much less how
to represent them, the camera's capacity to hold a mirror to this century becomes suspect. In Japan, the difficulty over how to remember the war leads
to sidestepping much of the twentieth century in representations of the
nation, and commandeering pre–twentieth century images as sources of
illumination for the present. The desire for amnesia creates pressures that
pervade arenas far away from international relations and school textbook
controversies where the issue of war remembrance is generally discussed.
The upshot is a disquiet that permeates the museum world as it tries to come
to grips with the art of the twentieth century through one of its most powerful media. With the fundamental basis of Japan's national identity at issue,
Japanese art museums will not be clean, well-lighted spaces abstracted from
their particular national locale.

The world of photographic exhibitions is as elusive and ephemeral as the
"decisive moment" that Cartier-Bresson worked to capture on film. Trying
to map this shifting terrain can be a lesson in the fragility of cultural production. Exhibitions in museums and especially in private galleries vanish,
sometimes in a week, leaving at best a difficult-to-obtain catalog, brochure,
or leaflet. The citywide conjunction of images at any particular time is also
very difficult, if not impossible, to reconstruct in retrospect. And yet, this
ephemeral world is the first line of engagement with issues at the heart of intellectual history: debates over the nature of history, the nature of the nation,

and history's relationship with culture. These issues were, and continue to be, vibrantly and forcefully explored in the catalogs and on the walls of Japanese photography exhibitions.[45]

Although curators rarely direct their criticisms at one another — never attacking another curator by name in print, at least that I have seen — the tension is palpable between those who resist historicity and those who wish to engage it. From their position in mainstream cultural institutions such as the TMMP, curators such as Okatsuka who wish to examine Japanese history can begin to change standard assumptions about national identity. They are unlikely to attract the blaring sound trucks and midnight threats of Japan's ultranationalist right wing as do direct critiques of the imperial house or of wartime atrocities.[46] Nevertheless, such exhibits and such curators offer an important challenge to the lure of wearied forgetfulness. They break the pall of silence that hangs over a national culture that, in refusing a modern past, stymies creative controversy about what it is to become in the future. If successful in suggesting a sense of national identity rooted in recent histories, these curators are poised to present many possible alternatives to Japan's image of itself.

7. Realizing Memory, Transforming History

Euro /American / Indians

> I identify myself in Language, but only by losing
> myself in it like an object. What is *realized* in my
> history is not the past definite of what was, since it is
> no more, or even the present perfect of what has been
> in what I am, but the future anterior of what I shall
> have been for what I am in the process of becoming.
> —Jacques Lacan, *The Language of the Self*

Several years ago I invited Native American Indians into three Los Angeles museums — the Gene Autry Western Heritage Museum (now the Autry Museum of Western History), the Southwest Museum, and the Los Angeles County Museum of Natural History — and videotaped their interactions with museum exhibitions of their own culture and history. Those persons who accepted my invitation were culturally and politically active in various Native American communities, and most are California Indians indigenous to the greater Los Angeles area, members of groups that have been regarded by anthropologists as *extinct*. All of these people speak English as a first language and share the material culture of late-twentieth-century Southern California. But these indigenous persons also live by separate realities that are in some ways invisible to Euro-Americans. These realities are grounded on the memory and knowledge that the European colonization of the land is not now, nor ever will be, complete.

My fieldwork resulted in a thesis in which I described how subtle differences in language use by the American Indians in the museums constitute fundamentally different theories about communication and representation. I focused on the viewers' responses to museum exhibits as part of the multiple contexts and meanings in which these exhibits, documents in a narrative of colonization, can be read from different standpoints.[1] Attention to differences in remembering was part of that work, and I intend to explore here how those different kinds of memory also constitute different standpoints within historical narratives.

I have continued to interact with indigenous people as they remember the land as their own and remember themselves as indigenous persons living in the present. Visiting museums, talking over kitchen tables, praying together in ceremonial circles, sitting by the pool, huddled together in sweatlodges, shopping with our children, and encamped on the radioactive ground of the Nevada Test Site, Native American Indians often have said to me: "We don't study the past, we live it." This statement is more than a platitude, it is a declaration of a culturally shared sense of a future anterior and of memory's strong agency for organizing the present and the embodiment of the future as well as representing the past.

In the English language, *memory* denotes a habitual knowing that allows us to *recall* the signs and skills we use in everyday life: words, names, techniques, locations, things. In a more specific sense, memory, together with language, is the knowing ordering, the *remembering*, of events in time. The narrative organization of remembering constitutes the temporal relationships of events and the possible and probable causality of their interconnections. Linguists and anthropologists are aware that humans have a wide range of ways of ordering time,[2] which in turn have specific consequences for social and psychological relationships.

For many American Indians,[3] even those who do not speak an indigenous language, remembering is understood as not only the passive recall or representation of events gone by, but also a creative action instantiating the present and prefiguring the future. Active or passive memory cannot be straightforwardly associated with either Euro-American or American Indian traditions; such sweeping generalizations will always break down when one looks at specific instances of memory use. But recognizing structural differences in memory practices leads to a more articulate recognition of subtle distinctions in what may otherwise be assumed to be similar memories of shared events. This recognition affords a more detailed and *reflexive* comparison of the psychocultural practices of memory.[4]

A reflexive, cross-cultural comparison of memory practices is the inversion of the assumption that the object of inquiry — memory — precedes the documents that produce it: texts, signs, images, things, bodies, and their culturally shared signification. When we compare memory practices, we are comparing different uses of networks of cognitive, representational, and communicative practices. Culturally specific memory practices can be compared not on the basis of a thing called memory, but on the basis of the uses of documents and signs and their significance, including temporal and causal strategies, and how memory itself is understood and categorized in specific cultural traditions. We can begin by noting that in European traditions, memory exists within a whole series of ways of knowing: cognition, thinking, memory, imagination, vision, creativity, fantasy, and dreaming, among many others.

In contemporary European and American traditions these ways of knowing are ordered hierarchically, from illegitimate through increasingly legitimate ways of knowing reality and the truth. This hierarchical ordering is also a process of constituting reality and truth as the singular, legitimate way of knowing. From a logocentric standpoint, memory, so necessary for the so-called higher cognitive practices, is also a potentially subversive mode of knowing because it so obviously uses as its medium not only the representational tools of words and images, but also all the senses, the body itself, to remember. In effect, memory denotes a process of somatic reflexivity that recalls for us that the object of its inquiry, the past (and/or present and future), does not completely precede the documents, or body, that produce it. A desire to avoid subversion may be why memory for many contemporary persons of European descent is primarily about elsewhere — the past — and is not explicitly a way of also knowing the present and the future, as it apparently was for some Europeans in the Middle Ages.[5]

In the European and American traditions, texts, and archives, the representations of history, and especially the institution of museums, make the past, and the memories of that past, possible. They do this by ordering material signs according to very specific assumptions about what memory is and how it may be used. Bringing American Indians into museums brought a potentially subversive memory practice into those archival institutions: materials memory. Richard Terdiman has taken up the topic of materials memory in the framework of Marxist analysis:

Just as Marx has claimed that under capitalism the power and creativity of the worker seem to pass into the tool, here memory appears to reside not in perceiving consciousness but *in the material*: in the practices and institutions of social life, which strangely seem not to require our participation, and still less our explicit allegiance. . . . The analogy of such a "materials memory" would be nothing more grandiose than the materials memory which keeps the crease in our slacks or allows plastics to resume their shape after they have been deformed. . . . "[M]aterials memory" [was] produced in the innovative form of the nineteenth century's increasingly powerful information media. . . . this structured experience of confusion naturalized new forms of non-organic cultural and perceptual contents. . . . "[The newspaper] is built by addition of discrete, theoretically disconnected elements which juxtapose themselves only in response to the abstract requirements of 'layout'. . . ." I could as well have said that what I termed "newspaper culture" produced a new and more abstract form of memory. Newspaper culture puts that paradigm of natural memory into crisis by excluding the context which makes memory function for us.[6]

Terdiman is describing two kinds of materials memory. The first is the literal sense of the materials memory of the crease in one's slacks. The second is the kind of materials memory in which materials have an agency (and power) that remembers. Terdiman recognizes the importance of materials in the process of labor and also in the process of memory. But he conflates materials memory with a particular kind of dissociated memory. Newspapers may predispose us to abstract, dissociated memory, but do not compel us; there are multiple ways to read the newspaper, and/or museum exhibits. It is precisely a *connected* reading of a newspaper-like juxtaposition of museum exhibits that at times made them so offensive, or so hilarious, to some American Indians. And these connected readings can be combined with an acknowledgment of the agency and power in materials themselves, resulting in substantially different ways to remember, and substantially different memories.

Differences

My work with American Indians was motivated by my own reactions to museum displays that I thought dispossessed American Indians of their culture and history by placing indigenous artifacts behind glass and by narrating their histories in the context of an ethnographic extinction. I invited American Indians into museums because I thought they felt dispossessed and could articulate those feelings with authority. But they did not feel dispossessed, they remembered and lived their past very actively, and with humor, in spite of some very grim circumstances they found in the museums. In fact, most of them managed to appropriate the images and words of the museums to their own ends, turning the museums inside out in the process.[7]

I found that many American Indians have a kind of "materials memory" that even the most ideologically objectionable exhibits cannot repress. This came across in particularly powerful ways at the Southwest Museum located in Los Angeles. The Southwest Museum was founded in the early part of the twentieth century and is dedicated to the exhibition of the culture and history of indigenous people of North America. Its mission-style building is a well-known landmark between downtown Los Angeles and Pasadena, and under its present leadership the museum has also become noted for support given to Native American communities nationwide. In a gallery installed in the mid-1980s called *The People of California*, fluorescent-lit vitrines line a medium-sized room, packed with artifacts, ritual paraphernalia, and every-day household items. Above the vitrines, large black-and-white photographs of California Natives, the ancestors of people I know, loom in an eerie ethno-graphic twilight. Without descriptive titles or names, these photos suggest an archetypal stasis, moments out of time. Across from the entrance, one corner of the gallery displays a fraction of the museum's collection of California bas-ketry. Near this corner is a vitrine in which are displayed three woven baby carriers. Next to these baby carriers, in the same vitrine, but displayed on a different panel, are artifacts from the genocide of Native people that coin-cided with the Gold Rush of Northern California: a handgun, an iron cruci-fix, a gold pan, a gold scale, a powder flask, handcuffs, and nesting weights. When one American Indian woman, Helen Herrera, came upon this juxta-position she startled me by exclaiming, "That's a fucking obscenity!" I looked toward where she pointed, but I saw only three baby carriers and some things from the California Gold Rush.

She told me that the baby carriers are made out of natural materials by pregnant women, who pray over them while making them; that the baby car-riers are used by infants for the first months of their lives; that the baby car-riers are still ceremonially connected to those people and their families; and that that kind of thing should not be next to things made out of metal, things made by a different culture, and things made for punishment and violence. Aside from the offense taken at the juxtaposition of these articles, I found none of the above to be new information. But Helen Herrera had obviously been deeply offended, and she was determined that I would, despite whatever cultural differences might exist between us, understand what she was tell-ing me.

Another woman, on another day, viewed the same exhibit and responded in a lower key: "That's weird." When I asked why, she replied: "Well, they don't belong together, the cradleboards. . . . [pause]. . . . they make it themselves."

Two American Indian men, on separate occasions, objected to the display by focusing on the Euro-American artifacts instead of the baby carriers. One man began by saying: "Shouldn't be here," a statement he turned into a joke (on me) after I asked exactly what he meant: "Shouldn't be here in the whole continent!"

A third woman, Cindi Alvitre, responded to this exhibit with the following: "That's even questionable to have baby carriers in here because — that's something that stays within the family. . . . there are a lot of prayers and when those are being made it's a ceremony. So the spirit of that child is there. Yes, it is a contradiction. I hope they are learning more — but I don't think the museum people realize the symbolism and the subconscious thinking and energies that are going into people when they are making this. This is saying that this doesn't matter — to jump from this to that."

If memory is a particular use of documents — the material signs — of the past, then it should be obvious from the above that there are fundamentally different ways to remember based on fundamental differences in attributing meaning and causality to material signs. For most Euro-Americans, things exhibited in museums stand metaphorically for events that took place in the past. For some American Indians, things exhibited in museums *are* events that took place in the past and are still taking place; they are artifacts that carry the material traces of events of the past into the present. Many Euro-Americans read exhibits like texts, as a series of discrete signs having an arbitrary but shared meaning. Placing baby carriers next to handcuffs, gun, and crucifix can mean nothing more than the juxtaposition of separate words or chapters, building blocks for a larger narrative. But for the consultants, the juxtaposition of artifacts that carry the living traces of that past means something else, something very obscene. The American Indian people I have quoted above understood this exhibit as not only having symbolic, metaphoric, or metonymic relations to events of the past, but also constituting an icon of events still taking place. Exhibiting baby carriers next to a gun has the same meaning as placing an operational gun in an operational (Indian) baby carriage — in effect, continuing the genocide the museum wished merely to record. To read the exhibits with the latter, iconic, meaning, as did some American Indians, is also to read these exhibits according to principles of contiguous causality rather than according to those of abstract similarity or association:[8] things that are touching are causally linked, and things that are physically separated are not. Time and again in my fieldwork, I was presented with surprising, and sometimes very humorous, readings of museum exhibits that made sense according to the principles of contiguity rather than those of similarity and association.

Roman Jakobson suggested in the 1950s that the principles of contiguity and similarity are used together at all levels of language structure, and in language use. He also recognized that one principle may be artificially privileged over the other by social and cultural conventions. Jakobson also suggested that European and American academic traditions, especially those dealing with the interpretation of texts, suffered (in the 1950s) from something akin to "contiguity disorder," which he described as an unbalanced focus on associative and metaphoric meaning at the expense of the metonymic, which "based on a different principle, easily defies interpretation."[9] Contemporary research in cognitive reasoning suggests, as did Jakobson, that associative thinking and contiguous thinking are inextricable. One study of "magical thinking" has been especially suggestive. Cultural psychologists Rozin and Nemeroff took up the problem of contiguous metonymy and found that laws of contagion do not operate in young children (at least in the domain of disgust) and therefore do not afford the assumptions of primitiveness in the sense of an early developmental stage. They find rather that the

cognitive basis for contagion is, in fact, quite sophisticated. Most certainly essence is invisible, and perhaps, insensible. Thus, the principle of contagion is built on the premise that things are seldom what they seem or that appearance is not equal to reality. As we will indicate in the discussion of the development of similarity, the equation of appearance and reality . . . is indeed a simple and primitive aspect of mentation.[10]

Both contiguous and associative thinking can be cognitively sophisticated, and both have logical traps inherent in their uses. Rozin and Nemeroff link this nominal realism with a developmental, or childish, way of thinking that becomes less salient but does not disappear with age: "Through the age of six years, children believe that the name is inseparable from the referent. Up to the age of nine or ten, children continue to believe that things must have a name."[11]

Nominal realism is based on the principle of similarity, not contiguity. Both associative and contiguous thinking can afford either cognitive mistakes or cognitive sophistication. Materials memory linked to contiguous casualty is not necessarily a cognitive pathology but is part of a semiotic continuum of diverse possible ways for communicating and making sense. Terdiman partially theorizes materials memory but does not acknowledge the always present possibilities of contiguous materials memories, no matter how dissociated the materials themselves may appear. This is perhaps an example of Jakobson's point: contiguous meanings have been systematically excluded from European and Euro-American interpretations. American Indians' statements suggest that contiguous materials memories have spiritual (Terdiman might say conservative) implications. The powerful agency and bodily experiences of the contiguous materials memories of some American

Indians suggest that these memory practices involve differences that have to be understood on their own terms. Memories are always partially created in the process of representation and communication, and this process of creation depends not only on what documents we use, but also on how we use them for sharing experience. Therefore, understanding how different people use different documents to share different meanings requires understanding the fundamentals of how we make sense out of things and events. Understanding how we make sense out of things and events, understanding materials memory practices on their own terms, entails understanding different ways of realizing memory as well as different ways of transforming history.

There are two relational and interdependent organizational functions that underlie all communication; *referentiality*, the distinction of subjects, objects, and qualities; and *transitivity*, the attribution of agency, causality, and context to subjects, objects, and qualities. In addition, there are two modes in which these functions can be fulfilled: *speaking*, the use of arbitrary symbols for communication; and *doing*, the attribution of meaning to actions and events. Speaking and doing, like referentiality and transitivity, are inextricable categories but also critical heuristic distinctions. Taken together, these four generate four conceptual strategies.

1. The *referentiality of speaking* is the use of codes of all sorts to distinguish subjects and objects. Speaking entails language, but language is not necessarily a linguistic code.

2. The *transitivity of speaking* is the attribution of causality, agency, and context. Transitivity is accomplished through language but not necessarily on the terms of linguistic structure. As a process it can be characterized as *thought*.

3. The *referentiality of doing* is the accomplishment of relationships through *interactivity*, and the shared cultural and social assumptions about the meanings of presence and process that mark out subjects and objects as distinctly as the referentiality of language.

4. The *transitivity of doing* is the realization and attribution of agency and causality to somatic sense, the transformation of the body into the bodily grounds of shared sense and meanings, including those of memory practices. The transitivity of doing, which I call *embodiment*, is the most reflexive, and also the most occluded, strategy of communication.

Language, thought, interactivity, and embodiment are all entailed in materials memory, and materials memory can fulfill these functions in very distinct ways. Euro-American literate memory practices—histories—have sometimes taken note of American Indian materials memories as practices, but such practices are usually regarded as that which simply fails to fulfill the functions of referentiality and transitivity in a correct or familiar way. However, the materials memory of some American Indians can be understood as positive differences for realizing memory.

Referentiality / Language

As America becomes more comfortable in redeploying its Indian myths, the more invisible we become as people. This is true even if— or more likely, especially if—we are allowed to participate. One wants, of course, to develop ideas for effective strategies for intervention in the American narrative. It is not a narrative about us. It is absolutely not about us. There is nothing to correct, no footnotes for us to add.
—Jimmie Durham, "Cowboys and . . ."

Another story of materials memory took place in the Spirit of Conquest Gallery of the Autry Museum of Western History (AMWH). The museum, a 150,000-square-foot institution, was established in Los Angeles in 1988 and is dedicated to a high-tech representation of at least three Western heritages: geography, cinema, and civilization. Indian history and culture are represented there in the Spirit of Conquest Gallery; not surprisingly, the AMWH can be a palpably anxious place for living Indian visitors.

For example, in the gallery's final audiovisual display a tall man with sharp features, dressed in fringed buckskin, appears on the screen to pronounce, with great dignity, lines that begin, "My ancestors once roamed free," and end, "Now we are scattered as dust in the wind." Watching this with Helen Herrera and indigenous Californian Marcus Lopez, I heard Herrera gasp at the moment of the man's appearance: "That's a white man!" while at exactly the same time Lopez said in a loud but descending intonation: "Oh shit!" The clean-cut middle-class family that was sharing the dark viewing recess with us decided at that moment to move out of the gallery into the light of the foyer.

At the AMWH, Indian people and their histories are subsumed into existing narratives of cinema and television that are based largely on the conflict between the federal government and Indian Tribes in the nineteenth century. The Spirit of Conquest Gallery, for example, is partially a shrine to

General George Custer, well known for his definitive defeat at the hands of a band of Lakota and Cheyenne warriors in 1876 who were defending their sacred Black Hills — theirs by treaties already signed, as well as by indigenous right. To the left of the entrance to the Spirit of Conquest Gallery are three wall vitrines dedicated to General George Custer and Captain Myles Keogh, both of whom died in the battle of the Little Bighorn. Perpendicular to the wall is a vitrine containing six mannequins in costumes from the late 1800s. The mannequins suggest how we might understand the relation of the historical figure of Custer to his contemporaries. In a not-so-subtle ranking of ethnicity and gender, the mannequins consist of an officer's wife (a Euro-American woman); a member of the cavalry (an Afro-American man); a "mountain man" (a Euro-American man who dresses and behaves like a Native American); a scout (a Native American man who makes himself useful to the army); a warrior (a Native American man); and a "forcibly adapted" person (a Native American woman). Following the Indian woman, but outside the vitrine, stands a desiccated but nonetheless anthropomorphic eight-foot-tall saguaro cactus. At its foot, this label:

When people of different cultures meet they often fight — especially if their way of life seems threatened. Sometimes individuals adapt to the newcomers, however, and attempt to live in peace. In either instance, change is inevitable.

The cactus visually suggests that the "inevitable change" in question is neither resistance nor adaptation but the inevitable desiccation of Native American culture altogether.

The rest of the gallery leaves little doubt as to the entelechy embedded in the "inevitable change" mentioned in the saguaro label: the Plains Indian way of life was finally transformed by the railroad, stage coach, pony express, and telegraph, subjects to which the second half of the Spirit of Conquest Gallery is devoted. The inevitability of change is suggested to be the inevitability of progress, the inevitability of the triumph of technological sophistication: the manifest destiny of the "civilized" races.

When I brought Helen Herrera to visit the gallery, I thought that perhaps she too would take offense at its condescending lineup. I watched while she examined the indigenous clothing very carefully and then moved on to the other vitrines. When it was obvious that she was not going to comment, I asked what she thought about the label copy at the foot of the cactus.

She told me: "Sometimes individuals adapt to the newcomers and in an effort to survive, because they have to, but I do agree that change is inevitable. The problem with a facility like this is that they perpetrate misinformation, and you know, children, especially children who are particularly vulnerable, will come in and internalize this, this may be all they see. They lump us together with Native Americans, just like they lump the South with the term Hispanics."

I asked her: "Wait a minute—you mean different tribes?" She answered: "Like what happened between the Lakota and the buffalo, and what happened to the Mescalero at the Bosque Redondo. They were not minor, they were major events, that have changed the whole face of this land as we know it, and it has carried on spiritually to not only our people, but their own today."

The memories evoked by this exhibit for Herrera are radically different from my own. I had *read* Native Americans as ciphers placed against others —those of civilization. I had read this gallery as based on metaphoric principles of similarity and equivalencies, as eristical, a form of dialectical synthesis in which one pole of the dialectic is subsumed completely. I had read them as the representations of the past, from a standpoint disconnected from that past, with rhetorical metaphors. Herrera too had read the exhibit, and she made a critique of its representation— "They lump us together with Native Americans" (they don't recognize the diverse and distinct groups we represent)—but she also *remembered* the figures as the effects of historical events connected to both our lives.

Helen Herrera does not only study history, she lives it, and she brings a problem of representation into focus: she realizes a distinction between referential representation and historical events for which she claims spiritual effects. She is addressing me within a system of representation in which the people and their events cannot even be properly named— "they lump us to together"—but she is also saying that, despite this repression and forgetting, there are effects: the Mescalero, her own relatives and ancestors, and the Lakota, the people of her teacher and friends, have survived events that "have changed the whole face of this land as we know it, and it has carried on spiritually to not only our people, but their own today." The arrangement of the figures in the vitrines was of little consequence for Helen Herrera: what interested her was the work, the production and craft, of the buckskins that several of those figures wore. Using the same documents for representing the past, she re-members differently, and consequently re-members a present in which I only partially share. She has a "materials memory" that I do not, which is not to say that the memory afforded by my perception of the organization of these figures is wrong, but only quite different, and affords a quite different relationship to colonization.

I was confused at the time of our conversation about the exact referent of "us" in "they lump us together." When I asked her for clarification, she said in part: "They were not minor, they were major *events*, that have changed the whole face of this land as we know it, and it has carried on spiritually to not only our people, but their own today."

This did not clear up my confusion but compounded it, because I took the referent of "it" (has carried on) to be the *events* she mentioned, which would naturally take a plural verb. Not only was "it" ambiguous, but her final use of "their" in "their own today" was equally ambiguous. Was "their" a pronoun referring to the Lakota and the Mescalero? Or to Euro-Americans? Or both? Herrera looked at me for a long while as if to gauge, or engage, my comprehension, which was slight.

In other transcripts of museum visits, I noticed that the word *it* was used as a singular pronoun for a plural referent by other American Indians, producing what for me was an unusual effect, but representing also the inimitable style of what has been called "Native American English." [12] Take, for example, the response of another American Indian woman to the baby carriers, quoted above: "Well, they don't belong together, the cradleboards . . . [pause] . . . they make it themselves." This "it" either takes an indeterminate referent, thereby producing a non sequitur, or is ungrammatical.

Ultimately I realized that the usage of an ungrammatical *it* in the transcripts from my fieldwork was always in contexts that constructed the referent of *it* as possibly *ceremony*. *Ceremony* is what "they make themselves." Helen Herrera's "it" refers to a historical / ceremonial process, one that has "changed the whole face of this land." The activity of ceremony makes sense of these *its*, but taking all these examples together the word *ceremony* itself is mentioned only once. These people may be using the word *it* as a referent for a process that is only partially glossed by the English word *ceremony*.

But *it* is not just a reference to something that the English language does not and cannot properly convey; *it* may also instantiate a way of knowing and remembering different from my own. This practice of memory may entail a different, indeterminate use of English: references aren't supposed to be clear, and *the process of referential indeterminacy itself may be the referent.*

It is important to understand this use of referentiality not as a lack or an absence, but rather as a positive difference. Indeterminate referentiality may be a necessary part of remembering specific kinds of events that mark the land and people in the present. But the consequences for Native uses of referential indeterminacy as a practice of remembering have to be understood in the context of choices about transitivity, participation, and embodiment.

Transitivity / Thought

Just as materials memory may involve a positive use of referential indeterminacy, likewise Native American Indians' materials memories may involve particular uses of intransitivity that are in effect a transitivity that is both passive and active, and yet different from either. This is most easily shown by comparing American Indian ways of framing the agency of materials with European and American practices. Recall Terdiman on materials memory:

Just as Marx has claimed that under capitalism the power and creativity of the worker seem to pass into the tool, here memory appears to reside not in perceiving consciousness but *in the material*: in the practices and institutions of social life which strangely seem not to require our participation, and still less our explicit allegiance. . . . The analogy of such a "materials memory" would be nothing more grandiose than the materials memory which keeps the crease in our slacks or allows plastics to resume their shape after they have been deformed.[13]

There are two obvious differences between Terdiman's analysis of materials memory and indigenous practices. First, for some American Indians materials memory may not be necessarily grandiose, but can be definitely more significant than a physical property of matter as this is normally understood. For example, Cindi Alvitre said: "I don't think the museum people realize the symbolism and the subconscious thinking and energies that are going into people when they are making this [baby carriers]."

Alvitre also commented on a shaman's stick in the Southwest Museum: "the simplest things are the most powerful." For some American Indians, materials memory is more than something that allows slacks to hold their crease, it is *energies* and *power* that emerge in reciprocal relations of participation between materials and humans.

Second, the nature of *reciprocity* between material and people marks a fundamental difference between how materials memory is understood by Terdiman and the material remembering of some American Indians. Terdiman's analysis recalls that in capitalist relations "the power and creativity of the worker seem to pass into the tool"; Marxist analysis links this passage with an agency in which the worker is not a conscious participant, resulting in alienation and mystification. Alvitre explicitly suggests that energies go from materials "into people," as well as implicitly suggesting that power goes from people into materials.[14]

The idea of energies going into people seems curious to most Euro-Americans, not only because it attributes agency and sentience to what are supposed to be inert materials, but like Terdiman's construction, it is an intransitive construction where we might normally expect a transitive one: energy is put into people *by* materials, or power and creativity are put into the tools *by* workers. Analogous to the use of referential indeterminacy, the use of intransitivity by American Indians can be understood as a lack, an ambiguous passivity. But certain kinds of intransitive constructions, not only in grammar but also in narrative interpretations of events, may be neither wholly active, passive, nor intransitive, but rather are a third way to attribute agency to the documents of the past. This kind of agency is called the *middle voice* by linguists and is intimately connected with ceremony:

According to the classic example, given by Meillet and Benveniste, the verb to sacrifice (ritually) is active if the priest sacrifices the victim in my place for me, and it is middle voice if, taking the knife from the priest's hands, I make the sacrifice for myself. In the case of the active, the action is accomplished outside the subject, because although the priest makes the sacrifice, he is not affected by it. In the case of the middle voice, on the contrary, the subject affects himself in acting; he always remains inside the action, even if an object is involved. The middle voice does not, therefore, exclude transitivity.[15]

A middle voice potentially displaces an active/passive polarity, with consequences for both philosophy and politics:

And we shall see why what is designated by "difference" is neither simply active nor simply passive, that it announces or rather recalls something like the middle voice, that it speaks of an operation which is not an operation, which cannot be thought of either as passive or as an action of a subject upon an object, as starting from an agent or from a patient, or on the basis of, or in view of, any of these terms. But philosophy has perhaps commenced by distributing the middle voice, expressing a certain intransitiveness, into the active and the passive voice, and has itself been constituted in this repression.[16]

The middle voice accommodates very specific kinds of recognitions of the reciprocal transformative effects between people and things, and the acknowledgment of a grammatically improvised middle voice in English is critical for the comparison of practices of memory. Documents, and other signs of the past, can be understood not only as the causes and/or effects of past actions, but also as subject to reciprocal transformation between people and things in the present. Some American Indians have persuaded some museum curators to ceremonially *feed* certain ethnographic objects that are kept in museums and that are regarded by American Indians as sentient beings. These sentient beings are treated as if they have energy and power that can turn destructive if they are not properly tended, and that is beneficial when they are properly tended. This ceremonial feeding is both a recognition and a remembering of power and creativity that has passed, and is still passing, between the object and the persons that have and will come into contact with it. These recollections, the passings of power and creativity between artifacts and caretakers, do not produce unconsciousness and alienation for American Indians. Euro-Americans usually assume that these ways of remembering, and the pasts they recall, are ahistorical fictions. Some may regard Western history in a similar fashion, but few regard the two traditions—American Indian and Euro-American—as equivalent in truth-fulness. I am not arguing that American Indian practices of memory are true, only that they are different, and that they need to be recognized, articulated, and understood, not only as relative but also as relational to European and American personal and institutional practices of memory.

Referentiality/Activity

Both indeterminate referentiality and middle voice transitivity are conducive to specific kinds of remembering, or in Helen Herrera's words, "carrying on spiritually." These ways of representing memory, and of giving significance to the documents of memory, are organized by cultural and ceremonial structures of participation that, like indeterminacy and a middle voice, can be hard to recognize and harder still for many academics to acknowledge as anything other than mystification. Again, recall Terdiman on materials memory:

[M]aterials memory" [was] produced in the innovative form of the nineteenth century's increasingly powerful information media. . . . this structured experience of confusion naturalized new forms of non-organic cultural and perceptual contents. . . . "[The newspaper] is built by addition of discreet, theoretically disconnected elements which juxtapose themselves only in response to the abstract requirements of 'layout'. . . ." I could as well have said that what I termed "newspaper culture" produced a new and more abstract form of memory. Newspaper culture puts that paradigm of natural memory into crisis by excluding the context which makes memory function for us.[17]

Newspapers do not necessarily exclude the context that makes memory function for us; they could alternatively be regarded as providing a new kind of context. The "particular abstract layout" of the museum exhibits is precisely what Alvitre finds both objectionable *and* meaningful, and her strategy for "reading" this juxtaposition depends on the same strategy of meaningful connectedness that attributes sentience to the baby carriers. What allows her and others to re-member artifacts as sentient is a kind of memory resistant to forgetting the context that is repressed, forgotten, or unconscious/unarticulated for the typical newspaper reader or museum visitor. She read *across* the exhibits at the same time I read them *down*, connecting panels that I isolated. Other consultants consistently read exhibits across; sometimes the results were considerably more amusing than they were in the case of the baby carriers.

American Indians are heirs to different traditions of literacy than are Euro-Americans, and many American Indians today have different ways of reading the past, which one could argue is more often experienced and represented as a "structured experience of confusion" than not. For example, American Indian material documents of the past constitute a continent-wide palimpsest; some artifacts and documents have been excavated and exhibited, but many are still in place. Native American Indians active in cultural resource issues would like to have a say in what happens to American Indian historical artifacts as increasing real estate value and future urban development inevitably encroach upon their present archival status. For these people, the cultural resource struggle is a struggle to use materials memory — to read and remember — in ways that are culturally significant for their indigenous traditions.

The materials memories of the indigenous past, present, and future exist all over the Los Angeles Basin, not only in the collections of museums and universities, but also at as yet intact dwelling sites, shrines, caches, pictographs, petroglyphs, cemeteries, caves, springs, and rock shelters — ultimately, everywhere underfoot. I once listened to a Chumash woman and practitioner of indigenous religion and medicine, A-lul'Koy Lotah, try to explain to an attorney how the Chumash interpret the legal meaning of "cultural resources of significance." Lotah, always an animated speaker, addressed the lawyer a bit more forcefully than usual: "Things that are there *are* significant. *They are there because the culture put them there, and they have to be there for the culture to be there.* And whoever lives there has to respect it. They either feel part of the place or they are going to be floating in and out."

When Lotah said, "Things that are there *are* significant," she was rejecting the law's, and the lawyer's, attempts to hierarchize significance. It was all significant to her, no matter how ubiquitous the objects might seem to the archaeologists, no matter how worthless and insignificant they might be to the developer with millions of dollars at stake. "They are there because the culture put them there, and they have to be there for the culture to be there." Lotah pronounced "for the culture to be there" in such a way as to make it clear that she meant "for the culture to be there *now*," as it has been *there* for several millennia, and will be there for several more, if she has anything to do with it. The artifacts, no matter how unspectacular from a scientific point of view, mark the land with the contiguity of occupation, from thousands of years ago to and through the present. The fact that the Chumash still retain a very specific claim to the land is made altogether clear in her following sentence: "And whoever lives there has to respect it." That is, whoever happens to hold abstract title to the land still has to pay respect to the caretakers and original occupants, who placed their things, their culture *there*, thereby linking those things and placings to present-day Chumash culture as well as present-day occupants. "They either feel part of the place or they are going to be floating in and out." Lotah was making a reference to the ways she expects the new residents to feel part of the place: historically, culturally, and *psychically*. Again and again A-lul'Koy Lotah and her husband, Kote Lotah, both indigenous religious practitioners and *a'tis-win*, indigenous Chumash medical doctors, have insisted they have the well-being of the future residents of the site in mind when they negotiate either the avoidance of artifacts or their proper ceremonial removal under the supervision of Chumash monitors and/or spiritual practitioners. To "be floating in and out," certainly a ghostly metaphor of unconnectedness and placelessness, is a condition Lotah intimates to be as potentially dangerous as it is unpleasant.

A-lul'Koy Lotah's statement also raises two critical points for the examination of memory practices. First, her assertion that the artifacts "have to be there for the culture to be there" presents an explicit theory about the use of the documents of the past. This statement includes both a *ceremonial* standpoint and the inversion of the assumption that the object of inquiry — indigenous culture — precedes the documents that produce it. A-lul'Koy Lotah's standpoint is explicitly ceremonial, that is, it explicitly acknowledges its own engagement in the participatory creation and accomplishment of the past and present as well as the historical or narrative representation of that past. But her statement is also implicitly ethnomethodological; it may be that both Western theory and indigenous practice have the potential for reflexive participation in the representation of the past. However, indigenous ceremonial traditions more actively take the position of the middle voice, "remaining within the action," as practices based more on contiguous causality than on abstract similarity. These differences result in radically different understandings of the transformative possibilities of memory by indigenous persons.

The second important point raised by A-lul'Koy Lotah's statement is that she assumes that the effects of present-day Chumash people's participation in indigenous remembering extend to those who are ignorant of indigenous memory practices. Many reflective Natives, including Lotah, do recognize different consequences for remembering according to their own cultural memory practices and according to those of nonnatives, but it is also undeniable that certain effects of indigenous memory practices are believed by many indigenous people, and by nonnatives as well, to constitute not only the cultural organization of reality, but reality itself. Among Chumash persons with whom I have spoken there are oral traditions about the disturbance of ancestral remains causing sudden torrential rains, illness, or in at least two cases, one Native and one nonnative, death. Natives are not the only believers; folklore among nonnative residents of the Santa Monica Mountains tells of families who have borne generations of ill luck due to their excavation and collection of indigenous artifacts. I can't vouch for the explanatory accuracy of these stories, nor is that the point. These remembrances of precontact realities are based on the same documents as those of empirical archaeology; the modes of interpretation vary greatly, but they share the belief that they both approach the truth.

It is critical to recognize these other memory practices, but they are not alternatives for the totalizing histories of the West, for they themselves are totalizing. But they do have different consequences for remembering, consequences that are inherently no more or less mystifying than those of written history, and no more or less illogical. The ultimate goal is to understand both traditions' practices well enough for individuals of each to engage in dialogue with each other. Such dialogue is critical, both theoretically and politically.

Transitivity / Embodiment

Native ways of remembering, their ceremonial traditions for memory, can recognize the embodied nature of memory more explicitly than do the most common contemporary memory practices of Euro-American persons and institutions. In this, perhaps, they can again be understood as truth-ful, but not as the truth.

We have many senses, and we learn from juridical procedures, social conventions, and cultural traditions, to depend to a greater or lesser extent on specific senses, sight for example, as the most reliable. Dennis Tedlock writes in *Days from a Dream Almanac* about learning a Mayan system of divination that requires becoming sensitive to the small electric charges that run up and down one's limbs. Once one is able to treat these impulses as representational signs within a context of dream images and timekeeping, they become part of a future anterior memory practice that is both prophetic and teleological:

Time and again while writing . . . I have felt a strange sense of relief as I liberated yet another experience from the insistence of chronology, of unilineal time. There are, of course, small-scale chronologies in the poem, with the lower limit at the interval between two successive images in the same dream and the upper limit at 260 days, but returns of day names and numbers make a palimpsest of time itself. Once the palimpsest is formed, events already in place have a way of evoking possible future events, and new events, once places have been found for them, have a way of seeming prefigured.[18]

Our bodies are instruments of knowing, and there are more cultural technologies and semiologies that allow us to know and remember than meet the eye. Obviously, different technologies of the sensorium will have an effect on practices of memory and temporal organizations. Embodied technologies produce bodily documents and signs that can be repressed or acknowledged as somatic sense.

Some Native American Indians say that "the political and the spiritual are the same thing." This conflation of the political and spiritual can be understood as a *ceremonial* standpoint: an explicit responsibility for the day-to-day creation of an indigenous past, present, and future anterior. This is a heavy responsibility, but one that many Native American Indians I have known have taken upon themselves for their people.

I recently heard one such person admonish a group of other Natives: "If you stay in touch with the ancestors, then there is nothing that colonization has taken from you that cannot be returned, including the land." To "stay in touch with the ancestors" signifies, I believe, to stay in touch with, or share, a particular kind of embodiment of the past in the present. Like the baby carriers at the Southwest Museum, the ancestral remains are sentient and living, they carry forward the traces of the past into the present. These ancestral documents of the past literally "stay within the action" of, and embody, an indigenous present, and their disposition powerfully affects that present and future for some American Indians. When some Natives remain in touch, literally, with the ancestors, they place themselves into a future anterior of "what [they] shall have been for what [they are] in the process of becoming," and in that place there is nothing that cannot be returned, including the land. This is a strong statement of the agency for indigenous meaning and remembering and for the subjective and political relationships it can produce. "Staying in touch with the ancestors" is staying in touch with embodied memory, and embodied memory is the use of artifactual documents, including the land itself, in ways that are primarily based on contiguous causality, organized according to multiplexing networks of reciprocal relationships, accomplished by means of ritual participation. One woman, whose ancestors were dispossessed of their material belongings by Spanish, Mexican, and American, colonizers, said to me, "Land *is* family . . . we have always felt so free in our own land."

Embodied knowing and memory is not necessarily *true*, and in fact it can seem quite false to Euro-Americans. The consultation that I and many others have done for the nationwide process of complying with the Native American Grave Protection and Repatriation Act (NAGPRA) has revealed at least several indigenous traditions for hearing bones speak. Talking bones are a kind of historical document that Euro-Americans are not normally prepared to deal with, and for them there is almost no critical or theoretical way to believe that such communication could take place. But talking bones may be a function of different uses and orderings of the sensorium, and not only "fabrication." These and other similar embodied phenomena are beginning to be taken seriously and theorized by medical and psychological anthropologists,[19] again, not as the truth, but as truth-ful and socially, culturally, psychologically, and physically consequential for subjectivity and experience.

Still, embodied knowing is not all-knowing. There are cultural and social standards for the validity of embodied memories, just as there are for referential, historical *facts*. The standards for the former are harder to discern because they are the results of accretions of knowledge resulting from long experimentation within esoteric cultural traditions; because they are dependent upon personal wisdom that comes from understanding and experiencing the fundamental principles underlying the organization of one's universe; and also because these traditions of knowledge and memory are adapting to rapidly changing contexts. The uses of contiguous technologies, like those of empirical knowledge, range from superstition to sophisticated, reflexive awareness. In the most sophisticated and creative uses of ceremony, both ritualized and everyday varieties, there seem to be both logic and consistency; in my own experience, ethnographers are nowhere near to understanding either. Both Native practitioners of indigenous traditions and some Elders ponder these same questions of use. We could attend to their answers which are given in their actions, as well as their words.

Two Traditions, One Continent

Psychoanalysis and historiography . . . thus have two
different ways of distributing the space of memory.
They conceive of the relation between the past and
present differently. Psychoanalysis recognizes the
past in the present; historiography places them one
beside the other. Psychoanalysis treats the relation as
one of imbrication (one in the place of the other),
of repetition (one reproduces the other in another
form), of the equivocal and of the quid pro quo
(What "takes the place" of what? Everywhere, there
are games of masking, reversal, and ambiguity). Historiography conceives the relation as one of succession (one after the other), correlation (greater or
lesser proximities), cause and effect (one follows
from the other), and disjunction (either one or the
other, but not both at the same time).
—Michel de Certeau, *Heterologies*

I have drawn out differences in American Indian and Euro-American memory practices, but only with the intention of intertwining them again. I have juxtaposed Western theory and American Indian theory, academic texts and consultants' speech, not to exoticize the latter but to put the former into context. I have tried to place the two traditions not only into a framework of simple relativism, but also into a dimensional relationality that takes into account the fact that the worlds we remember are in fact tied in secret knots.

From the beginning, my reasons for thinking about museums, memory, and American Indians were to think about the history and relations of colonization, and what roles museums play, and could play, in those relations. Euro-Americans/American Indians not only have different memories of the past, they have different pasts, and consequently, different presents and futures. These different histories and memory practices, and the resulting interrelations, are simultaneously complementary and contradictory. I don't have a solution for the colonization of a continent, but if we choose to work toward local solutions other than termination and extinction, we will have to involve both dialogue and ceremony in a reinvention of psycho-historio-analysis.

Dialogue itself is a material practice and also involves materials memory:

A compelling strain of more recent theory — Bakhtin's — derives its power from a reversal of this generalized decontextualization of social objects and signs. The effect of Bakhtin's theories is to reassert the mediation linking all social objects and signs to the larger cultural system in which their meanings are made meaningful. The basis of such a relations is a "materials memory" within the sign. . . . Bakhtin argues that "the word in language is half someone else's." But this is not conceived as a dispossession. It is rather a liberating recollection of the collective condition of possibility of any language, of any social communication.[20]

Like dialogue, ceremony is a sharing of the meanings of material signs; nothing on which I have written transcends material signs. Both ceremony and reflexive dialogue are memory practices using nonrepresentational, yet material, modes of communication, precisely to remember that representation does not present all that there is in communication while not forgetting that the object of inquiry does not precede the documents that produce it.

Dialogue and ceremony are embodied, material practices of memory holding the potential for effecting material transformations, in spectacular as well as incremental ways. The effectiveness of our participation in both dialogue and ceremony is dependent upon recognizing positive differences in memory practices. Recognizing those differences is related to acknowledging quantitatively different kinds of meanings and uses for language, thought, activity, and embodiment. In North America, for Euro/American / Indians, there are many opportunities to engage materials memories in museums not only as dissociated, and not only as dispossessed, but like the land itself, as shared contradictions: always already half someone else's.

8. Global Culture, Modern Heritage

Re-membering the Chinese
Imperial Collections

Little more than seventy years have passed since the massive wooden doors of the Wu Men (Meridian Gate) swung open to admit ordinary citizens into Beijing's Forbidden City, marking its transformation from imperial residence to Palace Museum. Construction began on this complex maze of imperial palaces in the early years of the Ming dynasty (1368–1644) during the "twilight years" of an imperial state that was born more than two thousand years earlier. Today, for the price of an admission ticket, anyone can walk through the central arch — the southernmost point on a north-south axis formerly reserved for the emperor alone — and wander through the vast complex of administrative and residential palaces that housed twenty-four Chinese emperors over the course of nearly five hundred years, from the fifteenth through the twentieth centuries. Once inside, few visitors notice the peeling vermilion paint or the weeds that grow wild among the bricks that pave the immense courtyards. Instead they strain and elbow their way among the crowds to catch a glimpse of an imperial bridal chamber or a gilded throne. Following a visit to the Forbidden City, Simone de Beauvoir commented on the sacred aura of imperial life that continues to permeate the palace:

The barriers have tumbled. The Forbidden City has become a public place; now everyone strolls freely through its courtyards, sips tea under its porches; Young Pioneers in red neckerchiefs visit the exhibits mounted in its hallways; certain buildings have been turned into palaces of culture and libraries; in another part of it the government has its seat. Beneath this new life invading it the original meaning of the palace remains unimpaired, I seldom succeed in forgetting it.[1]

For most museum visitors, the drama of the renovated late imperial palaces eclipses images of ancient China found in the displays of ancient art and antiquities in the nation's provincial museums — or even the blockbuster shows of rare imperial Chinese art and artifacts that tour major cities in Europe and the United States. In this museum, unlike any other of Chinese art or Chinese history, visitors tour imperial halls so magnificently well appointed that one imagines the emperor might return at any moment to take up where he left off when the monarchy was abolished almost a hundred years ago. Visitors to the museum encounter a simulation of daily life in the imperial court that glitters with opulence and elegance — an encounter that is, as I will argue in more detail below, skillfully orchestrated to guide visitors in re-membering China's imperial past.

The elaborate and imposing former palace complex provides an ideal site for remembering a Chinese past. Brilliant yellow-tiled rooftops present a striking contrast to a rapidly changing urban landscape of steel and glass skyscrapers. A moat fifty meters wide and thick walls ten meters high separate the palace compound from the crowds and chaos of downtown Beijing, lending an aura of mystery and suspense to the walled compound. Inside, the former imperial collections, commissioned and accumulated by Chinese emperors over the course of several millennia, offer material testimony to China's lengthy history of sophisticated technology and superior aesthetic sensibilities. Yet this display of wealth and power is not without irony — particularly under the auspices of a Communist state.

The museum embodies a central paradox of the construction of the past in the modern state: the need to sever the (postimperial) present from the imperial past while maintaining a sense of connection to and continuity with the ancient culture and civilization from which a modern identity is derived. In this essay I explore the ambiguities and contradictions that emerge from the recollection of China's imperial past in the exhibition halls and imperial chambers that constitute Beijing's Palace Museum. I argue that the museum offers a compelling site for asserting state hegemony over the construction of a Chinese past that simultaneously severs the present from an imperial past yet preserves a sense of connection to and continuity with ancient Chinese culture and civilization. The museum serves to resolve the contradictions inherent in constructing a past that is both distant and immediate through the inversion of two seemingly distinct discourses; on the one hand, a global cultural rhetoric of museums and monuments that, in this instance, legitimates local meanings and political processes and, on the other hand, the symbolic rhetoric of Chinese imperial rule, adopted to promote the universality of a Chinese cultural heritage suitable for global consumption. In the museum these multiple discourses intersect, and the state effectively constructs a collective memory of China's imperial past that successfully, but invisibly, re-sists the homogenizing forces of global "heritage" and remains deeply em-bedded in contemporary culture and politics.

A powerful instance of this can be found in the terms used to denote the museum. Only rarely does one hear the museum referred to by its full official designation, Gu Gong Bowuyuan (Imperial Palace Museum). Instead, the title is shortened to Gu Gong (the Imperial Palace) or abandoned in favor of the more "exotic" Zijin Cheng (the Forbidden City). The widespread usage of the latter term is further evidenced by the fact that it serves as the name of both the museum's internal publishing house and the bimonthly magazine it produces.[2] The casual substitution of these various terms collapses the dis-tinction between imperial palace and museum, thus forging a conceptual link in the continuum that will bind the present to the ancient past. These usages also blur the distinction between the imperial palace and the impe-rial collection, thus constructing a symbolic symmetry between the buildings, constructed little more than five hundred years before the collapse of impe-rial China, and the collection of objects amassed by Chinese emperors over the course of several millennia. The complexity of these metonymic usages suggests the range of possible meanings for both local and global representa-tions of the imperial palace and the imperial collections in the construction of a Chinese imperial past.

My inquiry into the construction of collective memory in Beijing's Palace Museum rests upon an understanding of museums as structured ritual spaces within which visitors engage in carefully choreographed ritual practices — generating a limited range of both personal and collective memories.[3] This is not to suggest that visitors do not see, experience, or interpret the museum in different ways. Visits to the museum often engender powerful personal memories, recorded in photographs or on video, or purchased in the form of memorabilia readily available to eager tourists in museum curio stands and gift shops. Yet despite the individual qualities of any particular visit, all visi-tors share the opportunity afforded by modern (postimperial) China — the opportunity for ordinary citizens from around the world to enter this sacred space, the palace formerly reserved exclusively for the emperor and the members of his household and staff. Strolling through the imperial gardens or peeking into the private quarters of the Empress Dowager, all visitors be-come part of re-membering a Chinese past that legitimizes — both locally and globally — the political, cultural, and historical authority of a modern Chinese state.[4]

Negotiating Ambiguities: Memorializing the Imperial Past

In his study of Beijing as a sacred city, Jeffrey Meyer points to the tensions inherent in the museum, noting that maintenance of the palace places the current regime ". . . in a strange and ambiguous position, preserving the elegance and grandeur of the decadent imperial past."[5] Meyer proposes that this dilemma arises in response to the demands of Western tourists, but he also notes briefly the potential symbolic significance of the Forbidden City for Chinese citizens: "I sense an ambiguity in the minds of Chinese who come to their capital. They do not want him back, but the emperor still lives in their imaginations, a reminder of the grandeur and glory of the old 'Central Kingdom.'"[6] Travel accounts by Western visitors—like the one by de Beauvoir cited above—suggest that the palace inspires imaginings of the emperor in many visitors, whether Chinese or not. Yet the question remains: how do contemporary visitors imagine this emperor? And what role does the museum—in the trust of the state—play in generating these images of a glorious imperial Chinese past?

In his highly romanticized account of the palace, Frank Dorn clearly identifies the political potentialities of the museum, as he bemoans the fate of the palace cum museum where the "curious and uncouth" roam unfettered on hallowed ground. This appropriation of the palace to the museum, he claims, clearly serves the interests of the state, "as [no more than] a theatrical backdrop for their own domination. To the present rulers the lacquered pillars and yellow tiles represent an era of history for which they have neither sympathy nor understanding—over five centuries of waste and frivolity that ignored an oppressed and downtrodden people."[7]

While Dorn attributes greater agency to the state—as the source of destruction of the elaborate ritual order and elegance of imperial court life— he fails to explain why the state would appropriate, renovate, and ultimately preserve this symbol of "five centuries of waste and frivolity." In other words, how can we account for the tremendous efforts made to remember—rather than to forget—those centuries of imperial oppression.

The process of remembering in the Palace Museum, in fact, centers around a considerable degree of forgetting as well. Amid the treasures of the imperial court, images of the moral, political, and financial decline of the last dynasty (the Qing, 1644–1911) remain conveniently forgotten.[8] Similarly, nowhere does the palace commemorate the victims of poverty and suffering that surely accompanied such vast accumulations of wealth, as well as the tales of those who fell prey to the corruption, self-indulgence, betrayal, intrigue and other abuses of power that marked imperial rule. Nor does the museum stimulate memories of the rigid hierarchies — between, for example, emperor and subject; gentleman and peasant; men and women; or Han Chinese and barbarian invaders — upon which the exercise of imperial power depended. Instead the museum celebrates centuries of achievement in Chinese culture and civilization — collapsed within the imperial palaces of the last dynasty.

Touted as one of the largest and most integrated pieces of imperial architecture remaining in the world, the museum attracts a broad range of visitors, from those who live only a short walk or bus ride away from the entrance to those who travel hundreds or thousands of miles to see the palace for the first — and perhaps only — time.[9] Entering through the main gates, one sees, for example, camera-clad, travel-savvy white Euro-American tourists, many with only a vague understanding of Chinese culture or history; Japanese visitors; ethnic overseas Chinese "returning" from North America, Europe, Southeast Asia, and even Taiwan, eager to see the wonders of China that they have so often heard or read about; barely literate Chinese peasants on package tours to the capital; as well as the occasional student or scholar of Chinese culture and history. Yet despite seemingly dramatic differences among them — in such terms as race or ethnicity, class background, or cultural knowledge — all the visitors seem to share a sense of awe at this grand imperial structure. As I will explore in more detail below, most visitors who come to the museum do not spend their time inspecting the former imperial collections systematically arranged in modern glass cases and marked with identifying labels. Rather, they seem preoccupied with "remembering" court life in imperial China, represented in this lavishly renovated imperial palace.

The tensions inherent in the construction of such grand memories of imperial China play out in a series of subtle contrasts within the museum. The most vivid contrast resides in the juxtaposition of inside and outside the palace — marking a visitor's passage into formerly forbidden spaces. Once inside, a marked contrast emerges out of the juxtaposition of renovated "period rooms" (*yuanzhuang chenlie*) and "conventional" exhibition halls (*zhuanti chenlie*). Museum guidebooks use the former term to describe those halls and palaces that have been restored to resemble daily life in the imperial households of Ming and Qing dynasty China, while the latter term designates those halls and palaces that now serve as exhibit halls, displaying an imperial collection of art and antiquities dating back several millennia, from oracle bones and bronze inscriptions to porcelain, painting, and calligraphy. The period rooms rest primarily along the sacred central north-south axis, flanked by conventional exhibition halls on the east-west periphery. Another contrast emerges between what is seen and what remains unseen, since a significant portion of the immense compound (as well as the collections) remains invisible — closed to casual visitors. Most visitors never see those buildings that have yet to be repaired or renovated, as well as those that are used as storage space, offices, or residences for museum staff — in other words, the circumstances of daily life in the Forbidden City today. Despite the sense that the palace is now open to public view, that view is carefully circumscribed, and the movement of visitors through the museum is choreographed to provide an unobstructed and unambiguous portrait of China's imperial past.

Constructing a Collective Memory

Visitors entering at the main entrance to the museum on the south must proceed directly north, where they encounter three of the most imposing palaces in the Forbidden City: Tai He Dian (the Hall of Supreme Harmony), Zhong He Dian (the Hall of Middle Harmony), and Bao He Dian (the Hall of Preserving Harmony). Resting upon a three-tiered marble foundation, the three ceremonial palaces that constitute the Outer Court rise dramatically above the surrounding buildings. Located along the sacred north-south axis, these palaces, as well as the three smaller residential palaces directly to the north, formed the locus of imperial ritual and power. Today, all six of these palaces have been renovated with museum period rooms, preserving the cosmological unity of the central axis. This is clearly evidenced in the modified guidebook map (Figure 1) that portrays these six palaces, the main north and south gates, and the Qian Qing Gate, which separates the Inner and the Outer Court, with distinctive architectural designs, in contrast to the other palace buildings, depicted as simple boxes. The schematic map [10] shown in Figure 2 outlines the path recommended to visitors to guide them through the maze of palace halls and courtyards and clearly shows that there exists only one route — along the central axis and traversing the Outer Court — that will lead visitors into the inner courtyards and palaces. [11]

While we begin our journey along a path that follows in the footsteps of the emperor, moving through the formerly forbidden central arch of the Meridian Gate, we quickly experience a subtle shift that moves us slightly off this central axis of power that begins at the foot of the stone foundation upon which the palaces of the Outer Court rest. The delicately engraved Imperial Dragon Carriageway, along which the emperor was carried as he moved in

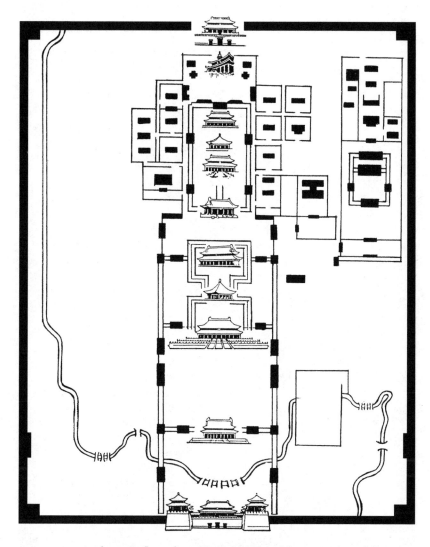

FIGURE 1. A schematic floor plan of Beijing's Palace Museum, adapted from museum and tourist publications, showing only those areas of the palace compound that are open to the public. (Adapted from museum and other local tourist publications. Drawing by Kang Mu.)

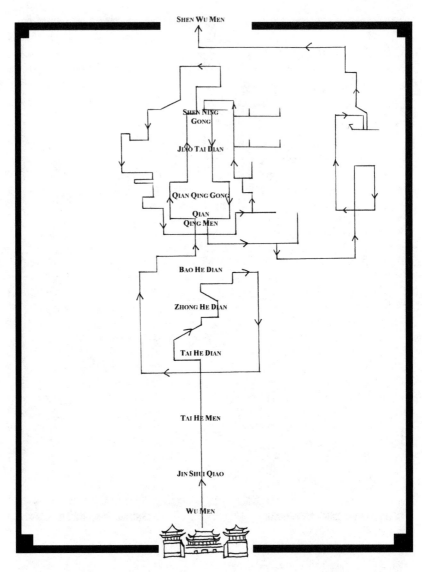

SHEN WU MEN

SHEN NING GONG

JIAO TAI DIAN

QIAN QING GONG

QIAN QING MEN

BAO HE DIAN

ZHONG HE DIAN

TAI HE DIAN

TAI HE MEN

JIN SHUI QIAO

WU MEN

FIGURE 2. A schematic depiction of the comprehensive tour recommended to museum visitors in local guidebooks. (Adapted from museum and other local tourist publications. Drawing by Kang Mu.)

and out of the Tai He Dian, remains cordoned off so that while we can observe the symbols of imperial authority, we are not permitted to imitate the emperors' ascent to the throne.

Similarly, waist-high latticework blocks the doorways of these palace rooms, allowing us to peer in from the outside but not to enter. Nor can we pass through these buildings from one to the next. Instead we must travel along the outside walkways, weaving back and forth across or moving parallel to the critical north-south axis. It is not until we reach the Qian Qing Gate—where the path through the museum grows more complex—that we can begin to make choices as to what we wish to see. However, the beginning of this journey—through the museum's period rooms—has already had a profound impact on both our perceptions and our expectations. Out of these carefully renovated period rooms emerges a "generic" image of imperial life, collapsing thousands of years of imperial China into a few immediate and powerful images.

Daily Life in the Forbidden City

The design of the *yuanzhuang chenlie* does not explicitly celebrate or condemn the twilight years of China's imperial order. It does, however, elicit a sense of imperial grandeur that inspires awe and mystery, most clearly evidenced by the crowds that gather to catch a glimpse of imperial brocade or calligraphy. There are few references—either material or textual—to the specific events that occurred in these palaces or to any of the individuals who inhabited these rooms over the course of several centuries.[12] Instead, the rooms evoke a sense of transcendent timelessness—despite the fact that the architectural style, the administrative order, and the bulk of the objects on display represent only a brief period in China's lengthy imperial history.

The absence of any references to life in the imperial palace on the eve of the emperor's abdication in 1911 further supports an ahistoric image of imperial China, constructing a sizable historical gap that effectively distances the present from a remote past. According to written and photographic accounts of the palaces in the period immediately following the appropriation of the Outer Court by the Republican government, the palace buildings were in a state of extensive deterioration and disrepair. This is in contrast to today, where, as a result of decades of continuous renovation (under both Nationalist and Communist governments), these same palace buildings now stand in better repair then when last inhabited by an emperor. The imperial collections seem to have suffered a similar fate during the final years of imperial rule. Published stories and histories of late imperial times portray the royal household in a state of chaos, with the emperor unwilling and unable to gain control of palace affairs. Rumors circulated that eunuchs and court officials routinely smuggled valuable objects out of the palace, replacing them with shoddy imitations. Many scholars regard the fire that destroyed an imperial storehouse following the establishment of the Republican government as evidence of efforts by palace officials to hide their extensive pillaging and looting of the imperial collections. None of this, however, constitutes part of the collective memory constructed in the exhibition halls of the Palace Museum, where the collections are now cataloged and sizable efforts are made to preserve and document these rare objects and buildings.

Bookstores and curio shops located both within the museum and in the antique and art market in a quaint "historic district" just outside Qian Men (the southern gate of the former Imperial City that enclosed the Forbidden City) offer a broad selection of books that further reinforce this sense of mystery and awe with detailed accounts of the opulence of daily life in the imperial palace. "Tell-alls" reveal the secrets of those emperors and members of the imperial household who inhabited these halls, and travel guides provide visitors with interesting anecdotes about the palace, from imperial architecture to imperial cuisine. A few volumes include a final chapter or two on the museum, although these chapters are generally markedly different in focus, shifting from an anecdotal to a prescriptive narrative that instructs the reader how to visit the museum and view the collections. Although some scholarly work on the founding and history of the museum provides documentation of continued "palace intrigue" among museum staff and government officials, this is noticeably missing from popular accounts, which depict a dramatic shift from chaos, mystery, and intrigue to an efficient and effective professional environment.

Most visitors clearly demonstrate a greater interest in representations of daily life in the Forbidden City than in the treasures of ancient China, as is evidenced both in the patterns that emerge from observing the movement of people through the museum and in the brisk business in books that deal with various aspects of life in the palace while weighty art-historical tomes on ancient art and artifacts gather dust. I gained a clear sense of this kind of "voyeuristic" interest in palace life when I had the opportunity to tour the museum in the company of a historian of late imperial Chinese history. As we toured the palaces of the Inner Court, his detailed account of the symbolism of architectural details, along with stories of the people who lived here and the events that occurred in these halls, attracted a flood of Chinese-speaking museum visitors who eagerly listened to the exotic details of court life and architecture that cannot be found on exhibit labels. But as we moved into the dusty quiet of the *zhuanti chenlie*, and my friend began to talk in similar detail about the calligraphic style evidenced in ancient bronze inscriptions, the crowds quickly became bored and dispersed.

Celebrating the Glory and Achievements of Chinese Civilization

Few visitors wander through the *zhuanti chenlie*; those who do can chat at length about the history or aesthetics of an object on display without being disturbed — or attracting the attention of even one other visitor, let alone a crowd. As I have already suggested, the whereabouts of these exhibit halls are generally poorly marked, and visitors casually wander in and out, perhaps stopping for a moment in a quiet courtyard to rest against an imperial tree. While they may, on occasion, pause briefly to inspect a specific object that has attracted their attention, I did not find visitors striding purposively through these corridors in search of a particular exhibit hall, let alone a particular object. Rows of display cases filled with a seemingly random collection of objects generally fail to stir a visitor's imagination with images of imperial grandeur or palace intrigue — despite the fact that many of these objects could, indeed, tell such tales. This sense of the mundane is further reinforced by the physical condition of the exhibits in these halls. Vitrines that bear the smudged imprint of a prior visitor's hand or nose pressed against the glass in an effort to view an object despite poorly placed and inadequate lighting constitute a sharp contrast to the elaborately renovated period rooms. The condition and location of the *zhuanti chenlie* — along the margins of the central axis constituted by the grand administrative halls that house the museum's period rooms — parallels the marginal position of these objects in the construction of collective memory in the Palace Museum.

Objects exhibited in these halls are generally grouped by "type" (for example, bronzes, porcelain, painting, and calligraphy), in contrast to the functional groupings of objects found in the period rooms. Within each grouping, objects are often then arranged to demonstrate historical developments in technology and aesthetics. In several of the halls the arrangement of these groupings further reflects even wider historical developments, for example, from Zhou dynasty (1050–771 B.C.E.) bronze inscriptions to Tang dynasty (618–906 C.E.) calligraphy or Song dynasty (960–1269 C.E.) porcelain. Other halls focus on objects from the Ming and Qing dynasties, the period in which this palace was in use, with particular attention given to objects of daily life and elaborate gifts presented to the emperor by European nations.

The Lidai Yishu Guan, the Hall of Ancient Art, located near the center of the palace in the eastern and western wings of the Bao He Dian (the grandest of the three ceremonial palaces of the Outer Court) represents one of the most powerful images of an ahistoric imperial past. The hall displays a variety of objects from throughout China's six thousand years of history, including such things as ancient engravings in bronze and bone and examples of the terra-cotta warriors from the grave of Qinshi Huang, the first emperor of China. In this hall, visitors "can be made to realize China's glorious achievements in ancient art and to understand its historical development." [13]

While this display of "ancient treasures" constitutes the largest (and most central) exhibition space in the museum, more than half of the permanent exhibition halls display artifacts from the most recent dynastic periods. The Zhenbao Guan (Hall of Rare Treasures), for example, houses a display of the material culture of ceremonial and everyday life in the Qing imperial household, including objects such as imperial seals, eating utensils, and combs made from gold, silver, and jade. In the Zhongbiao Guan (Hall of Clocks and Watches), extravagant and elaborate watches and clocks — largely of European manufacture — are displayed as evidence of China's history as a world power, able to elicit lavish gifts and "tribute" from foreign nations. In contrast to the broad historical portraits of the glory and achievements of Chinese culture and civilization found in exhibit halls such as the Lidai Yishu Guan, these exhibits inspire visions of the wealth, luxury, and power of imperial China.

The complementarity of these images — of thousands of years of cultural, artistic, and technical achievement on the one hand, that culminates in a brief but expansive period of global power and wealth on the other hand — contributes to dimensions of collective memory that are not found in the *yuanzhuang chenlie*: the construction of the imperial past as "a" time of technological innovation, increasingly sophisticated artisanal skill, and an ever-widening circle of global power and influence. Instead, the complexity of Chinese history — the context within which these objects were both made and used — is collapsed into an ahistoric, generic past that is re-membered in the seemingly random collection of material objects displayed in these halls.

The erasure of the meaning of individual objects, however, is not unique to the Palace Museum but rather a fundamental part of the conceptual structure of museums. In his critique of museums and tourism in Europe, Horne argues that

An art museum is not the place to attempt to see the meanings of old paintings in terms of those who painted them and of those they were painted for. There is not usually any intellectual theme in a collection of paintings. . . . Normally, paintings come together simply through the accidents of collection. For these reasons, tourists with little or no knowledge of painting are expected to pay their respects solely to the fame, costliness and authenticity of these sacred objects, remote in their frames. As "works of art" from which tourists must keep their distance, the value of paintings can depend not on their nature, but on their authenticated scarcity. The gap between "art" and the tourist's own environment is thereby maintained.[14]

As this passage suggests, objects within a museum take on a variety of meanings and become subject to a range of interpretations based on such "simple" technical factors as how, when, and where they are displayed. The polysemic possibilities presented by the museum as a mode of remembering provide for the construction of countless different narratives from a single collection. These narratives emerge out of the juxtaposition of objects, tangibly portrayed in the structure of the museum's exhibitions. As Horne suggests, museums do not offer much opportunity for "close readings" of specific objects, but instead evoke what Rubie Watson has described as "powerful and compelling images . . . [that] give people the sense that they are reexperiencing an event that may have occurred long before their birth."[15] This mode of collective memory clearly dictates *how* to remember — through the physicality of material objects carefully arranged in a set of "powerful and compelling" images, but it does not dictate *what* is remembered. This dazzling portrait of the glory and achievement of China's imperial bureaucracy effectively erases the "waste and frivolity that ignored an oppressed and downtrodden people."

From Imperial Palace to Palace Museum

The Palace Museum emerged out of the collapse of the Qing dynasty in the early twentieth century — an event that marked not only the end of Qing rule, but also the end of the dynastic cycles that had ordered the Chinese past for thousands of years. As the imperial order crumbled, a new generation of leaders sought to distance themselves from the chaos that had defined Chinese social and political life in the final century of imperial rule. They desperately struggled to unify a highly fractured society and to forge an image of a "modern nation," modeled after the sovereign nations of Europe and North America.

The success of this project rested heavily upon the construction of a collective memory that would clearly sever the present from the imperial past but would nonetheless preserve a sense of continuity with the distinctive heritage of ancient Chinese civilization. Amid the turmoil of the end of the empire the Chinese imperial collections emerged as a potentially powerful representation of this collective memory.[16] In the global context they would serve to represent the legitimacy of a modern Chinese nation possessed of a distinctive culture and a lengthy history. At the local level, both the extravagant walled palace and its mythical contents continued to inspire mystery and awe. It became clear to the leaders of the new nation that the political legitimacy symbolized in possession of the imperial collections should not be overlooked. The battered ruins of imperial China thus became a potent symbol of the strength and continuity of the Chinese people.

Early advocates of the museum consisted largely of those scholars who had entered the palace upon the departure of the emperor and had begun the process of sorting and cataloging the collections. In founding the museum they sought to celebrate a distinctive and exclusive cultural heritage, but this was *not* conceived of as *Chinese* heritage. Rather, the Chinese imperial collections were envisaged as part of a *global* cultural heritage, one instance of the collective memory of the horrors of feudalism and imperial rule that is shared by all modern nations. The preservation of a "generic" imperial past was ultimately required to ensure a place for China in the universal heritage of the global community.[17]

Though slower to realize it, the state also had a vested interest in preserving the palace, particularly the imperial collections. For centuries, the Chinese imperial collections had symbolized both political and moral authority. Throughout Chinese history, dynastic succession was marked, in part, by the appropriation of the imperial palace and its collection of art and antiquities. Thus the state's appropriation of the imperial collection legitimated its political power and authority. In the early years of the museum, however, critics contested the cost and energy required to renovate and maintain the former palace. In 1928 a member of the State Council characterized the collections as the useless remains of a treasonous and corrupt past, which should be abandoned rather than preserved. He argued that the effort expended in the restoration of the palace and the preservation of the imperial collections made it appear — to both Chinese citizens and foreign observers — as if the nation were preparing to install the next emperor. Despite this opposition, the museum was formally established and placed under the auspices of the state. Although government financial and administrative involvement in the museum was initially quite marginal, the state eventually recognized that public display of the collection—however limited the display might be— could significantly enhance the public perception of its cultural authority and historical legitimacy, and began to take a more active part in the construction of collective memory in the Palace Museum.

Explicit parallels between the museum and the nation were established at the opening ceremonies of the museum in October 1925. Newspaper reports that appeared the following day quoted at length the speaker who stated: "In the future this day [National Day] will have two levels of meaning. . . . Those who might seek to loot or plunder the museum, will also plunder the joyous festival that marks the founding of the nation. We must all share in its defense."[18] Within a year, metaphorical connections between the future of the museum and the future of the nation were transformed into historical realities when political instability within the state led to the temporary closure of the museum. Over the next six years, limited financial resources, coupled with a rapidly shifting political situation, prohibited a permanent reopening. By 1933 museum administrators and government officials, fearing the threat of advancing Japanese troops, had arranged for the imperial collection of art and antiquities to be packed up, removed from the palace, transported to Shanghai, and eventually put into storage in newly constructed warehouses in Nanjing. Over the next twelve years the collections were moved several times, following the retreat of the Nationalist government before the invading Japanese army and, later, before Chinese Communist forces. In 1948, the Nationalist government fled to the island province of Taiwan, taking with it two freighters carefully loaded with the most valuable objects in the collection. Pierre Rycksman argues that "at the time, Peking experienced this move as a bitter political set-back."[19] Indeed, most guidebooks to Beijing's Palace Museum include a brief chapter on the Palace Museum in Taiwan, detailing the impact of this rupture on the integrity of the imperial collections.

The greatest immediate impact of the Nationalist appropriation of the collections, however, can still be seen in the collections of Beijing's Palace Museum. Much of the "ancient art and antiquities" displayed in the exhibition halls of Beijing's Palace Museum was not part of the original museum collection, although it may have constituted part of the imperial collection at some earlier point in time. Some pieces could never have been part of the imperial collections, since they were excavated after the founding of the Republic — for example, the second century B.C.E. terra-cotta soldiers from the grave of China's first emperor or the incised "oracle bones" dating from the Shang dynasty (1500–1050 B.C.E.). Throughout Chinese history, emperors treated the collections with varying degrees of interest and enthusiasm. Some eagerly sought to expand them, acquiring desirable objects at all costs. For others art had little value, and they generously offered pieces from the collection as gifts to generals successful in battle or officials whose counsel was particularly pleasing. In the early part of the twentieth century, during the final years of Qing rule and in the early years of the Republic, it is widely believed that extensive looting occurred among the collections stored in imperial warehouses. During this period a portion of the collection was removed from the palace and moved to Manchuria, where the Japanese had installed the emperor as a puppet ruler. Yet despite the lack of material continuity, the former imperial collections became a central symbol in the struggle for political legitimacy between the Nationalist and the Communist governments.

Following the establishment of the People's Republic of China in 1949, the Communist government quickly sought to open the doors of the former imperial palace to the Chinese people again — despite the fact that much of the imperial collections was now gone. Pieces from the collections that had mysteriously disappeared in the final days of imperial rule were painstakingly tracked down and recovered (often at tremendous monetary expense) from provincial museums or private collections in other parts of China, Hong Kong, Taiwan, the United States, and other parts of the world. Yet despite these efforts to rebuild the collection, it soon became clear that it would be impossible to re-create the magnitude of the collection that had been shipped to Taiwan.[20] Instead, museum staff concentrated on what remained: the palace itself and all of the accoutrements of daily life in the Forbidden City. In other words, although the collections had been radically redefined by the events of the previous decades, the physical space of the museum — where the emperors of China had lived and worked for more than five centuries — remained largely the same.

Accounts of this period in the museum's history often focus on the extensive deterioration of the buildings and the enormous cost and effort required for restoration, citing the corruption and negligence of the Nationalist government as the reason for the dilapidated state of the palace. Interestingly, this discourse lacks any reference to the wealth of objects transported from the Chinese mainland to Taiwan by the Nationalist government.[21] Although the Beijing Palace Museum collections clearly could not rival the wealth of objects stored in the Palace Museum on Taiwan, a reminder of this unfortunate loss would only serve to undermine the Communist state's claims to political authority and legitimacy. This silence, as well as the criticisms leveled at the Nationalist state concerning the dilapidated condition of the palace, shift the symbolic locus of legitimacy away from the former imperial collections to the physical space of the palace, thus subverting Nationalist claims to political authority.[22]

Recent historical events provide further evidence of the Communist state's efforts to recover the sacred symbolism of the palace. During the early years of the Cultural Revolution, enthusiastic armies of young Red Guard soldiers sought to destroy any remnants of China's "feudal history," including displays of imperial art and architecture. Stelae engraved with the calligraphic inscriptions of Qing emperors were overturned and tossed into back alleys. The faces of Buddhist images carved into the temples of the Summer Palace were smashed. Yet the most prominent symbol of the feudal period, the imperial palace, remained untouched following orders from the central government to bolt the gates of the museum. While most of the country's scholars and intellectuals were "sent down" to the countryside to learn from the peasants, the museum staff remained in seclusion inside the palace continuing to conduct research, to catalog and to conserve both the palace buildings and their contents.[23] The intersection of universal heritage and local meanings appears particularly powerful here in the shrewd political maneuvering of the state and the heroic efforts of the museum staff to preserve the palace in the midst of a radical revolutionary movement aimed expressly at destroying the past.

New exhibits, additions to the collection, even changing definitions of what actually constitutes the museum's collections have sharpened but not significantly altered the images of the glories of imperial China represented in this museum. Despite radical shifts in the political structures that hold guardianship over this space, the imperial palace and collections remain a central symbol of political legitimacy and authority—a symbolism that is deeply embedded in the materiality of the buildings and the physical objects they contain. As the passage from Dorn cited above suggests, this elaborate site serves as a captivating "theatrical backdrop" for scripting a mysterious and engaging tale of the Chinese past.

Throughout Chinese history, occupation of the imperial palace and possession of the imperial collections symbolized more than political legitimacy —it signified the heavenly mandate that gave an emperor the cosmological authority to rule. The cost[24] and effort required to maintain this ancient architectural structure and to reassemble, research, conserve, and exhibit the collections point to the tremendous political significance the palace and imperial collections continue to possess. In an essay written in response to the 1989 massacre in Tiananmen Square, author Zhang Langlang alludes to the powerful symbolism of the imperial city:

The old men of the party who sent in the troops to slaughter the students and citizens who had been protesting in Peking were all provincials, people from outside the capital. *For the better part of forty years, they have occupied the ancient imperial city, living in its secluded princely mansions and palaces.* They never walk in the streets with their own citizens; the lost pleasures described in this essay are entirely foreign to them. These cadres, the old men and their toadies, come mostly from the rural south or the west; they are peasants who hate the self-sufficient, proud culture of the old imperial city and have connived to destroy it since 1949. (Mao once reportedly even contemplated tearing down the Imperial Palace.) They never felt at home in Peking, and when the city rebelled in May, albeit peacefully, they had their revenge, using as tools provincial soldiers who, like themselves, deeply distrusted and resented the city.[25]

For Zhang, the elegance of the former palaces symbolizes the sophistication and elegance of the capital city itself. While he scoffs at the awe and reverence the imperial city inspired among the former peasants who led China through such radical revolution, his disdain derives primarily from their forcible appropriation of the city and its imperial splendor without the necessary cultural/cosmological mandate. Like Dorn, Zhang condemns the current custodians of the imperial palaces for lack of sympathy with and understanding of the imperial splendor now in their possession. The constant stream of visitors to the Forbidden City, however, suggests that the Communist state understands only too well the mysterious attraction of the palaces for ordinary citizens. While Mao may in fact have contemplated tearing down the imperial palace, such an act would not have served his broader ideological interests to garner support of and legitimacy for a Communist state. Indeed, in the years since the Communist Revolution the palace has come to serve as a foundation for the construction of revolutionary memory in the nation's capital.[26]

The gates to the former imperial palace — leading up to the former geographical center of the imperial city — remain at the cosmological center of the nation. In the square area that extends beyond the Tianan Gate stand recently erected monuments to a postimperial modern Chinese nation: the Great Hall of the People, the Museums of Chinese History and Revolution, the Monument to the People's Heroes, and the Chairman Mao Memorial Hall. Immediately to the west of the museum, hidden behind massive walls, lay the residences of China's highest ranking officials. The Imperial Palace / Museum remains at the center.

The institution of the museum legitimizes the state's appropriation of the luxurious accoutrements of imperial power, while the appropriation of these accoutrements legitimizes the political authority of the state. The Palace Museum thus portrays an image of an imperial past that is clearly distant and distinct from the present but nonetheless preserves and legitimates the sacred authority of the palace and its contents. Ordinary citizens may now visit the palace, where they can admire this extraordinary display of power and authority from a position slightly "off-center," leaving the sacred central corridor intact and untouched. As I have already suggested, disruptions in the cosmological order that occur when commoners pass through the imperial gates are quickly remedied as visitors are moved to the margins, prohibited from entering the sacred central axis of the Forbidden City.

Making Modern Memories

A powerful global rhetoric of cultural heritage and identity, organized around the themes of collection, conservation, and display, renders the symbolic ambiguities embedded in the imperial palace and collections nearly transparent. The emperor no longer rules from his perch within the palace, nor does the current government explicitly use the palace to conduct affairs of state. The powerful political symbolism of this space is hidden by the open gates that give visitors a sense of privilege at the opportunity to catch a glimpse of that mysterious place which was, for centuries, forbidden to them.

Liu Yiran's short story "Rocking Tiananmen" provides an excellent instance of the erasure of the state in popular constructions of the former palace. When Liu describes break dancing where the old Qing emperors slept as a "real turn-on," he frames this sensual experience solely in terms of the former imperial inhabitants — speaking, at one point, directly to the emperor himself.

What could be better: dancing to rock music where the old Qing emperors slept. It's a real turn-on. . . . When I reach the Noon [Meridian] Gate the place is exploding with break dancing. Rock music hits me on all sides: ghetto blasters of every shape and size on the ground, stuck on the back of bikes, hung in the trees. Sorry, Your Imperial Highness, we couldn't be bothered to prostrate ourselves on the ground, kowtow, and cry out "Ten Thousand Years" tonight. Instead, our thunder is shaking you from your dreams. . . . There's this old fella there mumbling away, abusing our ancestors. . . . He's still carping on when this guy bops over and says, "What's eating you grandad? *The emperor left this for all of us. . . ."* [27]

The emotional intensity of the dancers described in the story stems in part from the rebellion implied in the unconventional use of a space seeped in ritual and tradition. References to disrupting the emperor's sleep, refusing to kowtow, and waking "Old Granny Cixi" (the empress dowager) all suggest that the story's narrator has at least a basic understanding of the history of the palace. Indeed, in his response to "grandad," the narrator makes direct claims upon the palace — an inheritance to be shared by all — effectively erasing the guardianship — and authority — of the state.

Liu addresses the question of the state's authority over the palace obliquely, carefully distancing it from the defiant narrator's impassioned account of break dancing at the Meridian Gate in terms of both narrative structure and voice. The gates of the palace lose the spirit of both imperial grandeur and wild freedom when the narrator's sweetheart becomes cold and detached, reprimanding him for "getting mixed up with the types that go *to a place like that!*" She goes on to interrogate the limits of his rebelliousness when she asks "What's next? Break dancing in Zhongnanhai?" — the walled compound on the west side of the imperial palace that serves as the residence for high-ranking Communist Party officials. [28] This passage clearly establishes a hierarchical link between the palace and the physically adjacent residences of Zhongnanhai — with both falling directly under the authority of the state. By giving voice to these more "conventional" sentiments through the narrator's girlfriend, Liu preserves the contrast to the radical sense of ownership of these monuments expressed by the narrator himself. The energy and wild abandon of the break dancers in this story effectively challenges the nostalgic, reverential commemoration of imperial life embodied in the museum and re-presents the space of the palace as a public space that should be used by all in the practice of everyday life in contemporary China. This is most powerfully expressed by the exchange between the old man and the anonymous dancer who claims that *"the emperor left this for all of us."* The use of this broadly inclusive first-person plural pronoun points to yet another dimension of ambiguity.

The Palace Museum in Beijing appears as number 439 on the UNESCO World Heritage List of natural and cultural sites deemed to be of "outstanding universal value." Following the nomination of the former palace by the Chinese state, the site won the approval of the World Heritage Committee in 1987 because it successfully satisfied a sufficient number of criteria as outlined in the World Heritage Convention. As custodian of this World Heritage site, the Chinese government must now regularly report to the committee on the condition of the museum and must document its efforts in the areas of both conservation and education. In other words, the universal criteria for evaluation of cultural sites detailed in the convention grant global legitimacy to local claims of ownership made by any of the states that subscribe to the convention.

This rhetoric of universal global heritage boldly enunciated by organizations such as UNESCO's World Heritage Center, its attendant conservation groups, or member states, recognizes and promotes the diversity of human societies and cultures through the construction of distinctive pasts that are possessed by, and ultimately definitive of, distinctive peoples. Yet despite the celebration of distinctive communities, this universalizing rhetoric ultimately rests upon the erasure of difference. We recognize and evaluate the distinctive qualities of any particular heritage only because they resemble the distinctive qualities of any other heritage, couched in terms such as precedence, antiquity, continuity, coherence, heroism, and sacrifice, the exaltation of unique heroes and virtues, and the celebration of success, stability, and progress.[29] Yet while this rhetoric seeks to demonstrate precedence and continuity that stretch from past to present, in fact it inverts the relationship, creating a contemporary identity out of the construction of a collective memory. This process of re-collection demands the proliferation of *modern* cultural communities since identity can be legitimated only with reference to a *distinctive* past.

Ironically, the contradictions embedded in heritage rhetoric — between the local and the global, the particular and the universal — also open up paths of resistance to the hegemonic and homogenizing ideology of heritage. Local appropriations of heritage in particular times and places demand a careful mediation of both local and global concerns — preserving local authority while constructing legitimacy within the global context. In these contexts, resistance remains invisible to the casual observer, more often embedded in heritage rather than rhetoric. As I have argued above, the rhetoric of global heritage provides a powerful tool for legitimizing the Chinese state's occupation of the former imperial palace as a symbol of political (and moral) authority.

The recognition of China as an equal participant in a global community of modern nations required the re-collection of a distinctive heritage, a heritage that is readily expressed in the elegance and splendor of the former imperial palace. Within the museum we find an imperial past remembered in exquisitely appointed period rooms and embodied in rare and unusual objects, from ancient calligraphy to a small gold stupa (a miniature Buddhist shrine) commissioned by a Qing emperor to hold his mother's hair. The coherence of this relatively random collection emerges out of the exhibition of its constituent objects as part of a larger and more glorious past. Through the collections we see the collective memory of a Chinese imperial past filled with glory and achievement—a generic imperial past deliberately and self-consciously constructed to resemble representations of "the" imperial past in museums throughout the world—distinctively Chinese, but only in ways that can be readily recognized in a global context. Drawing upon the possibilities of the museum to endow otherwise ordinary objects with sacred qualities and through the exhibition of these objects to thus re-member a community, the Chinese state constructs a set of compelling images of the Chinese past—a collective memory shared by all who pass through the massive wooden gates.

The elegantly reconstructed central axis of cosmological power remains "closed," however, and visitors look on with admiration from the periphery. It is here, along this central axis, that the state appropriates the rhetoric of heritage as a mode of resistance to the universalizing—and ultimately homogenizing—demands of a global community that erases difference at the very moment that it strives to promote it. What the state "preserves" is not the collections themselves but their symbolic significance as a sign of political authority and legitimacy. In resisting the hegemony of a universalizing heritage, the state asserts its own hegemony over the construction of the Chinese past, instilling in museum visitors a memory of imperial rule that ultimately leads directly to the legitimization of the current state. The elaborate rituals of the imperial state are reimagined in the ritual passage of eager visitors through the maze of palace halls and gardens. Visitors gain access to this sacred space only at the behest of the ruling elite, where they become a necessary component of the state ritual carried out within these walls. Their ritual journey through the museum constitutes a critical component in the construction of collective *memory* but remains marginal in the making of history.

PART III

Collectors and Institutions

9. The Modern Muses

*Renaissance Collecting and the
Cult of Remembrance*

I have heard some with deep sighs lament the lost
lines of Cicero; others with as many groans deplore
the combustion of the library of Alexandria: for my
own part, I think there be too many in the world
and could with patience behold the urn and ashes
of the Vatican.
　　　— Thomas Browne, *Religio Medici* (1642)

During the sixteenth and seventeenth centuries, humanist scholars and their patrons increasingly favored the museum as a key site for a wide variety of cultural endeavors. Setting aside a room or series of rooms in their houses or palaces, they filled them to capacity with objects — books, manuscripts, paintings, sculptures, medals, scientific instruments, *naturalia* and *exotica*, the bric-a-brac of the learned world. No object was too trivial to be excluded from the Renaissance museum, and those that were too large — a rhinoceros perhaps or an Etruscan tomb — were simply divided up into pieces, like the relics of saints, in order to satisfy the voracious appetite for things that characterized the activities of early collectors. While some museums were entirely private, created for the eyes of the collector alone, the majority enjoyed regular visits from princes, clerics, scholars, and curious patricians who publicized the qualities of these museums in their letters, travel journals, and conversations. By the end of the Renaissance, the museum had become a standard feature of the cultural itinerary of any learned person, giving collectors enormous status in European society, as the people charged with the formidable task of preserving and displaying knowledge.[1] In their museums lay the memory of an entire society — "remembrances of infinite things," as one Renaissance collector put it[2]—as well as their reflections on the past they claimed to possess and revive.

Memory was a central feature of the birth of the museum in Renaissance Europe. Cicero described it as the "thesaurus of inventions," while sixteenth-century scholars labeled it the "mother of knowledge" or, as Vico later put it, the "mother of the Muses."[3] It was not coincidental that the revival of the ancient arts of memory and the appearance of collections occurred at the same time.[4] Knowing how to retain knowledge and acquiring the objects that represented knowledge were shared endeavors. Both attempted to visualize culture, whether through a set of symbols in an imaginary theater that represented the encyclopedic potential of the human mind or through the arrangement of key artifacts in a room. As Walter Ong eloquently observes, "The mind has its spaces, too, and at the time of the Renaissance, nothing is more evident than the role which spatially oriented conceptualizations begin to play in the notion of knowledge itself."[5]

In the work of the Venetian Giulio Camillo (c. 1480–1544), these different activities seemed to unite. Writing to Erasmus from Padua in 1532, Viglius Zuichemus reported that Camillo had actually built a theater of memory "into which whoever is admitted as spectator will be able to discourse on any subject no less fluently than Cicero." Zuichemus traveled to Venice to meet the mysterious Camillo and see his creation. He walked through the concentric circles of the wooden structure, absorbing the astrological and mythological images pasted on the walls, no doubt trying to understand the secrets they contained. Camillo, he informed Erasmus, "calls this theater of his by many names, saying now that it is a built or constructed mind and soul, and now that it is a windowed one."[6] Whether inside the mind or simply looking into it, Camillo's metaphor aptly summed up the desire to make knowledge a tangible and visible object. One had to see to remember, and remember to know. Such advice demanded an entirely new sort of scholar whom Camillo placed squarely in the center of his amphitheater in order to command an all-encompassing view of his mnemonic secrets. "Let's turn scholars into spectators," he advised in his *Idea of the Theater* (1550).[7]

Less than a decade later, one of the greatest collectors of this generation, the Bolognese naturalist Ulisse Aldrovandi (1522–1605), brought Camillo's image of the humanist spectator to its logical fulfillment. Reflecting on the process by which he had written his *On Ancient Statues* (1556), one of the first guidebooks to antiquarian collections in Rome, Aldrovandi described it as being formed through "writing and collecting, as if in a Theater" (*scrivere et raccogliere, come in un Theatro*).[8] While Aldrovandi expressly critiqued the Hermetic approach to memory that Camillo advocated, he nonetheless shared the new image of learning that privileged the theater as a site of knowledge, placing himself at its center. He also viewed memory as the central cognitive faculty, writing in 1581: "by memory in the depths of time one conserves every sort of knowledge and wisdom in the human mind."[9] The fact that Aldrovandi owned all of Camillo's works further suggests that this Renaissance collector engaged with the Venetian occultist's ideas even if he did not entirely approve of their philosophical origins.[10] In the midst of his notebooks, he recorded that he had been reading "some books that spoke of artificial memory."[11] They were one of the many sources Aldrovandi eagerly consumed in his quest to bring order to his museum.

Other collectors who read Camillo incorporated his ideas more directly into their own schemes of knowledge, sharing his utopian vision of memory. Fifteen years after the posthumous publication of Camillo's description of his memory theater, a Flemish physician, Samuel Quiccheberg, decided to write an account of an ideal museum that drew heavily upon his knowledge of the collection of his patron, Duke Albrecht V of Bavaria. Quiccheberg also visited the museums of other princes and leading scholars in Renaissance Europe, signing the visitors' books of Aldrovandi and the Swiss naturalist and bibliophile Conrad Gesner of Zurich (1516–65) along the way.[12] As has been often mentioned, Camillo was one of Quiccheberg's key sources of inspiration. Imagining a prince at the center of his museum, in imitation of Camillo's spectator, Quiccheberg filled it with five different classes of objects, beginning with an archive of histories, genealogies, maps, wars, festivals, and other noteworthy commemorations of the patron's glory and adding rooms of *artificialia*, *naturalia*, instruments, and paintings to complete the microcosm, which he labeled a "theater of knowledge" (*theatrum sapientiae*).[13]

Elsewhere Quiccheberg described a collection devoted to curiosities as a "promptuary of miraculous things" (*miraculosum rerum promptuarium*). Such an image surely underscored the mnemonic potential of the museum as a setting in which the sight of objects elicited learned discourses that were as various as the artifacts themselves. Like Camillo's theater, Quiccheberg's Vitruvian theater was an imaginary space in which one could become a better Cicero through the flawless manipulation of all forms of knowledge.[14] Collecting and remembering facilitated the control of information that lay at the heart of a well-ordered polity. Both activities contributed to the image of the learned ruler whose wisdom emanated not only from communion with God but also from an active engagement in the production and expansion of the humanist encyclopedia.

Camillo's dream of a perfect theater lived on in the utopian literature of the Renaissance, which continued to fantasize about a world in which all knowledge might easily be organized and recalled at will. Almost one hundred years after Erasmus enjoyed a description of Camillo's memory theater, the Dominican philosopher Tommaso Campanella described a city in which six walls containing the sum of natural philosophy and human invention ringed a temple of knowledge. These walls would allow the inhabitants of the *City of the Sun* (1623) "to know all the sciences pictorially before they are ten years old." [15] Campanella's solarian temple was yet another paper museum that presented collecting as a solution to the problem of knowledge. Conjoined with the art of memory, it offered the youth of his utopian society the sort of knowledge that one gained, however imperfectly, only in full maturity after years of reading, seeing, and traveling the globe. It was a permanent museum that assumed a fixed and eternal body of knowledge whose open display responded to the growing sense of the imperfection and incompleteness of knowledge; it was, indeed, this sense that fueled the Renaissance passion for collecting.

The Legacy of Alexandria

The vision of a museum as a site of complete knowledge evoked a specific set of cultural images in the minds of Renaissance Europeans that allows us to understand more precisely what it was that they wished to remember. *Musaeum* traditionally defined "the place where the Muses dwell." [16] Very quickly the image of the museum expanded from that of a temple dedicated to the subjects of these nine goddesses to that of a house of knowledge. "[A]lthough a great portion of the Ancients approved of the name 'Muse' only for the guardianship of Song and Poetry," wrote Teodoro Bondini in the preface to the 1677 catalog of Ferdinando Cospi's museum in Bologna, "nonetheless many others wished to incorporate all knowledge under such a name." [17]

Expanding the definition of museum beyond the disciplines of the Muses satisfied a deeply felt need to connect the activities of the humanist republic of letters to those of its most illustrious ancestor, the Museum of Alexandria. The best image of this center for ancient scholarship comes from the mouth of the Greek author Timon of Phlius, who wrote: "In the populous land of Egypt they breed a race of bookish scribblers who spend their whole lives pecking away in the cage of the Muses." [18] The story of the Museum of Alexandria and its spectacular demise, whether in the flames set by Julius

Caesar or the ones set by Muslim rulers over six centuries later, haunted the dreams of late Renaissance humanists. Rather than being the utopia that could be, it was the utopia that *was*, a perfect moment of knowledge carelessly wiped away by the callous maneuvers of ambitious leaders. Timon's metaphor had its uses: the cage had been unlocked, the birds had flown. One had to create a new cage for the Muses in order to lure them back into their rightful resting place.

Even as popular writers began to refer to museums as "cabinets" and "galleries," in order to describe the physical locations in which they existed, more philosophical interpreters of museums insisted on retaining the original word to maintain the connection to Alexandria. Thus the seventeenth-century Roman College museum, maintained its Jesuit curator Filippo Bonanni, was no gallery:

One should more properly say Museum, a term originating from the Greek according to Pliny, which means the same as the "Domain for the Muses dedicated to the housing of learned men," which Strabo refers to in his last book, "at Alexandria there was the most celebrated Museum." Spartianus discusses it in his life of Hadrian, saying: "At Alexandria in the Museum he proposed many questions to the professors. . . . Or, as *musaeum* alludes, one says a place dedicated to the Muses.[19]

Such definitions made explicit commonly understood views of the cultural meaning of the museum. As Marion Rothstein observes in her discussion of Renaissance etymologies, "Sources, origins, are perceived as active guides to how a thing is to be regarded, and how it may be expected to perform. The source functions as something perpetually present, though at any specific moment of the continuum it need not be overtly expressed."[20] Both the knowledge that Alexandria represented—which to the Renaissance mind suggested the writings of Aristotle and his disciples—and the difficulties of preserving this patrimony served as an essential starting point in virtually every discussion of what a Renaissance museum could become and how it might avoid the fate of the original Museum.

Loss of knowledge was a central theme informing the evolution of the Renaissance museum from its inception. Prior to worrying about the demise of the new museum, the process of reconstruction had to begin. Ironically the cause of Alexandria's demise was also its genesis: rulers were both necessary patrons and fierce enemies of culture. Without Alexander the Great, Aristotle's writings would not have existed. Without Ptolemy of Egypt, the Museum could not have housed them and been a haven for other intellectuals who continued this sort of philosophical inquiry. In this spirit, Renaissance collectors invited patrons to reinvent an ancient relationship between knowledge and power. Addressing the Grand Duke of Tuscany, Ferdinando I de' Medici, in the late 1580s, Aldrovandi urged him to be like "great Ptolemy, King of Egypt, who spent millions to collect the most noteworthy efforts of writers of that time in his most memorable Library."[21]

More frequently Aldrovandi invoked the image of Alexander who had initiated the process of creating the knowledge that Ptolemy had collected.[22] After all, it was Alexander whose patronage gave Aristotle the opportunity to gather data from the length and breadth of the Macedonian empire, transforming it into the books that shaped the encyclopedic goals of many Renaissance collectors. Quite unintentionally Alexander's fame existed principally in the words of his tutor, a paper legacy that Renaissance readers examined intensively not only for knowledge of the Greek world that they cherished but also for clues about how they, too, might win immortality. Like the fall of Alexandria, the fate of Alexander seemed to offer yet another lesson in the contest between learned civilizations and the "barbarians." Soon after the fall of Alexander's empire, argued humanist interpreters, his cities were destroyed and "inhabited by barbarians." These seemingly eternal architectural monuments no longer bore the imprint of their founder and, accordingly, did not cherish his memory. Noting what he was certain would have been Alexander's surprise at the fragility of his empire, Aldrovandi remarked in 1572: "If Alexander were alive today, he would marvel [at the fact] that, among the multitude of famous works that he did, those books of animals acquired greater glory than any other."[23]

Alexander's eternity through the works of Aristotle seemed to be much on the mind of this particular Renaissance collector who appropriately fashioned himself as a new and better Aristotle. During an attempt to interest Philip II of Spain in patronizing his museum, Aldrovandi wrote to the cardinal protector of the Spanish College in Bologna that this sort of contribution to knowledge was not simply long-lived but potentially eternal. "But the memory of the animals described by Aristotle in Alexander's name already has been preserved for more than nineteen hundred years until now and, God willing, it will be preserved until the end of the World." Through his accumulation of objects, Aldrovandi felt that he could offer an even more lasting gift for a willing patron. As he told the cardinal protector, in addition to his thousands of other artifacts and numerous manuscripts ready for publication, he had a herbarium that already numbered thirteen volumes — an archive of plants for their "perpetual memory."[24] Thus the museum eternalized objects in addition to securing the immortal reputation of its creators and patrons.

In Aldrovandi's reading of the combination of events that had preserved Alexander's fame, the interaction between words and objects played a central role. Like most humanists, men of the book, he saw words as playing a particularly important role in the survival of any human endeavor. "The preservative arts of memory that one can leave to posterity are writing, painting, sculpting and forging," he observed in 1581, "among which writing and books preserve memory best and are the most universal among all the other arts that preserve the memory of things."[25] To support his argument, he cited the Egyptian papyri that had outlasted all the paintings Pliny had seen in Rome and described in his *Natural History*; they had been reduced to words after they themselves had vanished while the papyri — both words and objects — survived.

Yet writing alone did not preserve one's memory (a fact that Aldrovandi knew well from his own experience since he found it so difficult to get his treatises published).[26] Others besides Aristotle had memorialized the feats of Alexander without bringing him glory and therefore eternity. "[M]any writers of his works and deeds came to nothing, and no memory exists of them save for one or two of his last writers."[27] Words did not automatically guarantee immortality, Aldrovandi suggested, without being connected to a substantial project that the future might care to preserve and even continue. The project of Aristotelian knowledge had endured for almost two thousand years because it was not confined only to the Museum of Alexandria but transcended it. Timon's bird had flown and would fly again. From this perspective, Aldrovandi saw his own reinvention of Aristotle's natural history in his museum in Bologna as a project that would repeat the successes of his ancient model and become part of the eternal edifice of knowledge. By putting the objects in his museum into print, using the tools of modern scholarship unavailable to Aristotle, he hoped to make them permanent. By making his museum a public monument in which he hoped a wide variety of people would invest their objects, joining them with his, he hoped that it would avoid the fate of the original Museum, which had fallen not only due to the brutality of conquest but perhaps as a result of civic indifference on the part of the local citizens who had not participated enough in the creation of the Museum to care about its end. Individual accomplishments had to be cherished by society in order to last. The museum provided the ideal means for publicizing the humanist program of knowledge in the hope that Renaissance society might come to share the collector's passion for preserving those objects, images, and words deemed memorable in the long march of history.

In 1603, Aldrovandi donated his enormous collection — some twenty thousand natural specimens, several thousand illustrations of flora and fauna, approximately thirty-five hundred books and one hundred and fifty manuscripts, and several hundred woodcuts for his publications — to the Senate of Bologna. His decision to make this gift to the city came from a wish "that my many labors continue after my death in honor and for the use of the City, and that they have not occurred for nothing." [28] Like many collectors, Aldrovandi wished to be remembered for his efforts to bring all knowledge together in one place, realizing the promise of imaginary memory theaters such as Camillo's. Just as each of his objects had a story to be told, so the history of his museum itself needed to survive. Aldrovandi was more successful than most of his Renaissance counterparts at preserving the memory of his collection. Between 1617 and 1742 the Studio Aldrovandi existed, virtually intact, in the Palazzo Pubblico of Bologna. [29] After that, even its reorganization as part of its incorporation into a new museum for a local scientific academy and its transportation to Paris at the hands of Napoléon's troops did not entirely destroy it. By the early twentieth century it had been reconstructed in the university library of the city, a nucleus within a labyrinth of books, a fitting site for the work of a collector who aspired to solve the problems of the Alexandrian Museum.

"That Their Memory Be Preserved"

Renaissance collectors demanded nothing less than immortality for their museums, which they hoped would transcend time itself. But what exactly would the museum preserve? The museum housed a specific sort of cultural legacy that connected the present to the past by creating a genealogy of knowledge so as to make the humanists heirs of Egypt, Greece, and Rome. At the same time, it wrote the history of collectors and their patrons by ensuring their fame through the celebration of the objects that they had assembled. Such concerns informed the popularity of certain artifacts in Renaissance museums, especially portraits, and shaped the presentation of objects by emphasizing the various means by which one could be remembered through things. Without such tangible gifts, collectors argued, the permanency of one's legacy was never truly assured.

The use of portraits in Renaissance museums offers another opportunity to see how ancient models informed early modern practices. In 1625 the archbishop of Milan, Federico Borromeo, informed readers of his *Musaeum*, the catalog of his collection, that he had included images of men of letters so "that their memory be preserved with portraits." [30] Both Cicero and Pliny the Younger had stressed the importance of decorating libraries with images of the Muses or famous men. During the fourteenth and fifteenth centuries such princely collectors as Leonello d'Este in Ferrara and Federigo da Montefeltro in Urbino created "Temples of the Muses" (*Tempietti delle Muse*) in or near their studies. At the same time, no less notable a figure than Petrarch advised his patrons on the creation of a room of illustrious men (*sala virorum illustrium*) that realized his fantasy of bringing the ancients back to life. [31]

By the sixteenth century both models became incorporated into the material culture of museums. Between 1538 and 1543 the humanist Paolo Giovio built his villa near Como on the alleged ruins of Pliny's fabled villa at Borgo Vico, attempting to reconstitute this ancient *musaeum*. Visiting the villa shortly after its completion, Anton Francesco Doni particularly praised "a most miraculous room depicting all the Muses one by one with their instruments. This," continued Doni, "one calls properly the Museum." [32] Completing this room was a portrait collection Giovio had begun by 1521 that attempted to reconstitute historical memory through the images of famous men, thereby taking Machiavelli's famous desire to "enter into the ancient courts of ancient men" through his study to its logical conclusion. [33]

Beginning with Giovio, the selection of subjects for portraits gradually began to emphasize the present over the past. Collectors made the portrait gallery a highly dynamic container that actively interpreted and judged the present for posterity. Images of Renaissance humanists, artists, popes, and princes joined and, in some instances, replaced busts of Socrates, Plato, Cicero, and other famous men (*viri illustres*) of antiquity. Toward the middle of the century, Ludovico Beccadelli decorated his villa on the island of Sipan, off the Dalmatian coast, with portraits of Pietro Bembo, Jacopo Sadoleto, Reginald Pole, Michelangelo, and other humanists. Beccadelli chose these figures not to invoke a vanquished antiquity but to remind him of the lively cultural atmosphere he had left behind in Rome during his tenure as archbishop of Ragusa. By the time he returned to Bologna in the 1560s, where he created a *studio* in his family palace, he had added portraits of Paul III and the Holy Roman Emperor to his collection. [34] Portraits, as Giovio had suggested to his contemporaries in his famous collection, created a microcosm of society. One could not only remember the past through such images but also shape the image of the present by determining who deserved this sort of commemoration.

Collecting and displaying portraits made it possible to tell a history of a community, a discipline, or even a society through the selection and arrangement of this one type of object. Increasingly collectors placed portraits in the entryways and first rooms of their museums. The apothecary Francesco Calzolari (1521–1600) followed this model, placing portraits of famous naturalists and important patrons in his Verona museum. Around 1592, he wrote his friend Aldrovandi requesting a portrait of the Bolognese naturalist to add to the collection. Aldrovandi had previously written a testimonial of the importance of Calzolari's museum that not only appeared in the 1584 catalog of the museum but also was on display there.[35] Yet Calzolari did not cultivate his friend's fame at the expense of his own. Two years earlier he had had his portrait painted, wearing a gold chain given in appreciation for his services by the duke of Mantua. During the same period his image found its way into the entrance of the museum of the Pisan botanical garden sponsored by the Medici grand dukes, joining the portraits of other famous naturalists who had reshaped natural history in the late sixteenth century.[36]

The portrait was a reciprocal commodity that collectors exchanged routinely. Princely patrons displayed portraits of their scholarly clients knowing that their own images would circulate widely in Renaissance museums. Images of the Medici, for example, appeared in the homes of collectors such as Aldrovandi, who placed portraits of Francesco I and Ferdinando I next to those of himself and his wife in his villa.[37] Such private acts of commemoration, not unlike the portrait of Cosimo I that hung in the *studiolo* created by Francesco I in the Palazzo Vecchio in Florence between 1575 and 1586, had their more public counterparts. By the mid–seventeenth century, Medici portraits had become a centerpiece of the Cospi museum in Bologna, annexed to the *Studio Aldrovandi*. As one contemporary observer recounted: "In the gallery of the Marchese Ferdinando Cospi, Bolognese Senator, are the portraits of eight princes of the royal house of Tuscany, from the hand of Sustermans, presented to the Marchese by these princes. Underneath the portraits can be read the distich, "A famous hand of the age painted the Medicean faces, these royal gifts record the Medicean mind."[38] Portraits, in short, were highly mobile and reproducible objects whose circulation in Renaissance society testified to the importance of remembering people as well as things.

The active function of such portraits becomes evident in a rather curious episode in the life of the humanist Giovan Vincenzo Pinelli (1535–1601). A friend of many other collectors, including Aldrovandi, Pinelli had one of the largest private libraries and museums in Europe and routinely welcomed scholars into his study in Padua. One day in the 1590s two men appeared at his home, dressed as simple priests; they declared that they wished to tour his museum and engage Pinelli in learned conversation. They did not identify themselves but, in the tradition of humble pilgrims, asked Pinelli to perform an act of charity through his hospitality. Pinelli, however, was undeceived by their disguise; he knew he was in the presence of the ecclesiastical historian Cesare Baronio and the reforming cardinal Robert Bellarmine. Rather than simply ending the deception, however, he used his collection to indicate his own understanding of who they were. As he later told the French scholar Nicolas Claude Fabri de Peiresc, "I brought them into that part of my study where the Pictures of famous men hung, and theirs among the rest." [39] Portraits were not simply historical objects but often contemporary interpretations of the cultural life of a society. Baronio and Bellarmine could not be anonymous in such a world because they had already earned the status of Muses.

As portraits became a popular form of commemoration, collectors increasingly insisted on the presence of their own images in museums. Such images helped to increase the visibility of collectors as a group, implicitly elevating their status through their addition to the galleries of famous men. [40] Often a collector's portrait was the centerpiece of a museum. In Aldrovandi's instructions specifying the posthumous arrangement of his museum by the Senate of Bologna in 1603, for example, he recommended that it be displayed "with my Portrait which I leave to them." [41] Ten years later, the members of the Accademia dei Lincei in Rome echoed the desirability of such commemorative acts when they promised the Neapolitan natural magician Giovan Battista della Porta (1535–1615) that donating his museum to the academy would ensure his fame. "[W]e would place an inscription with a marble portrait in the Lyceum," wrote the Lincei's founder, the Roman noble Federico Cesi, "and he would obtain the honor and title of First Benefactor." [42]

The contents of the Della Porta museum, which contained not only the materials of Giovan Battista but also those of his brother the famous antiquary Giovan Vincenzo, made the idea of a marble bust especially fitting. As the 1615 inventory reveals, the room in the family palace in Naples that housed this museum contained niches for sixteen ancient marble busts. Among them were portraits of Cicero, Caesar, and Alexander the Great; on the walls, paintings of various moderns — the Della Porta brothers, Cesi, and another famous Lincean, Galileo Galilei — looked down upon the giants of antiquity. [43] The bust of Della Porta that Cesi proposed followed in the wake of a medal of the Neapolitan collector that Cesi had previously commissioned and presented to him, imitating the practices of many antiquarians who saw numismatics as an ancient form of material commemoration worthy of revival. Already immortalized in a medal and a painting, Della Porta only needed to be carved in stone to complete his transformation into a modern Muse.[44]

By the mid–seventeenth century, baroque collectors formalized the role of the portraits, imitating the arrival of printed galleries of famous men such as Giovanni Imperiali's *Musaeum Historicum et Physicum* (1640) and Gian Vittorio Rossi's *Pinacotheca* (1643).[45] When the Roman senator Alfonso Donnino donated his collection of art, antiquities, and exotica to the Roman College in 1651, he left instructions specifying that the Jesuits would not only build a tomb in his memory in the church of San Ignazio but also place his portrait in the museum. "I hope that the gratitude that the Fathers have shown to their other benefactors will be exhibited with me, remembering me in their holy sacrifices and orations."[46] Shortly after Donnino's death in 1657, the curator of the museum, Athanasius Kircher (1602–80), received a letter from Donnino's cousin regarding the completion of the image and recommending an artist for the commission. By then a portrait gallery had become an important feature of the Roman College museum, displaying images of the Hapsburg emperors, Italian and German princes, and popes who patronized the collection, as well as of famous Jesuit missionaries. Donnino would be in illustrious company indeed.

In time, Kircher himself achieved the status of modern Muse through the addition of his own collection of natural and technological wonders to the museum. His portrait circulated widely throughout the republic of letters as Aldrovandi's and Della Porta's had done before him. Patrons and collectors as far away as Hungary and Poland requested copies of it to adorn their museums. One admirer of Kircher's wrote in 1677, "[A]lthough it is an inadequate and inauthentic countersign of the veneration in which I hold the merit and singular virtues of you, Father, I wish to preserve some of this in my little Museum with a copy of your portrait."[47] Portraits transformed individuals into objects, completing the process of materializing knowledge that lay at the heart of the museum. In this expanding world of things, even the collector could be collected.

"Immortal Cadavers"

Museum objects, as humanists suggested repeatedly, were not ordinary things. They enjoyed a special status that made them a different kind of artifact, transformed by their setting and their purpose. As the physician Paolo Terzago wrote in the 1666 catalog of canon Manfredo Settala's museum in Milan, museums contained "immortal cadavers."[48] Seemingly without the fragility of any mortal remains, museum specimens existed beyond the flow of cultures and the decline of civilizations. A society might disappear, but if it participated in the culture of collecting, its best objects would remain.

Nowhere was this philosophy better articulated than in Federico Borromeo's *Musaeum*. A connoisseur of the Renaissance "art of memory" (*ars mnemonica*) and reader of Camillo, Borromeo crafted his description of the objects in his museum with an eye to the debates about the immortality of culture. Discussions about the fate of various objects at times became moralized tales about the lack of foresight among many collectors in the preservation of their patrimony. Describing the complicated history of Titian's *Adoration of the Magi*, Borromeo recounted its sale to his uncle, Carlo Borromeo, when the unexpected death of the original owner, Cardinal Ippolito d'Este, had left its status in doubt. Exhibiting the fatal flaw of many a collector, lack of foresight, d'Este had made no specific provisions for the painting's donation to the French king, for whom he had intended it. It disappeared into the open market to find its way into the Borromeo collection. "And this is the ordinary end of objects which decorate the great houses," commented Borromeo, "to be put on sale and to be dispersed and torn apart like the cadavers of their patrons which are consumed by worms."[49] Only the intervention of his uncle had saved Titian's painting from this ignominious fate.

Prudent acts of gift-giving offered collectors an opportunity to avoid the mistakes of Cardinal d'Este, who had not anticipated the death of his museum. Patrons enjoyed immortality not only through portraits but also through a wide array of objects that, as gifts, preserved their memory in the eye of the beholder. Returning from a trip to Florence in 1577, Aldrovandi wrote immediately to Grand Duke Francesco I requesting a memento: "I remember seeing many beautiful silvery shells in your Palace from which, among four or five, I desire one in memory of Your Highness."[50] One year later, Aldrovandi wrote to the papal nuncio in Florence, Monsignor Alberto Bolognetti, requesting other artifacts—paintings of various animals by the court artist Jacopo Ligozzi and a crystal and porcelain vase made by the grand duke himself in his artisanal workshop. "I reminded His Highness . . . ," wrote Aldrovandi, "so that the things which he promised me on other occasions will be placed in my Theater of Nature in his perpetual memory."[51] When Francesco I complied with Aldrovandi's repeated pleas for objects, the Bolognese naturalist thanked him profusely, describing in detail how such gifts heightened the memory of the grand duke in his museum. "Words cannot express how dear to me are the things sent by Your Most Serene Highness . . . ," he wrote in 1586, after receiving plants from the Medici gardens. "I have placed part of them in the ground and reserved part of them in my Museum in your perpetual memory, as I always do with all the things you send me in which, as in a mirror, I gaze at and revere Your Highness from afar." [52]

Gradually Aldrovandi convinced the Medici grand duke that he could enjoy no better monument to his reign than the one erected in Bologna to complement the Uffizi galleries in Florence, which were then under construction. By the time Aldrovandi wrote his own autobiography in 1587, one year after declaring that his museum was a mirror for princes, he stated confidently that Francesco I gave him "part of anything that fell into his hands from foreign lands," and one of any object for which the grand duke had a duplicate. "One can see this in the Museum of Doctor Aldrovandi and likewise in his histories, where he remembers the Grand Duke, as he does with all others who have liberally enriched his Theater of Nature." [53] With this policy established, the grand ducal collection in Florence and the naturalist's collection in Bologna began to approximate each other, the latter becoming a copy of the former. The triple life of a collection — the original, the copy, and the published description — further ensured the immortality of Aldrovandi's patron, since the eternity of objects lay not in their simple existence but in their ability to circulate in society.

Through such statements, Renaissance collectors established the idea of gifts as the surest means of commemoration. Whether donating an individual object or an entire museum, patrons demanded reassurance that they would live on through their acts of generosity. "I am content that you promise to remember your affectionate [friend] Imperato in your most learned work," wrote the Neapolitan apothecary Ferrante Imperato after donating many objects from his museum to Aldrovandi. [54] Likewise Aldrovandi flattered even his ordinary correspondents that they could share immortality with princes and great scholars through their less spectacular gifts to his museum. After prying some fossilized fish teeth out of one acquaintance, he wrote that his sole desire was to "enrich and embellish our theater of natural things in your memory." [55] Indeed Aldrovandi's reputation as a collector generous to patrons and friends — this was the man, after all, who signed all his books with the famous humanist phrase *et amicorum* — facilitated the entry of thousands of objects into his museum by men who hoped that their contributions to the new Alexandria might place them among the Olympian gods of culture.

By the seventeenth century the need to publicize gifts led collectors to affix labels to various objects in their museums and to celebrate them in museum catalogs. When Raffaele Maffei presented Kircher with a marble squid for the Roman College museum, he was informed that "it is exposed to all those who come to see it, together with the name of the benefactor." Similarly the gift of a silver incense burner from Duke Ernst August of Brunswick-Lüneberg in 1665 prompted Kircher to declare that he would "keep it in my Gallery to his eternal memory." [56] As collectors refined the exhibition of objects, words became an important part of their display so that the memory of the gifts and deeds surrounding each artifact could not disappear casually. Objects without memories were not eternal but inert. Their loss was as irrevocable as the loss of empires without monuments.

"No Memory of It Remains"

In a letter of 1613 to his fellow academician Francesco Stelluti, Federico Cesi recounted the history of various Renaissance collections after the death of their originator. The libraries of Lorenzo de' Medici and Fulvio Orsini had ended well, Cesi concluded, because they had been donated to great institutions — respectively the convent of San Marco in Florence and the Vatican Library — that understood the value of what they contained. By contrast, the famous *musaeum* of the Venetian humanist Pietro Bembo had disappeared: "left to the discretion of his heirs, it was dispersed immediately so that no memory of it remains." [57] Without proper guidance from the Accademia dei Lincei, Della Porta's collection would suffer a similar fate. Cesi's pleas that an academy would preserve a museum better than the family heirs — echoing the phrase used by Aldrovandi, he wrote that Della Porta should know that it would be "in his perpetual memory" [58] — fell on deaf ears. After 1615, the museum closed its doors to the republic of letters, and its objects quietly disappeared into the Neapolitan book and antiquities market. Within a few decades, the world neither knew nor cared what had befallen the collection of this great scholar.

The metaphorical fate of Alexandria awaited many other Renaissance museums. Ironically, Cesi was so busy tending to the affairs of the Accademia dei Lincei that he forgot to consider the afterlife of his own collection (no doubt expecting to live to a ripe old age). When he died unexpectedly in his forties, no provision had been made for the Linceans to inherit his museum, and the objects passed to his family. In 1632, Stelluti mournfully informed Galileo: "Even more, it grieves me that he had not provided the things for the Academy, to which he wished to leave his entire library, museum, manuscripts, and other wonderful things. I don't know into whose hands they will fall." [59] Very quickly, Cesi's museum joined Della Porta's, Bembo's, and thousands of other forgotten museums in the dustbin of history.

The transitory nature of the seemingly eternal task of collecting inspired Borromeo, in the same decades of the seventeenth century, to continue the project of writing the museum that had commenced with his humanist predecessors. Echoing Aldrovandi's statements about words outlasting objects, Borromeo wrote that the ancients had commemorated their cultural monuments in writing in order "to let them live a double life." He continued:

Experience has demonstrated that this second life is longer than the first. In fact, while entire cities, let alone palaces and museums, are destroyed by fire, writings hidden in obscure and abject places have escaped fire and ruin. . . . With the passing of time, grandiose buildings decay, the most stable bridges disintegrate, obelisks fall and fragment, while the writings of even the more obscure scholars escape from the universal massacre and enjoy, so to speak, the privilege of immortality. [60]

Words survived, Borromeo argued, because they were easily duplicated. While Aldrovandi might keep a second copy of the best objects in the Medici gallery, books reproduced themselves in the hundreds and thousands. This was immortality indeed.

Borromeo wrote these lines with the problem of art preservation in mind. He wished to offer great pictures the same eternity as great ideas through the production of copies of famous works. In order to facilitate achieving this end, he did not hesitate to display copies of Renaissance works of art in his museum. Anticipating the scorn of true connoisseurs who might not see the value in this project, he described his encounter with one of the famous local paintings in Milan, Leonardo da Vinci's *Last Supper*. Already displaying in the early seventeenth century the multiple problems that twentieth-century art restoration has made famous, Leonardo's crumbling fresco was in danger of disappearing altogether. Making his way through the pieces of plaster that had fallen to the floor of the monastery refectory, Borromeo was "taken with an ardent desire to save that masterpiece as much as was humanly possible." [61]

From the start, the project of saving the *Last Supper* connected Leonardo to the Borromeo museum. Borromeo hired an artist, Bernardino Luino, to make a copy, meticulously researching details that the ruin of the fresco had begun to obscure by comparing it with Leonardo's sketches. Upon the copy's completion, he hung it in his museum. By 1625, a number of years after he had first seen the horror that time had wrought on Leonardo's masterpiece, Borromeo could remark proudly: "Therefore this *Last Supper* is among the most precious things in our Museum and will increase in value daily because the work of Leonardo, which was always esteemed as a treasure, is ruined and by now entirely lost."[62] Of course Borromeo's predictions about the fate of this object did not allow room for the development of new techniques of preservation that slowed the damage he saw. Yet his utterance testified to the increased consciousness about the fragility of the very objects that collectors most prized. Many natural objects often had an even shorter life than paintings and sculptures, so we can only imagine the effort expended by collectors such as Aldrovandi to keep the memory of his patrons alive. Similarly, we should consider anxiety about cultural loss as one of the motivating factors that led the Jesuit Kircher to create miniature replicas of the ancient obelisks he had helped to restore in Rome during the 1650s and 1660s.[63] Like Borromeo's duplicate paintings, they made perfect and whole objects that existed in an incomplete and fragile state outside the imaginary world of the museum.

As museums became more permanent institutions, their utopian aspirations only increased. Despite the legacy of Alexandria, which left Renaissance collectors in fear that their precious piles of goods would not last, they remained perpetually optimistic that they would not repeat the mistakes of the past. Confident that modern technologies of knowledge, embodied most visibly by the printing press, and the growing general interest in museums would vault them to the Olympian heights, Renaissance collectors theorized their relationship to objects in increasingly complicated ways. Memory mediated the relations among collectors, patrons, and objects on many different levels. From the formal art of memory as a philosophical pursuit to the social uses of memory as part of the patronage relations of Renaissance elites, the pursuit of memory made the museum a rich and enduring institution, even as its contents changed.

Such ideas necessarily shaped the vision of the collector as a transcendent figure who conserved culture by investing body and soul in the project of the museum. Just as museum objects enjoyed a unique artifactual existence, the body of the collector resembled that of no ordinary human but allegorized the traits of the museum. In the bedroom of Francesco I in the Palazzo Vecchio in Florence, adjoining his famous *studiolo* that was filled with precious objects from the Medici collections, Giorgio Vasari painted a portrait of Solomon sleeping. Waking, Solomon found himself responding to God's question: what did he most desire? Solomon chose wisdom and was rewarded with the riches of knowledge, infinitely vaster than the material wealth and power others craved (and, as many Renaissance scholars would have said, the key to obtaining the latter two).[64] This image of the late-sixteenth-century collector as the possessor of wisdom found its counterpart a century later in a letter written to Kircher by one of his missionary correspondents. Writing of his isolation and despair, far away from Rome, Eusebius Truchses confessed: "I see myself in a rather more privileged place, that is, in the memory of Your Reverence, whose memory is a gallery in which the rarest and most exquisite things of the world are conserved."[65]

Giulio Camillo's "built mind" lay not in a rickety wooden theater, already rotting for a good century and a half by the time a lonely missionary penned these lines. Instead it persisted in the cognitive practices of Renaissance collectors whose museums externalized their visions of knowledge. The mind of the collector was a privileged site indeed — an unbounded space for objects, people, and ideas that overcame the problems of mortal knowledge. In that setting, memory coexisted happily with the two other mental faculties, according to the Aristotelian schema, reason and imagination. Untouched by the ravages of time, it housed everything one would ever care to know or recall, a perfect museum that one might roam with abandon, a true temple of the Muses. And in that temple, the Saracens were always turned back from the port of Alexandria, saving the original Museum from the flames.

10. The Quarrel of the Ancients and Moderns in the German Museums

"It's not over until it's over" is a phrase that has been applied to baseball games, elections, and failing business ventures, but not, to my knowledge, to the stuff of intellectual history. In this essay, I would like to make a case for the endurance of one specific cultural figuration: the quarrel between the ancients and moderns. This dispute, beginning in seventeenth-century France, pitted the defenders of the wisdom of the ancients against the advocates of the superiority of the new. In the natural sciences, the discoveries of Robert Boyle and Isaac Newton seemed to prove the moderns' case, while the "battle of the books" showed off the skills of the modern philologist to the embarrassment of those who believed ancient models of history writing could not be surpassed.[1] But in the plastic arts, the ancients reigned supreme late into the nineteenth century—almost, it can be maintained, until its end. Their dominance in the aesthetic realm was bound up with the exemplariness of classical sculpture, an intellectual credo that continued to be pervasive—despite the challenges of Impressionism, Expressionism, and Cubism—until sometime just before World War I.

Historians, usually partisans of the modern, have largely treated the decline of aestheticizing classicism as a more or less inevitable result of the advent of avant-garde art and the opening up of museums and galleries to a "bourgeois" public. In this essay, however, I want to emphasize the slow and halting "modernization" of nineteenth-century aesthetic experience and to underline the role played by scholars, of various types, in this process. The longevity of antiquity's appeal has, it seems to me, been seriously underestimated, making it difficult for us to understand both the travails of those outside classicism's charmed circle and the cultural unity that, until very recently, classical eductaion conferred. If one can now presume the "quarrel" to have ended, it is time we assessed with a critical eye the contingent circumstances that gave the moderns their final victory.

The historicization (or "modernization") of aesthetics, I argue, proceeded very slowly from the seventeenth to the mid–nineteenth century and was only accomplished in the first half of the twentieth century as a result of interdependent developments in museums, schooling, scholarship, and international relations. I focus here on museums because it seems to me that the museum, better than any other cultural institution, reflects the complicated and often contradictory changes in the scholarly treatment, state patronage, and social function of classical antiquity in the nineteenth century; furthermore, it was the museum, this essay will claim, that helped to launch a critical attack on humanist scholarship. I concentrate here on Germany, because during that critical period between 1750 and 1880, German scholars were generally acknowledged to be the leaders in classical scholarship and aesthetic philosophy, as well as the inventors and loyal partisans of historicism.[2] The home of such influential figures as G. W. F. Hegel and J. J. Winckelmann — both of whom simultaneously historicized art and idealized classical sculpture — should prove an instructive field for an examination of the later stages of the "quarrel," particularly as this double commitment — to scholarly historicism and to Greek superiority — was embodied by prestigious new institutions backed by the state.

The Berlin Museums, a series of public museums developed in the course of the Napoleonic Wars, expanded enormously over the course of the nineteenth century, thanks largely to the backing of the Prussian and then German state; relative latecomers in the international contest to possess the widest array of art treasures, German officialdom was especially eager to bring that most prestigious of genres, Greek sculpture, to Prussia's capital city. But museums, in Germany, were bound not only to state initiatives; overlapping personnel, social circles, and intellectual aims also bound the museums to academia and the prestigious classical secondary schools, the *Gymnasien*. Here, then, "modernization" threatened a whole array of cultural institutions and succeeded only to the degree that social hierarchies, political priorities, and scientific norms could also be transformed. To examine the fate of neoclassical aesthetics in the Berlin Museums, then, is to link the late-nineteenth- and early-twentieth-century forms of the "quarrel" to other "modern" phenomena, the rise of specialized sciences, the bureaucratization of cultural affairs, and the post-1880 escalation of nationalist chauvinism, without presuming that any of these processes happened naturally, triumphed completely, or can be understood in isolation from the others.

Acknowledging the persistence of the ancients' aesthetic exemplarity late into the nineteenth century should allow us, correspondingly, to identify more clearly the social forces and intellectual currents that ultimately demoted the ancients from lofty exemplars to the status of one among many past cultures. In the second half of this essay, I want to argue that a combination of "modernizing" forces — from school reform to specialization — was necessary to break classicism's stranglehold on national cultural institutions. Intellectually, no "modernizing" force contributed so much as the rise to prominence of a collection of disciplines whose primary function was the interpretation of artifacts, not of texts (the central occupation of humanist scholars since the Renaissance). For the sake of conciseness, I will refer to these fields (including historical geography, ethnology, art history, folklore studies, prehistory, archaeology, and paleontology) as the "ethnological sciences"; for all aspired, in one way or another, to convert material evidence into historical narratives, and usually expended their energies on the study of more or less exotic societies and eras with little in the way of written records. My claim, baldly stated, is that we have overlooked a crucial shift in the way we define "culture"; though the older definition (culture as acquired refinements) still exists, we now much more frequently presume an anthropological definition (culture as a complex of traits and styles). This process began in the late nineteenth century and remains incomplete; it is bound up with the rise to prominence of the artifact-based ethnological sciences and the relative decline of the prestige of the text-based humanities — and of their aesthetic proclivities. It is the nearly universal adoption of an anthropological definition of culture over the older, aristocratic view that marks what for all intents and purposes can be called the end of the "quarrel."[3]

The centrality of museums to this cultural transformation will become clear and, I hope, complicate the picture of museums as purely reflective institutions. Museums provided the institutional and material support-systems for the development of courses of study based on the comparison, organization, and explication of artifacts. I consider them here mainly in the role as enabling institutions but also as sites in which to observe the continuing aesthetic appeal of the ancients and the power of the humanistically trained elite. This essay opens, then, with a short history of the Berlin Museums down to the third quarter of the nineteenth century. We then turn to a consideration of a series of "modernizing" forces, and the essay concludes by assessing the extent to which these forces were able to displace the culture of humanistic learning and its museological complement, aestheticizing neoclassicism.

The Berlin Museums

The Berlin Museums were not built in a day. Planning for a large Royal Museum began as early as 1797, in the midst of the Napoleonic Wars. Its first advocate, the antiquarian Alois Hirt, argued that a museum would help to cultivate public taste, thereby improving the quality of Prussian manufactures and curtailing dependence on imported goods. Hirt, as Steven Moyano has shown, wished to organize the collection historically, but K. F. Schinkel, the architect of what came to be known as the Altes Museum, put visual effects ahead of historical instruction, and it was the neoclassical architect whose plan won the day.[4] Wilhelm von Humboldt, appointed to oversee the installation of the works of art in 1829, insisted that only classical sculpture and Renaissance painting were appropriate for inclusion in the museum's displays.[5] Sculptures, for this Grecophile nobleman and his contemporaries, were especially important; for the Romantic generation, inspired by Winckelmann, the visual arts culminated in Greek sculpture, in which the human body (the highest content) was simultaneously given its most ideal and perfectly natural form.[6] And it was this generation whose tastes shaped nineteenth-century German cultural institutions, museum collections, and even museum buildings. K. F. Schinkel, for example, designed the entrance hall on the model of the Pantheon, complete with niches in which exemplary sculptures of the Greek gods would be placed. This devotion to statuary, however, entailed a further problem: how was the impecunious Prussian state to finance the furnishing of the museum with objects of international renown?

Already in the seventeenth century, the German art academies had developed a solution to this dilemma: when one could not afford the real thing, a cast would do just as well.[7] Casts—whiter than marble, and often amended to compensate for damaged originals—embodied the Winckelmannian ideal: the grandeur and serenity of the Greek (male) nude. There was, it seems, some opposition to casts already in the Vormärz era, but the desire to populate the national museum with classical sculptures won out, and when a new museum building opened in 1859, the cast collection occupied its entire first floor. By 1909, Aby Warburg estimated Berlin's collection of casts at 2,271.[8] Most of these, of course, were casts of classical works; as late as 1893, the catalog of the museum's cast-making worshop in Charlottenburg offered reproductions of 807 Greek and Roman works, more than all other styles combined (the breakdown is telling: the catalog also offered 165 Egyptian, 337 medieval and Renaissance, 141 ethnographic and prehistorical, and

64 Near Eastern works for purchase).[9] Increasingly, in museum displays, casts were made to fill in gaps, to create evolutionary, stylistic series for audiences to follow: from objects of aesthetic admiration and imitation, then, they became an intermediary means of historicization. At the same time, however, they underwrote the exemplarity of classical sculpture and continued to do so—while taking up a great deal of exhibition space—until they were at last shipped off to the University Museum in 1911 by archaeologist Theodor Wiegand, who had his own finds to exhibit.[10]

Of course, the Royal Museums were by no means the only museums in the German states. In addition to the private or semipublic galleries and libraries owned by various of the German princes, in the aftermath of the Napoleonic Wars scores of local museums were founded by regional associations (*Vereine*) to display the heritage and treasures of Germany's diverse hometowns.[11] Many of these priovincial museums were more historically than aesthetically oriented and exhibited in their cramped, ill-lighted, and ill-tended galleries, diverse curiosities largely unappealing to those engaged in planning the contents of the national museums.[12] Interestingly, in the immediate aftermath of the wars, it appeared that the central state might take an interest in helping to cultivate these local institutions. But, as the reform era gave way to Metternichian reaction, Prussian bureaucrats retracted their support from projects like Wilhelm Dorow's Museum für Rheinisch-Westfälische Altertümer in Bonn; German national sentiment, essential to the defeat of the French, in the 1820s became a dangerous threat to the sovereignty of the German princes. The collection of Germanic antiquities that Dorow had amassed fell victim both to political reaction and to the rising prominence of the classical philologists, who now enjoyed enhanced institutional power as a result of Humboldt's reform of the universities and secondary schools.[13] In the early 1820s, Prussian officials allowed classicists from the University of Bonn to advise them on the dispensation of the museum of Rhenish antiquities; these scholars suggested it be cleared of nonclassical artifacts, which they thought overly large and ugly.[14] Dorow's position as museum director was eliminated, and thereafter his collecting and digging enterprises had to be accomplished during vacations from his new post at the Foreign Ministry. Reflecting on this period of classical hegemony, Dorow described the frustrations of the patriotic amateur: "People then had . . . no sympathy for national antiquities; they dreamed only of art works, of museums of Greek and Egyptian antiquities."[15]

Thus, after about 1821, collections of local or regional artifacts survived on private donations and provincial subsidies and concentrated their energies on the cultivation of provincial or local pride.[16] The exclusion of Germanic studies from prestigious cultural institutions undoubtedly reinforced the field's antiestablishment self-conception and localist preoccupations; political sanctions, combined with low status in the emerging intellectual hierarchy, compelled these museums and the *Vereine* that supported them to retreat from grand claims and nationalist rhetoric into data collection. Interpretation of artifacts — presumed to be either politically dangerous or beyond the intellectual capacity of the amateur — was left for later experts to complete. This situation produced a typologizing meticulousness and anti-speculative propensity that remain characteristic of German prehistorical and folkloric thought today.[17] The collections — and the number — of such museums continued to expand over the course of the century, providing the material and the antiestablishment personnel for fin de siècle challenges to the Royal Museums.

If, as I will argue, major changes in aesthetic experience at the turn of the century were largely the result of external social and scholarly forces pressing in upon the world of humanistic learning, the specialization and increasingly positivist orientation of the humanities themselves, after 1850, also helped to prepare the way for our modern, nonnormative assessment of the art of the past. It is instructive, in this light, to note that it was a classicist turned "orientalist" who brought a new infusion of museological historicism to the Royal Museums. Karl Richard Lepsius acquired from his mentor, the redoubtable classical philologist K. O. Müller, a strictly historicist approach to the study of the history, language, and writing of Egypt.[18] Trained as a linguist, Lepsius made his first contribution to his chosen field in 1837 by perfecting Champollion's decipherment of hieroglyphics. He accomplished this feat not by studying monuments in Egypt, but by making the circuit of European libraries, while employed as a research assistant to the pious polyhistorian and diplomat C. J. Bunsen.[19] But by 1841, Lepsius was anxious to make his own expedition to Egypt, to collect new inscriptions, and if possible, to bring back some monuments for Berlin's tiny Egyptian museum.[20] Lepsius's three-year sojourn in Egypt (1842–45) was one of the first of such expeditions to be state-supported and proved extremely profitable both for Lepsius and for the Prussian museums.

When the Egyptian artifacts were moved to August von Stüler's Neues Museum from the Monbijou Palace in 1859, Lepsius played a major role in the new exhibit's design. His final product combined scholarly concern for the geographical and historical accuracy of murals and displays with aesthetic appreciation for symmetry, color, and the integrity of works of art. These murals — adapted from drawings of actual Egyptian wall paintings Lepsius had made during his travels — were copied by other museums as well, including the Viennese Egyptian Museum. Strict historicist that he was, Lepsius filled in spaces in the Berlin collection with plaster casts; his re-creation of an Egyptian court scene represents a transitional phase between the cast museums of the past and the period rooms of the future. Tellingly, Lepsius's successor at the museum, Adolf Erman, would denounce Lepsius's aestheticizing additions and complain bitterly about the early administrators' decision to forgo the purchase of originals in favor of casts.[21]

Lepsius was not the first scholar to take part in the designing of collections; Wilhelm von Humboldt, as we have seen, was involved in planning the museum from the first, and in Bonn, Otto Jahn and F. G. Welcker were centrally involved in administration of the Akademisches Kunstmuseum and the Museum für Rheinisch-Westfälische Altertümer. But museum administrations, in the years before unification, still contained significant numbers of nonspecialists, court favorites, and connoisseurs; administrators spent little time on museum business, and their assistants were poorly paid. Wedded to a byzantine organizational structure that fostered internal rivalries, "this fatal administrative arrangement," as the Roman historian Theodor Mommsen described it, impeded acquisitions even when funds were available.[22]

Lepsius, born in 1810, not only was a devoted professional academic, but belonged to a younger generation of more positivist mien, and he and his fellows were eager to rid the museums of these amateur administrators and expand the museums' collections.[23] Their chance came only with German unification and the appointment of the young bureaucrat Richard von Schöne to the general directorship of the Royal Museums. Upon his appointment in 1880, Schöne, trained as a classical archaeologist, undertook a full-scale reform of the museums. As we have seen, at its founding, the Altes Museum was meant to house only classical antiquities and paintings, but over the years, several subsidiary "collections" or "departments" were added. Schöne was especially aggressive in creating new departments (there were six in 1880 and seventeen when he retired in 1905), including departments for ethnography, Islamic art, and Near Eastern art. If Humboldt wished to display great art, Schöne's mission was to keep up with scholarly developments. To this end, he hired prestigious scholars like Alexander Conze, Adolf Bastian, and Friedrich Delitzsch to direct the museums' departments. These figures — an archaeologist, an explorer-ethnographer, and an Assyriologist — were not likely to put beauty ahead of *Wissenschaft*.

Schöne oversaw the enormous expansion and diversification of the collections during his quarter-century tenure (1880–1905). But perhaps his most consequential innovation was the linkage he created between the museum and three scholarly organizations: the Deutsches Archäologisches Institut; the Berliner Gesellschaft für Archäologie, Ethnographie, und Urgeschichte; and the Deutsche Orient-Gesellschaft. By allowing these "disinterested" scientific associations to do the collecting, Schöne could keep his acquisition costs down and the museums' prestige high; he could also placate the Foreign Ministry, which was continually anxious lest German acquisitiveness appear to verge on colonialist rapacity.[24] The postivist orientation of these three agencies by the 1890s encouraged their excavation or purchase of a wide variety of rather more prosaic artifacts, in addition to items believed to be of real aesthetic interest. As the collections grew more scholarly and extensive, the beautiful was increasingly swamped by the typical.

This positivist-historicist trend was evident, too, in the antiquities departments of the museum, despite the ongoing exhibition of casts. Of course, the meaning and even the conventional picture of Greek sculpture had not remained static since Humboldt's time. Even in that philhellene's later years, admiration for the austerity of the Elgin Marbles had begun to undermine eighteenth-century conceptions of the classical ideal and to call into question the propriety of considering casts and Roman copies typical of Greek art. Only slowly, however, did European museums move to acquire their own examples of "real" Greek art. For Grecophiles, the Greek War of Independence and Byron's *Pilgrimage of Childe Harold* had made Elgin a villain; for eager collectors and dealers, Elgin's sufferings and financial ruin served as admonitions not to repeat his endeavors.[25] Having won its independence from the Ottomans, Greece remained politically unstable and rather dangerous until the 1870s. But, as the lure of originals grew, so too did German scholars and bureaucrats develop greater longings to acquire original Greek art. In 1875, a German team at last received permission to begin excavations at Olympia, and, using the latest "scientific" techniques, uncovered huge quantities of Greek artifacts. Regrettably for the excavators, however, this expedition found little in the way of exemplary statuary, with the exceptions of the much-publicized Nike of Panaios and the Hermes of Praxiteles. Even more regrettably, the Greek-German excavation treaty specified that the Greek government retain all finds, and the Germans, while proud of their magnaminity, had nothing but casts and doubles to put in their museums.[26]

This disappointing upshot and the unsatisfied longing to possess and display real Greek monuments account in large measure for the series of excavations undertaken by German archaeologists in Asia Minor between 1879 and 1914. In petitioning the Foreign Ministry for three hundred thousand marks for the completion of excavations at Miletus in 1894, the German ambassador in Constantinople, Count Radolin, explained that the dig was of vital importance, "because here is perhaps the last point where sizable art treasures in the area in question [Greek settlements on the Turkish coast] are to be found."[27] In 1896 the kaiser extracted a secret concession from the Ottoman sultan, specifying that the Reich was to receive half of all finds excavated by German archaeologists in Asia Minor; this provision, which contradicted the official Ottoman antiquities law, was designed initially to legitimize German plundering of Ionian (Greek) sites, though it was later applied to Mesopotamia as well.[28] Schöne, of course, was instrumental in the planning, funding, and execution of these excavations, for the finds were all to come into the possession of the Royal Museums. His close relationship with Germany's leading archaeologists testifies to his eagerness to acquire originals and novelties, in spite of the irksome difficulties of arranging expeditions, and the criticisms of aesthetic unworthiness that his prize acquisitions — including the Pergamon Altar — frequently suffered. Excavations, and Schöne's untiring pursuit of original artifacts, accelerated the trend toward museological historicism begun by Lepsius.

So far, so "modern" — but the striking thing about Schöne's archaeological and ethnographic collections is just how little of this diverse material was actually exhibited during his directorship of the museums. The Pergamon Altar — surely the best-known monument in Berlin's museums — was initially exhibited in fragments in the rotunda of Schinkel's Altes Museum; in 1902 a special museum opened to display a reconstruction of the altar, but it was soon found to be structurally unsound, and closed again in 1907. The altar was not displayed again until the opening of the new Pergamon Museum in 1929. When the Kaiser Friedrich Museum opened in 1905, space was available for some new exhibits, but its galleries were quickly filled with Renaissance and Germanic art, leaving only one room for orientalia and consigning the monumental (early Islamic) Mschatta Gate to a dark basement. The many monuments excavated by German teams in Mesopotamia languished for decades in storage rooms — partly as a result of diplomatic snafus, but partly also due to lack of exhibition space. The Asia Minor department of the museums, which included the celebrated Ishtar Gate from Babylon, opened to the public only in 1931. Storage rooms were so stuffed with oriental carpets, Byzantine mosaics, and Renaissance furniture that in 1921 art critic Karl Scheffler accused the museums of *Anhäufungspolitik*, a policy of heaping things up.[29]

Though Schöne was aggressively active in the acquisition of new sorts of artifacts, his heart was not in their exhibition — and especially not in the exhibition of less than exemplary works of art. The Museum für Völkerkunde (Ethnographic Museum), finally completed in 1886, had been built many blocks away from the "Museums Island" on the Spree (directly across from the imperial palace), and, though it housed Schliemann's Trojan collection, in the eyes of Schöne and the academic elite it clearly took a backseat to the antiquities collection, which, thanks to the excavations, continued to expand at a rapid rate. In 1921, Scheffler quipped: "If the era of the *Kaiserreich* had lasted fifty years longer, if the war had come later and excavations had continued, we would surely have had to make room in the museum for an entire Greek city."[30] Indeed, when engaged in planning a new series of museum buildings to house the burgeoning collections in the years just before his retirement, the museums director advocated giving over the whole Museums Island to the display of Mediterranean antiquities.[31] One might easily have said of Schöne, as he did of the excavator Carl Humann in 1896: "Above all, the grandeur and sublimity of Greek culture filled his soul; to bring its monuments out of oblivion into the light of day, to make them accessible for scholarly study and awe-filled contemplation in the present, to ornament the capital city of the restored Reich with them — that was what he strove for with all his heart."[32] Although, for the glory of the nation and the benefit of science, Schöne had promoted the extension of the collections into unfamiliar aesthetic realms, to display great art, for this classically-trained bureaucrat, still meant to display Greek sculpture.

Schöne's successor, Wilhelm von Bode, also belonged to this generation of half-scholarly, half-aestheticizing administrators. An employee of the museum administration since 1872, Bode had largely obtained his art-historical credentials by independent study and on-the-job experience; his tastes were heavily shaped, in his early years, by the work of the Swiss cultural historian Jakob Burckhardt, and as the dominant voice in the paintings department after 1872, the director of the Christian art section after 1884, and the general director of the Berlin Museums from 1905 to 1920, he was able to embody his preferences in the nonclassical galleries of the Royal Museums. Bode's first love was Renaissance art, which he made the focus of the new Kaiser Friedrich Museum (after World War II renamed for Bode himself), but his horizons broadened over time. Unlike Schöne, Bode esteemed paintings as highly as sculptures and was a great advocate of Germanic art (of the Renaissance era) as well as a collector of oriental carpets. An aggressive nationalist, Bode wished the Royal Museums to display works of singular beauty of all eras, as did the Louvre and the British Museum, and in 1911, he complained bitterly that the state was not contributing enough to the support of the Museums' Near Eastern, medieval, East Asian, Egyptian, Islamic, and Germanic departments.[33] Bode did not by any means wish to establish parity of departments or objects—he continued to champion Renaissance art above the other forms.[34] But his eclectic tastes and commitment to style-historical organization of the museums must certainly be considered more "modern" than Schöne's classicizing orientation, and as general director from 1905 to 1920, Bode operated in, and helped to elaborate, an aesthetic empyrean that had enormously expanded since his formative years in the 1850s and 1860s.[35]

We have now to consider the conditions for and consequences of this expansion, both promoted and hampered by establishment bureaucrats and academics like Schöne, Bode, and Lepsius. The conditions underlying these changes include the school reform movement, the sharpening of cultural competition among the great powers, the specialization of scholarship, and the rise of historicist style analysis. The collection of self-congratulatory and chauvanistic traits that usually falls under the heading "nationalism" forms an integral part of all of these developments, but I would prefer not to treat it as a separate (or separable) cultural entity. Let us start first by examining the wider social setting in which humanism began to lose its social prestige and the museums' social status and functions increased. We then turn to a consideration of the rise of the ethnological sciences and attempt to assess the ways in which this new complex of disciplines contributed to the decline, if not total disappearance, of an aristocratic, text-oriented conception of culture.

The Ancients and the Moderns, 1870–1914

Undoubtedly, the linchpin of the nineteenth-century German educational system was the secondary schools; they created the credentials upon which an educated bourgeoisie would create semimeritocratic social distinctions and a new, white-collar elite. Not surprisingly, then, they continued to be, throughout the century and beyond, the site of fierce battles between those whose interests and ideology had been institutionalized, and those who demanded recognition for their own projects of "reform."

It was, of course, a school reform movement of a sort that ushered in the reconfiguration of German schooling under Wilhelm von Humboldt. During his tenure as head of the Prussian Interior Ministry's Department of Educational and Cultural Affairs in 1809–10, Humboldt sought to secularize secondary education and take it out of the hands of local officials; he also sought to institutionalize a sort of nonutilitarian general education, one that emphasized the cultivation of individual talents—and the learning of classical langugages. In practice, this "neohumanist" education was never made universally available or accessible; girls were not invited to share Bildung's riches, nor was the underclass able to forgo work or vocational education for nine years of *Gymnasium* instruction. The churches gave up their role in secondary education reluctantly if at all, and in most places retained control at the elementary level. But for the elite, the *Gymnasium* became the school of choice, partly because its graduates were accorded unique privileges (like a monopoly on university entrance, which opened the door to careers in the bureaucracy and free professions), and partly because nonutilitarian, humanistic education was thought to be indispensible to the shaping of a (male) member of the cultured classes.

Even in Humboldt's day, however, there had been groups who advocated different sorts of universal schooling and many who opposed the implementation of his plan. For our purposes, the most important of these groups was the loose confederation of those who found *Gymnasium* schooling too abstract and old-fashioned; these men, frequently members of the so-called *Besitzbürgertum* (propertied middle class) as opposed to the *Bildungsbürgertum* (educated middle class) protested the lack of *Gymnasium* attention to "modern" subjects like German literature and history, the applied sciences, and geography. They resented bitterly the exclusion of students trained at the *Realschulen* (secondary schools that taught Latin and modern languages but no Greek) from the universities, and denounced the *Gymnasien* for stuffing students' heads with useless knowledge. By the 1860s, several associations had been formed for the advocacy of a new sort of school reform; in the ensuing decades, this movement took on new urgency and acquired new social legitimacy as unification created demands for economic modernization and "spiritual" unity.[36] By 1890, Kaiser Wilhelm II himself was defending school reform; at an important school conference held in that year, the emperor announced his support for the modernization of schooling. "We want to educate our pupils into young Germans," he affirmed, "not young Greeks and Romans." Classical education formed physically inferior, decadent thinkers rather than healthy, patriotic doers; the *Gymnasien*, he implied, menaced the success of the Reich's *Weltpolitik*.[37] Significantly, it was also this fin de siècle kaiser who befriended the Assyriologist Friedrich Delitzsch and the ethnologist Leo Frobenius and even undertook his own archaeological excavations on the island of Corfu.[38] The monarchy itself was beginning to promote the dual causes of national modernization and aesthetic eclecticism.

School reform was vehemently opposed by the Prussian bureaucracy, and by academic humanists, who feared that the demise of the *Gymnasium's* monopoly on university entrance would destroy German *Geist* and *Wissenschaft*. Ulrich von Wilamowitz-Moellendorff, the premier classical philologist of his day and a keen opponent of school reform, in 1892 argued that school reform posed "a grave danger to the intellectual and moral health of our *Volk*, or indeed, to all human culture."[39] Wilamowitz himself, however, was not an aestheticizing philhellenist, but a determined historicist. Just as perspectives on Greek art in museological circles had changed over the course of the century, Wilamowitz and his fellow philologists had abandoned classicizing nostalgia for advocacy of the historical significance of Greek culture. But they still insisted that classical language training remain central to the curriculum and rejected out of hand complaints that antiquity had become irrelevant to the lives of their students. The specialization of scholarship had impressed on them the potential historical import of diverse places and eras, but the humanistic establishment was not yet ready to admit the equal interest of, for example, classical and "Oriental" history.[40]

Two additional factors, however, were eroding even this defense of the "ancients": the rise of international competition among scholars and the continued attractiveness of academia to young intellectuals. Since the Revolutionary Wars, the Germans had prided themselves on belonging to a land of "poets and thinkers"; after about 1820, German scholarly prowess became a central bragging point for liberals discontented with German weakness and disunity. Even before unification and more aggressively afterward, Germans had begun to think of scholarship as the realm for the demonstration of their nation's fitness for a premier place among the civilized nations. The excavations at Olympia were launched in this spirit; supported by Kaiser Wilhelm I, Crown Prince Friedrich, and quantities of ambassadors, administrators, and scholars (but not by Reich Chancellor Otto von Bismarck), the excavations were intended to crown the military victory over the French with a peaceful triumph in the realm of classical scholarship.[41] As competition between national "schools" for new excavation sites increased, the exhumation of past cultures became more and more a means to display German power, intellectual and actual.

Nowhere was this eagerness to keep up with the other Europeans so evident as in deliberations about the future of the museums. Schöne, as we have seen, oversaw a colossal expansion, diversification, and academization of the Royal Museums, but others played their part; the pleas directed to the Education, Finance, and Foreign Ministries by scholars and amateurs of all descriptions invariably stressed the enhancement of German prestige abroad that would result from the granting of funds for new acquisitions or expeditions. The Academy of Sciences, for example, in 1897 pled with Education Minister Robert Bosse to authorize and fund excavations in Mesopotamia. "It could only befit the cultural significance of the German Empire," they wrote, "if German work in the future no longer remains unrepresented where there is a world lost from human memory to resurrect and millennia of human histories, sculptural works, and inscriptions to recover." Dispelling fears that Germany might receive no concrete recompense for these labors, the academy averred: "treasures of the previously mentioned types, like those that fill the halls of the British Museum and the Louvre, are still there . . . in great quantity."[42] It was probably Schöne's keen desire to bring the German museums up to the level of the Louvre and the British Museum, and not his interest in the multiplicity of beautiful forms, that led him to establish some of the more exotic branches of the museums. Even if Czech altarpieces or Assyrian seals did not enhance the aesthetic appeal of the museums, they did function as proofs of Germany's adeptness at acquisition. Yet, however unwittingly, their study and collection did open the way for this century's expansion of aesthetic experience and the multiplication of our sources of knowledge about the past.

Academia's continued appeal, ironically, also contributed to the diversification of aesthetic experience. Part of the legacy of the post-Napoleonic and post-1848 reactions surely included the academic elite's attempt to secure fortress *Wissenschaft* against both governmental and popular intrusions. The advantages of cultural invincibility (as well as the social prestige and privileges of academics) attracted, over the century, an increasing number of acolytes; the disadvantages for these young aspirants, however, included a diminishing number of dissertation topics in fields of recognized importance (especially classical philology) and increasing pressure to serve as the lowest data collectors in evolving hierarchies of knowledge making. Yet, even after romanticism waned in the world of fiction writing, the fetishization of novelty lingered on in academia, and scholars, to earn respect, were required to discover, create, or invent something new. In these circumstances, both students and professors could hardly help but be attracted to less-plowed fields like medieval art or Indology. The decipherment of scores of new scripts led to the rise of new competitors (notably Egyptology and Assyriology), which eventually became powerful enough to claim their own university chairs. Where once humanists had to be content with biblical and classical texts, a much richer and more complicated world was now available to the scholar. But if specialization and diversification occurred rather naturally, integrating new knowledge about past cultures into a coherent worldview and into existing institutional arrangements was not so easy; and in practice, classical antiquity largely retained its normative status in secondary schools and university humanities faculties at least as late as the founding of the Weimar Republic.

Although national rivalries and humanistic specialization had begun to erode the foundations of aestheticizing classicism, it was, I believe, the rise to prominence of a new sort of knowledge that handed the ancients their final defeat. We have to consider here the rise of what I described at the outset as the "ethnological sciences," a collection of specialist fields that had in common the attempt to organize and explain material culture or human remains (including historical geography, ethnology, art history, folklore studies, archaeology, paleontology, and physical anthropology). Of course, none of these subspecialties was new in the post-1870 era, but all of them underwent great expansion, elaboration, and at least attempted professionalization in this period. Historical geography is perhaps the most obvious example. Developed in response to Darwinism's historicization of natural history, historical geography sought to unite the descriptive study of the earth's features with ethnology on the one hand and the geopolitical aspirations of the Reich on the other. The stategy proved successful, and in the wake of unification, a series of geography chairs were created at the top German universities. New sorts of publications appeared, advertising geography's ability to mediate between the natural and the human sciences. In a series of essays and books written in the 1870s and 1880s, Friedrich Ratzel almost single-handedly converted geography into what he called "Anthropo-Geographie," the study of human prehistory by means of tracking the diffusion of material culture as a zoologist would trace the migration of species.[43] Ratzel used analyses of style (most famously, of bow types) to write a new, more inclusive form of *Universalgeschichte* than that written by the Rankeans.[44] His half-scientific, half-historical method would appeal widely to the next generaton of cultural geographers and ethnologists. The Austrian ethnologist Wilhelm Schmidt, for example, would convert Ratzelian descriptions of "culture circles" — areas of shared traits — into a theory of global cultural diffusion and would organize a journal and a vast network of missionary data collectors to flesh out the story.[45]

Increasingly, geographers asserted the political importance of their discipline. Ratzel, a proponent of migrationist colonialism, penned numerous essays linking his geographical insights to Germany's future role in world history. More subtly, Ferdinand Freiherr von Richthofen contributed to the linkages between geographical science and patriotic pride. As a young man, Richthofen—trained as a geologist—had traveled to East Asia as part of a trade mission led by Graf von Eulenburg; when Eulenburg's party sailed home, Richthofen stayed to continue his studies, which included an arduous four-year survey of the geography of China. He returned to a position at the University of Bonn in 1875; in 1883, he received a chair at the University of Leipzig, already home to Ratzel; and three years later, he finally received a call to Berlin. Here he conveyed to the students in his renowned geography seminar—including the intrepid adventurers Sven Hedin, Leo Frobenius, and Ernst Drygalski—his ferocious will to find and conquer unmapped expanses.[46] He also published a revised version of his extensive (745 pages) manual for amateur surveyors, which he hoped would give missionaries and travelers the tools to "read" the landscape scientifically.[47] And finally, of course, he wished to found a museum. But typically, too, Richthofen's Museum für Meereskunde, completed after the founder's death, as Sven Hedin reported, was little frequented by Berliners: they preferred, Hedin lamented, to visit the antiquities galleries of the Royal Museums.[48]

Richthofen's successor in the Berlin chair, Albrecht Penck, exemplifies the transition from positivism to activism, from underappreciated discipline to politicized science characteristic of many of the ethnological sciences in early-twentieth-century Germany. Trained as a mineralogist, Penck became a geographer by virtue of his intensive studies of the Ice Age in Europe, a subject that also took him into the realms of prehistory and physical anthropology. As early as 1886, Penck published *Das deutsche Reich*, a half-popular, half-scholarly study intended to give the Reich's new boundaries scientific legitimacy and to explain away opposition to Prussia's dictates as a function of superficial, historical contingencies. During the Great War, Penck published a series of essays on the volatile topic of the "natural" borders of Germany and its neighbors; after his retirement in 1926, he devoted himself to the propagation of a "national geography."[49] In a 1916 essay, entitled "The War and the Study of Geography," Penck insisted that while the Napoleonic Wars had produced a German humanism based on history, this new, greater war would establish the prominence of a new set of more future-oriented disciplines: "This war will assure us of a place in the sun. In the future we will live more in the present than previously and true humanism will consist in clear recognition of this. The cultivation of geographical knowledge will make an essential contribution to furthering [this new humanism]."[50] A natural scientist and a fervent nationalist, Penck exemplified the new confidence of the ethnological sciences, now eager to find their own "place in the sun."

Geography was by no means the only discipline to expand its purview, body of practitioners, and claims to patriotic usefulness. Ethnology also experienced expansion as the doctors and amateur travelers of the 1850s and 1860s gave way in the next generation to an enlarged cohort of specialists. Archaeology and paleontology made their respective breaks from philology and comparative anatomy, and folkloric studies flourished as leisure time, middle-class wealth, and urbanization increased. In all these areas, new activity spurred the launching of new journals, new collecting ventures required the creation of new museums, and once created, new journals and museums encouraged new inquiries and acquisitions. In 1927 there were still at least 143 local history museums in Germany, despite the centralizing efforts of state-funded institutions.[51] Many of the attempts made by scholars in these fields to reach wider publics were successful; the mid-nineteenth-century geographic journal *Petermanns Mitteilungen* boasted a circulation of thirty thousand but soon other, more popular journals joined the competition.[52]

Some university chairs were created in these fields, but the end of the century brought a closing off of jobs for young aspirants just as the new fields began to produce trained experts. The disappointments engendered by this constriction of the job market were deeply felt and tended to exacerbate the aggressive nationalism (and antiestablishment sentiment) of practitioners in these fields. These conditions shaped the careers of men like the Germanic prehistorian Gustav Kossinna and the Byzantine art historian Josef Strzygowski, both of whom eventually received academic posts, but only after serving long and low-paying apprenticeships in libraries and museums.[53] Resentful that their specialities and their talents had gone so long unrecognized, these two cantankerous individuals developed sincere hatred of what Strzygowski called "the humanist faction," as well as ultranationalist defenses of their scholarly legitimacy. The university scholars' hostility toward amateurs like Schliemann, popular pursuits like folkloric studies, and fanatics like Kossinna and Strzygowski also aggravated tensions between the older humanities and the newer ethnological sciences. During the war and in the years following, attacks on the classicizing humanities — like that of Penck — began in earnest, incorporating the criticisms of the school reform movement into a general, often *völkisch* assault on the narrowness, superficiality, and suspiciously "cosmopolitan" orientation of German humanists.

For most members of this generation of ethnological scholars, the museum remained the central institution around which their work revolved. The expansion of museum activities had in fact encouraged the elaboration of many of these fields; as German expeditions hauled home artifacts from the African jungles, the deserts of Chinese Turkestan, and the vast plains of Assyria, museum assistants were called upon to describe, date, and catalog unfamiliar forms. This museological context, as well as the half-humanistic, half-natural-scientific training of the participants, helps to explain the central methological conviction these disciplines developed: the principle that stylistic features constituted reliable clues to the historical and often ethnic origins of the artifact in question. Articulated most clearly in the revelatory "readings" of paintings by the Italian doctor-connoisseur Giovanni Morelli, this principle was elaborated for the purposes of "reading" material remains by the Viennese scholar (and curator of oriental carpets) Alois Riegl.[54] But the multitudes of local prehistorians and folklorists did not need Riegl or Morelli to tell them that stylistic typologies could stand in for texts where documents were scarce or nonexistent: these latter-day antiquarians, as we have seen, had been perfecting their formal chronologies at least since the 1820s.[55]

Raised on classical philology, however, German scholars found it difficult to accept attributions or chronologies based exclusively on the stylistic analysis of artifacts. Long into the twentieth century, archaeologists as well as treasure hunters recognized an unwritten order of significance for their finds, as applicable in the Mediterranean as in Babylon or Tun-huang: (1) manuscripts and inscriptions; (2) monumental sculpture; (3) wall paintings or mosaics; (4) pottery; (5) figurines, articles of daily life, etc. This order was partly dictated by official patrons—the academies of science demanded manuscripts, the national museums pursued monumental sculpture—but even most of those devoted to the recovery of the material life of the past, it seems, shared the historians' presumption that only texts could generate legitimate scholarly interpretations, while artifacts supplied at best indirect, ambiguous proofs. Initially, it seems, Heinrich Schliemann had believed that he would need to find inscriptions to prove that he had discovered the remains of ancient Troy at Hissarlik. In a personal letter of 1872, he wrote: "Even if I uncover the palaces of Priam, Hector, and Paris, I will not be credited with having solved the Troy question. Inscriptions are what is desired, and I must and will find inscriptions of that age; I will find them if I have to dig fifty feet deeper."[56] "The prehistorian," wrote Moriz Hoernes in 1893, "is like a doctor who treats a child and must diagnose its condition, without being able to speak to the patient."[57] Both Hoernes and Schliemann hoped that by borrowing methods from the natural sciences, they might develop a systematic means for the study of primitive culture; but both also recognized that in their day, material evidence was, as it remains today, an inferior sort of historical testimony. It did not help the case that some members of the group made outlandish claims; in the years just before the First World War, the ethnologist Leo Frobenius, a great admirer of Schliemann, made a valiant attempt to prove that he had found the lost island of Atlantis—in southwest Africa. Although a widely respected and exceedingly energetic collector of African art and artifacts, Frobenius had little but some vague passages of Herodotus and a few Etruscan clay masks on which to base his claims.[58]

Yet, for a number of reasons, by about 1910 conclusions reached by stylistic analysis had achieved greater intellectual and especially social respectability than they had previously enjoyed. Morelli had demonstrated that style criticism was indispensable for authenticating works of questionable provenance, date, or authorship—precisely the sorts of artifacts that continued to pour into German museums. Frobenius, for example, had returned from his travels in central Africa in 1906 with a collection of eight thousand artifacts, which he turned over to the Hamburg Ethnography Museum as reimbursement for its support of his trip.[59] Nationalist prehistorians like Kossinna and Felix Dahn had made the publishing of the "ur-history" of the Germanic tribes popular—and their extensive knowledge of sword types and pot styles impressed even the dubious humanists.[60] Increasingly, private collections or privately funded museums were transformed into professionally directed, public galleries; this permitted new groups access to artifacts and also raised the status of collectors and curatorial experts. Finally, the immediacy of the appeal of objects to a society increasingly able to buy illustrated journals or visit museums should not be discounted, and it was not ignored by the classicists in the wake of rising challenges to their cultural hegemony. In the mid-1890s, Alexander Conze, the director of the Deutsches Archäologisches Institut, undertook to distribute an array of what he called "Anschauungsmittel," visual teaching aids intended to impress students having little interest in grammar with the glories of the Greeks.[61] The visual, it might be said, was replacing the literary as the primary source of aesthetic experience and norms.

Ethnology Comes of Age

The rise to prominence of stylistic analysis and the ethnological sciences had a transformative effect on aesthetics and ultimately on museum design and content. Increasingly, originals drove out casts; in 1907, George Swarzenski, founder of the Städtische Galerie in Frankfurt, sold the gallery's collection of two hundred casts in order to be able to buy originals—at first chiefly Renaissance and classical pieces, but soon Gothic and baroque pieces, began to dominate the collection. By 1919 the museum was seeking to integrate new acquisitions of East Asian and Coptic works with its prized Roman copy of the Athena of Myron and its other prewar masterpiece, a grand majolica altarpiece by Andrea Della Robbia.[62] Swarzenski, pressed by limited funds and a more historicist aesthetic, was undoubtedly typical of the museum directors of the 1910s and 1920s; Bode's tastes, too, diversified over time.

Changes in art-historical writing played a crucial role in the establishment of a nonnormative discussion of art forms, allowing Heinrich Schäfer, director of the Berlin Egyptian Museum, to argue in 1925 that Egyptian art was not inferior to classical art but was simply the result of a different sort of "seeing."[63] But art historians' ability to jettison old ideals for a new, more comprehensive understanding of style was itself in large part a response to the new experiences offered by the acceleration and diversification of public and private collecting and to the broadening of *Universalgeschichte* by geographers and ethnologists in the wake of the Darwinian revolution. All too often, in assessing this "modernizing" process, the centrality of the museum—as the site that permitted the elaboration of the scholarly study of artifacts—has been overlooked, leaving us with what seems to me an overly philosophical history of art-historical ideas.

Clearly, the nonnormative study of style could not easily be squared with neohumanist faith in the aesthetic exemplarity of the ancients—it is telling that Bode himself deeply disapproved of the Morellian method.[64] But by about 1910, it was evident that Bode's generation was losing its cultural potency—if not its institutional dominance. As parts of the school reform movement's complaints were taken over by nationalists weary of the ascendancy merely of German *Geist* and by youths longing for meaning disencumbered from the weight of historical and linguistic adiaphora, the era of text-based, Grecophile culture appeared to be nearing its end. Scholars who trafficked in archival notes or grammatical nuances, especially philologists, were parodied; artists and writers sought inspiration from India, Africa, Germanic prehistory, and a natural world untouched by Adam or the Greeks. Oswald Spengler predicted the imminent decline of the West, and in 1921, Germans flocked to hear Rabindranath Tagore, hoping that the Indian poet might offer some sage "oriental" solution to their nation's ills.[65] In 1923, Leo Frobenius reflected on the changes that had occurred since the publication of his first ethnographic studies of Africa in the 1890s. "At that time," he wrote, "philology and the natural sciences reigned. Culture in general, and especially the culture of such a 'wild' continent as Africa, was anything but popular. Today, in the streets, in salons, and even in the lecture halls, nothing, it seems is so much discussed as culture. Today, Buddhas, African figurines, and Oceanic masks are highly valued, in intellectual as well as monetary terms."[66] If not all of those eagerly discussing "culture" in the Weimar era understood it in the same way as did Frobenius and Spengler, it is certain that the aristocratic definition no longer predominated; an anthropological, geographical, and sometimes racial understanding of "culture" had largely replaced the elitist, but universalist, humanistic conception.

Museums played a central part in the demise of classical humanism, although their exhibition areas often reflected the partial and incomplete progress of modernization. It is worth noting that an enormous series of quarrels over exhibition space convulsed Berlin as late as the 1910s and 1920s, and it is instructive that here, once again, the classicists by and large won the battle. Even the Nazi regime — so solicitous toward the more aggressively nationalist exponents of the ethnological sciences — sought to prove the nobility of its aims by underlining the dual aesthetic and racial exemplarity of the Greeks. But perhaps the classicizing faction won its last battles under this regime — thanks to Hitler's preference for classical forms — for in the years since 1945, and especially since the mid-1960s, the classicism of Winckelmann or even of Schöne has come to seem cold, remote, and even lifeless. It seems safe to wager that the quarrel between the ancients and moderns has now been decided; but as we savor the "exotic" wings of our museums, we would do well to recall just how recently this battle raged.

11. The Museum's Discourse on Art

The Formation of Curatorial Art History in Turn-of-the-Century Berlin

The community of scholars of art falls into two different groups, if not two parties. The academic chairs
are occupied by gentlemen who like to call themselves historians, while in museum offices you meet
"connoisseurs." The historians preferably start out
from the general to reach the specific, from the abstract to the concrete, from the intellectual to the
visual, while the connoisseurs move in the opposite
direction. Both usually get stuck half way through,
without actually meeting each other.
— Max J. Friedländer, *Von Kunst und Kennerschaft*

When the German museum curator Max J. Friedländer attempted to describe the field of discourse in which he situated his art criticism, he confronted two different attitudes of art-historical scholarship and associated
them with clearly distinct images of professional behavior.[1] There is good reason to assume that Friedländer intended to create the impression of an archetypal metaphor for his audience of 1920. Yet, besides its function as a literary
device, the juxtaposition that he offered to his readers referred to a specific
experience in contemporary reality. As exemplified by Friedländer's account,
the appearance of two different and potentially conflicting discourses on the
history of art at the turn of the century was well registered by contemporaries
when reflecting on their position within the cultured public.

The emergence of this fundamental rift within the community of art historians can be traced better in Germany than elsewhere, through a series of controversies that characterized the problematic relationship between professors and museum administrators under the *Kaiserreich*. Germany was among the first countries to establish art history among the academic curricula, and its museums were foremost in introducing effective management. Since the discourse on art both as promoted by academic art history in the universities and as contained in the practice of curatorial connoisseurship came to engender an advanced degree of professional self-esteem at approximately the same time, the tensions between their practitioners increased considerably. Up to then museum administrations had been dominated largely, if not exclusively, by artists and amateurs, while "scholars of art" had defined the theoretical framework that constituted the museum. The scholars eventually managed to introduce a new field of studies into the fabric of academic discourses on culture and history during the latter half of the nineteenth century and from this vantage point defined standards of professionalism for the administration of art museums. After about 1880 the leading positions as museum curators were restricted entirely to academically trained art historians. But at the turn of the century exactly this successful attempt to oust amateurism was to upset the previously balanced relationship between the university and the museum.

For many reasons, the struggle over the administration of art museums became particularly acute in German society during the decades that followed the creation of a national state under Prussian hegemony in 1871. Under the impression of a serious "belatedness" in comparison to the long-established nations of the West, in particular the rival powers of France and Britain, influential sectors of the German public shared the preoccupation of the state authorities, claiming that their policy had to compensate for the time spent in political disunity. Through a series of diverse discourses, ranging from historical self-reflection to considerations of economic competition, members of the intellectual and financial elite continually voiced this concern.[2] A latent feeling of inferiority extended to the public art museums, which had traditionally been under the protection of the state. More than any other German government, that of Prussia adopted a policy of intensified support for their art museums, concentrating on the Royal Collections in Berlin, hoping to compete with the established museums in Paris and London. Within a few years after 1871 the amount of subsidies to these collections for acquisition and installation more than tripled and thereafter remained continuously on a high level. Under these circumstances the conflict concerning the administration of public museums was as much a conflict about the control of large-scale state subsidies as it was about definitions of cultural identity.[3] The first incident to be considered here occurred in 1891, when two of the foremost representatives of the Prussian art administration were involved in an argument about museum policy. For the first time, Herman Grimm, the leading art historian at the University of Berlin, and Wilhelm von Bode, the most successful museum curator in the capital, appealed to a broad public audience to promote their rival claims.

Wilhelm von Bode, who became director of the department of paintings of the Berlin Royal Collections in 1890, must have seemed the obvious choice for this position. His international reputation as a connoisseur and his abilities as an administrator, both well known to his superiors, were exactly the qualities required of a director whose mandate was to raise the status of the museums in Berlin. However, this appreciation was not universally shared by contemporaries, and the new director attracted harsh criticism within a year of assuming office. In fact, the promotion of Bode to this prestigious position was taken as a provocation by a particular group among the cultured public, the academic art historians, who saw their influence over art museums being eclipsed by the emergence of a new brand of professional museum managers.

Bode had made his career entirely within the museum administration, which he had joined in 1872 as an assistant in the sculpture department. He himself stressed the almost autodidactic manner in which he had acquired his competence as an art historian and a connoisseur. After having taken his first degree in law, he changed to art history only to present a doctoral thesis at the University of Leipzig within little more than a year after enrollment. Characteristically he submitted a *catalogue raisonné* of the work of Frans Hals, who had only recently become fashionable. The knowledge Bode could deploy in this type of research relied upon extensive firsthand experience of works of art in the major European collections rather than upon continuous adherence to the academic curricula. This particular competence was required in order to establish the authenticity of those paintings that were traditionally assembled under the name of Frans Hals. Connoisseurship was based on detailed visual comparisons between well-documented works of art, which served as points of reference, and a large number of other works whose provenance was uncertain, and which might have been significantly altered as a result of later restorations. In discerning deviations from what could be considered with reasonable certainty as the master's own work, the connoisseur adjudicated whether a given work of art could have emanated from his

FIGURE 1. Right to left: Wilhelm von Bode, Max J. Friedländer, and Anton Hauser (the head of the conservation department) in a gallery of the Berlin painting collection. The photo dates from before 1904. Courtesy of Stiftung Preußischer Kulturbesitz Berlin.

workshop or not. For a *catalogue raisonné*, however, a more specific decision about the personal involvement of the master of the workshop was required that could be based only on the quality of execution. As a consequence, successful connoisseurship displayed a combination of highly specialized versatility in empirical observation and a certain amount of self-assurance in advancing aesthetic judgments.

During his years in the museum administration Bode fused this connoisseurial attitude to art with a detailed knowledge of the international art market that allowed for many successful acquisitions on a limited budget. This success was based on a close observation of Europe's main marketplaces, achieved through extensive traveling and contact with confidential agents, as well as on gathering firsthand information about the holdings and circumstances of private collections that might appear on the market one day. In order to supplement the state-funded budget of his institution, Bode began to organize a close interdependence between museum curators and local collectors that would eventually generate additional funds and donations. With this entrepreneurial approach, Bode epitomized the new type of museum manager more than any of his colleagues. His success in achieving an unprecedented expansion of the state collections seemed the more spectacular to the contemporary public since most of the transactions on which it was based remained hidden in the realm of commercial discretion.[4]

Bode's antagonist in the controversy of 1891 had started his career almost at the same time that Bode entered the museum service. In 1873 Herman Grimm became the first regular professor of art history at the University of Berlin. This was the fifth chair of the new discipline in the country, for its establishment at German universities had only begun in 1860.[5] He had recommended himself thanks to a thorough education as an academic historian, as well as through his descent from a family of famous scholars.[6] Grimm's understanding of art history was based on the philosophy of Hegel and on Goethe's essays on literature and art, rather than on the positivist school of historiography then prevailing in Germany. He regarded the newly established discipline he was to represent in Berlin as part of a much larger project that he believed would eventually include in its scope the evolution of human culture and ideas in general. This envisaged integration of art, music, and literature into the history of ideas amounted to a new conception of cultural history (*Kulturgeschichte*). Grimm praised its most eminent representatives, Jakob Burckhardt and Carl Justi, more than any of his more specialized colleagues in the newly created art history departments.

Within the framework of *Kulturgeschichte*, art would have to be under-

FIGURE 2. Herman Grimm's official portrait as chairholder. Engraving made from a photograph, dating from the 1890s. Courtesy of Humboldt University, Berlin.

stood as one manifestation among others of the human spirit in history, although a particularly privileged one. In the tradition of Hegel and idealist aesthetics, Grimm believed that works of art were especially expressive of the *Zeitgeist*, the spirit prevailing in a particular period of the past, as long as they were the manifestations of real genius. For that reason he concentrated his efforts entirely on the achievements of what he regarded as the great men in the history of art, displaying in the process a distinctly conservative taste for High Renaissance art in Italy, specifically that of Leonardo, Michelangelo, and above all Raphael. In his lengthy monographs on the life and works of these artists he tried to portray them as titans, larger than life in their ambitions and achievements, against a broad panorama of contemporary culture that served to highlight the preeminence of his protagonists.[7]

Occasional remarks by Bode concerning a lack of cooperation between the museum and the university infuriated Grimm, who took the opportunity to launch a fundamental attack against the new director and his methods. Interestingly, he chose to include this riposte in an examination of the prospects and the place of art history within the field of academic discourses on culture and history, which he submitted to the respected periodical *Deutsche Rundschau* in 1891.[8] Here he expanded on his concept of *Kulturgeschichte*, into which art history would ultimately merge, and explained his pedagogical principles. He argued that the new trend of positivist expertise, concerned predominantly with securing correct dates and attributions for hitherto un-identified works, was entirely misconceived: "The task of the university teacher is neither to treat students as professional connoisseurs, nor to educate them for this role, but to heighten their awareness of the spiritual values embodied in those works of art, out of the enormous mass that is preserved to us, that are the most important through being richest in their content — not those works that are most debated among experts, but those that are most representative of their period."[9]

According to Grimm, connoisseurship, as represented by Bode's administration of the museum, reduced art history to secondary questions of authenticity and style at the expense of the most important issues of cultural tradition embodied in the "spiritual content" of the masterpieces that Grimm preferred to discuss in his lectures. Therefore the Berlin painting collection could not provide the material basis for his teaching, since its selection of artifacts was largely due to chance, depending on the predilections of curators past and present and the whims of the art market. While second- and third-rate masters had been acquired in large numbers, the major artists were underrepresented at best. In accordance with his traditional taste, Grimm felt the lack of major works by artists of the "classical phase" of the Italian Renaissance like Raphael or Michelangelo, while disregarding the extensive and systematically assembled collection of earlier, Quattrocento painting in Berlin, which he still regarded as a primitive and preparatory phase in the development toward artistic perfection.

The reason for this mistaken approach, Grimm argued, was that museum curators acted as if they were private collectors and followed their personal tastes, unrestrained by the fact that they were spending public money. Yet he had a remedy at hand that would counterbalance the inaccessibility of "those works of art which are the most important" and reduce the dangers of unrestrained collecting. Grimm proposed a scheme for an exhaustive museum of reproductions, which he called the *Museum für vaterländische Kunst-*

geschichte ("Museum of the Art History of the Fatherland"), although it was by no means restricted to German art. Rather than glorifying a national tradition in art, its purpose was to demonstrate the preeminence of art-historical scholarship in Germany. Housed in large open spaces similar to those of industrial architecture, the collection was to contain a systematic survey of sculpture in plaster casts and a similarly comprehensive selection of painting in modern oil copies, arranged by individual artists, whose development could be represented in minute detail, including every single work known to be by their hands.

Although essentially utopian in its scope, this proposal was part of a well-established nineteenth-century tradition of assembling vast collections of plaster casts, even if the practice had only rarely extended to copies of paintings.[10] In Berlin a collection of plaster casts had been created in the 1840s and was the fastest-growing department of the Royal Collections until well into the 1880s. Yet with the ascent of curatorial connoisseurship, the high status of plaster casts among museum administrators was eclipsed by a new interest in original works of art and an equally new ability to trace down previously undesired parts of the cultural heritage that were still available. More than anybody else, Wilhelm von Bode stood for this paradigmatic change in collecting, proving his predecessors wrong in asserting that no more major works could be bought. The shift of interest toward original works increasingly marginalized the collection of plaster casts. In 1887 a new building with more space for this department was still part of the building program, but it was to be erected separately from the main core of the institution in the center of Berlin, at a location in a suburb. In 1896 the plan was entirely dismissed in favor of a new building to house the growing number of original works, the Kaiser Friedrich Museum, and finally in 1911 the department was dissolved and most of its holdings handed over to the university to form a study collection.[11]

At the time Grimm put forward his ideal museum of reproductions, this proposal already had the character of a rearguard action, in keeping with his conservative taste, which made him unable to appreciate new areas in which the museum was collecting. The reaction to his critique made it unmistakably clear that the argument was one between necessary modernization and outdated traditionalism. Bode chose not to answer personally but delegated his justification to an anonymous author, who published under the pseudonym "W. Koopmann."[12] Koopmann, who defended Bode's museum policy in the periodical *Die Gegenwart* ("The Present"), deliberately underestimated the importance of different and at least partly conflicting interests within the two institutions involved. Since Grimm had embedded his attack in a consideration of the methodology of art history, Koopmann rejected his concept of *Kulturgeschichte* from the outset:

We cannot even begin to speak of a science of art in the strict sense, or of a philosophical inquiry into the nature of art, or even of understanding of a work of art in terms of cultural history, as long as the best representatives of art criticism disagree about which is a genuine work by Dürer and which is not, and what can be recognized as being by Leonardo's own hand and what cannot. For the foreseeable future there is no possibility that the most important questions of that kind will be resolved.[13]

To Koopmann it was inevitable that art history had to limit itself to a positivist, critical evaluation of its material, postponing any further considerations to a distant future. In his concept there remained virtually no room for the "spiritual content" of art, while he confronted the educational ideals of the academic world with a utilitarian approach to the university's role in society. Instead of disinterested exchange of ideas among men of letters, who refrained from any practical instrumentalization of their theories, the purpose of academic art history should be, above all else, the training of future connoisseurs and museum curators. Here Grimm's teaching at the university had proved to be utterly inadequate and furthermore demonstrated his lack of any real experience of art, according to Koopmann.

In repudiating Grimm's utopian museum as a "monstrosity," Koopmann asserted that the primary function of the art museum was to foster and develop an aesthetic appreciation of art in the general public — exactly the kind of appreciation that Grimm lacked. This aim could be attained only through an encounter with the aura emanating from original masterpieces. The educational purpose of the museum, its role as a home for art expertise, would come second. But that also could be achieved only through a broad selection of original works, which would enable a comparison of stylistic differences between the various masters and within their oeuvres. Bode himself argued this point with Grimm in personal conversations over and over again: "I used to respond in these instances that even a mere fragment of a beautiful original work was of more importance to our museums than the cast of the most magnificent monument or a copy of a famous painting."[14]

Clearly the two antagonists had a fundamentally different notion of the function of the art museum. Whereas Grimm envisioned a didactic institution devoted to the transmission of academic knowledge to an audience supposedly in need of traditional *Bildung*, Bode promoted an aesthetic concept that made the museum one of the cornerstones in a larger effort to improve taste in general. Within the framework of the German arts and crafts movement, the *Kunstgewerbebewegung*, the position of the art museum was complementary to the function of institutes for applied arts. While their collections were to display models and examples of successful design past and present as stimulus and model for artisans, the departments of "fine arts" were to raise the aesthetic standards of future consumers by educating their taste through objects of the highest possible quality. In this respect Bode had gained the support of the Prussian Emperor Friedrich III, who had sanctioned his reform program explicitly in a memorandum on cultural policy intended to promote Germany's economic development.[15]

There is no doubt that the essay in *Die Gegenwart* presented a convincing justification of Bode's museological practices and prevented further onslaughts by exponents of academic art history. While the overt conservatism of Grimm made it easy to counteract his criticism as long as it concerned strictly museological questions, the controversy of 1891 brought to light an underlying issue of far-reaching importance. For the first time the emerging conflict between a discourse on the history of art suited to the needs of the administration of a museum and quite another discourse suited to the practice of academic learning became visible to a larger public.

From the moment that Grimm's statement opened the dispute over methodology, both adversaries were prompted to venture into the territory of the other, far exceeding their specific competencies. Although this foray proved to be a failure for Grimm, since the future belonged to that curatorial attitude toward museum management which he despised, the designation of academic art history as training for future curators, as expounded by Koopmann, would have meant a serious and probably fatal limitation of the newly established discipline. According to the ideology of German universities during the nineteenth century and well beyond, the defining feature of academic learning was seen as disinterested discourse, as opposed to practical training that was relegated to less prestigious institutions of higher education. Only those discourses that kept a certain distance from their possible practical application had a chance to enter university curricula. The discourse of art history had achieved this status after half a century of struggle and could not afford to hazard its success.

Furthermore, in order to gain access into the academic world, art history had made itself the inheritor of a broad range of older discourses on art and culture. By reducing it to a positivist accumulation of facts, as proposed by Koopmann, these traditions were destined to be lost. Among those discourses the concept of *Kulturgeschichte*, as it had evolved in the period of political restoration before 1848, was the most prominent, featuring two interrelated agendas at the same time. Insofar as it was concerned with the material culture of "ordinary people," it offered a republican alternative to the monarchocentric historiography of state affairs. Insofar as it promoted cultural values, it supported the goal of national unification as prefigured in the ideal of the *Kulturnation*.[16]

Until the defeat of the revolution of 1848, the creation of national identity and the urge for democratic participation went hand in hand. In the latter half of the nineteenth century, these political agendas were separated, as a large part of the German public reconciled itself to the establishment of a national state without a complete parliamentary system. In view of the further need for constructions of national identity in a country divided by different cultural and religious traditions, aspects of *Kulturgeschichte* were integrated into the academic curricula at the expense of all traits that could remind their audience of its original political agenda. In Grimm's proposal for a *Museum für vaterländische Kunstgeschichte*, this program of cultural integration was not limited to definitions of a particular German culture but extended toward the promotion of idealist values embodied in the culture and the social rituals of German universities. While Grimm's version had a particularly conservative appeal, his insistence on an understanding of cultural tradition was justified. It proved to be the way in which academic discourses developed, when the next generation of art historians emancipated themselves from the methodological assumptions of the nineteenth century.[17]

One of the most prominent representatives of this generation was Heinrich Wölfflin, the successor to the chair of Herman Grimm at the University of Berlin from 1901. Although Wölfflin became known as one of the great innovators of art-historical methodology, he did share certain features with his conservative predecessor. Like Grimm, he came from a family of academics, underwent a thorough academic education, and preferred an influential teaching position to a secluded existence as a research scholar. This similarity went even further, since both men gained their reputation through a theatrical style of lecturing that was intended to captivate their audiences. Both used the new technique of slide projection, which Grimm embraced enthusiastically when it first appeared in his later years; Wölfflin's method of detailed stylistic comparison was unthinkable without it.[18] Moreover, during his formative years, Wölfflin's understanding of art history was also shaped by the ambitions of *Kulturgeschichte*, to which he remained devoted all his life, although his endeavors never quite lived up to his own expectations. His idea of cultural history, influenced by his teacher Jakob Burckhardt and by

FIGURE 3. Heinrich Wölfflin in his Berlin study. The photo dates from around 1900. Courtesy of Humboldt University, Berlin.

Hyppolite Taine's environmentalism, differed decisively from Grimm's in its attempt to understand cultural tradition as determined by climatic, geographical, and racial conditions. Yet in contrast to the connoisseurial attitude toward art, both shared the belief that their discipline could eventually account for the development of culture.

What prevented Wölfflin from completing a comprehensive project of this type, which he took up and abandoned at various stages in his career, was the recognition that current art history still lacked a systematic and well-grounded methodology of its own. In his 1886 doctoral thesis for the University of Munich, he had already applied current psychological theories to the aesthetic appreciation of architecture. At this time he was one of the first art historians who tried to use Robert Vischer's term "empathy" (*Einfühlung*) for the understanding of aesthetic perception.[19] Some years later Wölfflin came in contact with a group of neo-Romantic German artists, then living in Italy, in particular Hans von Marées and Adolf von Hildebrand, who shaped his taste for contemporary art and impressed him with their own contributions to art theory. Consequently Wölfflin dropped his psychological idea of aesthetic perception in favor of a strictly formalistic approach toward art. This was indebted in particular to Hildebrand's description of artistic production as a search for the right form to express images of nature situated in the imagination of the artist.[20]

From this point on Wölfflin's academic work centered on an attempt to clarify and define the categories used in art history to describe and explain its objects. On the basis of detailed stylistic comparisons between works from different periods, he singled out those formal properties that could constitute a definition of a particular "style of a period" (*Zeitstil*), associated with a specific way of visualizing nature through art. While still believing that the differences between these "forms of perception" (*Sehformen*) could ultimately be accounted for by cultural history, Wölfflin moved away from Grimm's concern for the "spiritual content" of art. His endeavor to define the "common optical denominator" (*gemeinsamer optischer Nenner*) of a given period in history culminated in his most influential analysis, of what he called "Fundamental Categories of Art-Historical Apprehension" (*Kunstgeschichtliche Grundbegriffe*), published in 1915, a year after he left Berlin for a professorship in Munich.[21]

While modern scholars usually stress the similarities between Wölfflin's formalism and the emergence of curatorial connoisseurship, both apparently being part of the shift toward aestheticism at the turn of the century and its insistence on a formalistic apprehension of art, the academic methodologist and the museum administrator were poles apart.[22] Bode's reputation for anti-intellectualism — a disinterest in anything outside his administrative reach — and his lack of any methodological reflection on his connoisseurship must have been conspicuous to the academic chairholder and severely limited the possibilities of cooperation between the two.[23] More important, Wölfflin's endeavor to discern basic laws of visual change, to provide what he termed "art history without names," collided with Bode's predominant interest in authorship at the expense of any further consideration. Wölfflin never repeated Grimm's mistake of coming out with a general attack against curatorial art history, yet the relationship between the university and the museum by no means improved after 1901. There were various instances in which Wölfflin called Bode's acquisitions into question — for instance, the sculpture of the so-called *Giovannino*, which he thought Bode falsely attributed to Michelangelo.[24] Even so, a remark of Bode's about his successor, reported by Ludwig Justi in his autobiography some thirty years after he had spent time as an intern at the museum in 1902–3, shows astonishing malice: "No less did he ridicule colleagues, in particular those in university positions who did not understand anything about buying. For example, he once showed me a newly arrived, somewhat mysterious picture: 'This buffoon was here the other day, what's his name, oh, Wölfflin. Of course he had no idea whatsoever; my little daughter (the fourteen-year-old Mariale) identified it immediately.'"[25] This statement shows to what extent Bode's dislike of Wölfflin was motivated by methodological considerations. Apparently it was Wölfflin's inability to identify the author of the painting in question that made him a "buffoon" in the eyes of Bode and discredited his theories, revealing that "art history without names" was due to a lack, not of concern but rather of visual sensitivity.

That Justi's recollections are in fact reliable on this point is confirmed by a similar criticism leveled at Wölfflin by another eminent Berlin connoisseur. In 1920 Max J. Friedländer, assistant at the Berlin department of paintings from 1896 and a specialist in the early Dutch and Flemish schools, gave a comprehensive account of the principles of his art criticism.[26] The main concern of these rather unsystematically assembled reflections was to defend his and Bode's intuitive method of attribution against Giovanni Morelli, the archenemy of the Berlin school of connoisseurs. Whereas Morelli claimed to have found a scientific approach to identifying authorship by concentrating on nonexpressive details of pictorial representation, Friedländer insisted on the importance of aesthetic evaluation while taking into account the overall effect of an artist's creation.[27] This justification of his methods brought him to a general consideration of the dangers and advantages of connoisseurship and its relation to academic discourses on art. He was willing to admit certain limitations inherent in the critic's attitude toward art, namely, the unverifiable and subjective nature of his judgments derived from intuition. At the same time, however, he addressed the failure of current academic art history, which had lost contact with its material basis by creating lofty theories about the development of art. According to Friedländer, it was exactly this theoretical impulse that had blinded his academic colleagues and made them lose the ability to actually encounter works of art. This skepticism was no longer aimed at outdated traditionalists like Grimm; its targets were the highbrow representatives of methodological innovation now dominating the academic world. From some only slightly disguised hints in the text it can be inferred that Friedländer had an opponent in mind when he argued against academic inadequacy, and that this was none other than Wölfflin:

I pass over the old controversy among philosophers of history as to whether the "accidentally" appearing heroes had a greater or smaller effect on the course of events. Longing for an "art history without names," I must still have arranged the monuments according to time and place and brought them in line with the biographical tradition, so far as possible, before I can begin to say something about the general development of the *Kunstwollen* [period style]. . . . When the Monforte Altarpiece of Hugo van der Goes came to Berlin, a sensitive art historian, for whom "art history without names" is a dear intention, shocked me by remarking that the picture was obviously a work from the sixteenth century and therefore could not have originated in van der Goes's time, since he died in the fifteenth century. [In my view] the limits of a period style ought to be drawn only when everything created has been investigated. And when will that be?[28]

The incident reported by Friedländer occurred in December 1913, when the altarpiece attributed to the Flemish painter Hugo van der Goes (1440/ 45–82) finally arrived in Berlin after long and difficult negotiations with the Spanish government. The painting was the central panel of a triptych preserved in the church of the monastery of Monforte de Lemos in northern Spain, where it must have arrived at an unknown date in the sixteenth century, considering the existence of various Flemish copies from the late fifteenth and early sixteenth centuries as proof of its original location in Flanders. When the Monforte Altarpiece was offered on the London art market in 1910 Bode sent Friedländer to Spain, where the painting still remained, in order to evaluate its authenticity and condition. The following year the Berlin department of paintings acquired the panel at auction in Madrid for the considerable sum of approximately 950,000 marks but could take possession of it only two years later after coming to an agreement over export regulations with the Spanish government.[29] Friedländer attributed the Monforte Altarpiece to Hugo van der Goes through stylistic comparison with his only securely attributed work, the Portinari Altarpiece in the Uffizi in Florence of around 1475. The oeuvre of van der Goes was still in the process of reconstruction by connoisseurial art historians, who were trying to bring the monuments "in line with the biographical tradition." Therefore Friedländer's association of his acquisition with van der Goes and a date after 1475 was by no means self-evident at the time, although it is now generally accepted.[30]

When Wölfflin proclaimed the Monforte Altarpiece to be characteristically sixteenth century within its period style, he was responding to what is now considered Hugo van der Goes's anticipation of a new mode of representation that became common artistic language in Flanders only after 1500. The precociousness of the painter in question escaped Wölfflin, true as he was to his search for the typical style as a "common optical denominator," while at the same time he was sensitive to the formal properties that made the painting influential for the next generation of painters. Feeling on secure ground with his attribution by 1920, when it was no longer in dispute, Friedländer could denounce Wölfflin's judgment as an instance of shortsightedness. The supposed inadequacy of the theoretician seemed to prove Friedländer's point that academic art history had reached an unprecedented level of detachment from its objects. Furthermore, by introducing the term *Kunstwollen,* he associated Wölfflin with the Viennese art historian Alois Riegl, thereby making sure that this particular instance would be understood as a symptom of a methodological problem that transcended the individual shortcomings of Wölfflin.[31]

Friedländer's criticism was obviously not supported by the actual circumstances of December 1913; he deliberately underestimated the strength of Wölfflin's arguments and the reasonable doubt he threw upon an attribution based entirely on stylistic comparison. Wölfflin responded to Friedländer indirectly a year later in 1921, when he defended himself against common curatorial prejudices:

In my *Kunstgeschichtliche Grundbegriffe* I attempted to demonstrate the typical steps in the stylistic development (*Gestaltungsstufen*) in the modern period in art. People have often misunderstood the book as an effort to replace "art history with persons" entirely, or at least to outdo it. Nothing could be more wrong. Personalities will always remain the most valuable aspect and must attract the greatest interest. However, it is my opinion that the achievements of a personality cannot be understood if we do not consider the general stylistic options (*Gestaltungsmöglichkeiten*) of the period in question, that ultimate foundation (hence the term "fundamental categories" [*Grundbegriffe*]), in which is anchored the creative imagination of someone who belongs to a particular era.[32]

The incident of the Monforte Altarpiece involuntarily points to one problem that made the gap between academic and curatorial art history almost unbridgeable. Wölfflin's questioning of his attribution must have particularly alarmed Friedländer, since a revision of authorship and date would cause the newly acquired painting to lose its value. His unacknowledged fear—that the large amount of money spent by the museum could turn out to be a bad investment—underscores the fact that curatorial connoisseurship had a hidden agenda that could not be separated from its methodology. Every judgment of a professional or recognized critic had serious effects on the price the object involved could fetch on the market. The intimate relationship that tied connoisseurs to the art market has now surfaced in the case of Bernard Berenson, one of the most successful followers of Morelli and a major rival of Bode, who made a fortune as an art dealer.[33] As opposed to freelance critics like Morelli or Berenson, museum curators used their abilities mainly in favor of the public institutions they represented, trying to expand the scope and enhance the quality of the collections they were in charge of.

Nonetheless they were constantly asked for assistance by art dealers and collectors, cooperating in a way that supposedly benefited the museum as much as the private interests. To this end connoisseurs like Bode or Friedländer not only provided expert reports and catalogs in exchange for donations or other considerations, but acted as agents and dealers in their own right. The extent to which commercial and curatorial activities were actually combined in Berlin escapes our knowledge, although it must have been considerable if we take into account the more than occasional remarks by contemporaries. The recollections of Ludwig Justi are particularly interesting in this respect, as he relied on firsthand knowledge:

> That commercial considerations colored his [Bode's] attitude toward art took me by surprise, and I still do not understand it. When looking at a work of art his first word always concerned the price valuation. . . . From a family tradition going back for centuries, passed on to me by my father and my uncle, I had inherited the fundamental idea that art, like music and poetry, means giving to intellectual and spiritual values a form that is to be revered, and cannot be measured by any external standard. And now I was continually hearing about prices, prices.[34]

Justi remembered well how disturbed he was, as a young student, proud of his descent from a family of academics and scholars and imbued with German idealism during his years of university study, when he was for the first time confronted with the unrestrained pragmatism of museum managers. From the point of view of academic idealism, the administrative concerns of curators appeared to be materialistic to the point of caricature. Bode and Friedländer were well aware of the ever-present danger that their activities would collide with their role as civil servants, insisting time and again that they did not profit personally from their commercial undertakings. Yet they could not dispel suspicions to the contrary, voiced above all by academic art historians. To some extent this mistrust was the result of different mentalities, but beyond that it can be understood as inherent in the distinction between curatorial and academic discourses on art. For a man like Wölfflin, the correct identification of the Monforte Altarpiece could have nothing but methodological consequences; for Friedländer it could have above all material consequences.

The distrust museum curators felt toward university teachers and vice versa had by no means diminished with the disappearance of traditional idealism in favor of a new interest in formalistic investigations. To the contrary, the disputes over attributions between Wölfflin and the Berlin curators highlight the degree of alienation that the two parties had reached in the meantime. Whereas Grimm's attack could still be dismissed as the rearguard action of obsolete conservatism, the issue of the Monforte Altarpiece finally revealed the existence of two mutually exclusive discourses. While the development of art history as represented in German universities between 1890 and 1914 is characterized by the replacement of projects based on traditional concepts like *Kulturgeschichte* by theories of visual change specifically linked to the visual arts, its discursive features remained essentially the same. The academic discourse generally tended to transgress its own boundaries to promote large-scale concepts of cultural evolution, which were characterized by their detachment from practical application. In the same period of time it had to face its mirror image in curatorial art history, which developed an unprecedented standard of proficiency in the empirical evaluation of particularities, based precisely on the pragmatic necessities that were excluded from the academic discourse. While remaining unable to account for more than a limited amount of aspects in the description of its objects, the curatorial discourse closely reflected the needs of museum administrators. Its appearance is linked immediately to the institution it served and can only be evaluated as an interaction of discourse and institution.

When the specific character of the museum as a medium is taken into account, curatorial connoisseurship can be understood as the "museum's discourse on art." Based on an accumulation of separate artifacts that remain isolated entities whatever discursive conception they are submitted to, its concern is with the precise identification of these artifacts within the relevant taxonomy rather than with overall concepts of cultural evolution. This preoccupation of the museum with the object is underscored by a second inherent feature, the need to present the results of curatorial art history not only in a textual form, but in the visual form of an exhibition. Curators invented different strategies of display in an attempt to recontextualize their holdings, thereby trying to mitigate the shortcomings of isolated vestiges of the past that resisted subsumption into any envisageable context. It remains for further analysis to show how and why the emergence of a discourse on museum installations went hand in hand with the appearance of curatorial connoisseurship in the last two decades before 1900.[35]

The rise of curatorial connoisseurship was part of a paradigmatic change in the manifest purpose of the art museum at the end of the nineteenth century. For most of the first hundred years of their existence, public collections were closely linked to the development of academic discourses that defined their taxonomies and formulated the basic assumptions on which their particular fields of study were grounded. Scholarly art history thus affected the museums long before its establishment in universities. As a consequence, art museums were arranged as large-scale representations of art history, demonstrating the evolution of artistic expression throughout history in a rigidly systematic way, allocating each object to a particular time and place.

In the last decades of the nineteenth century this paradigm was subjected to fundamental criticism that rearranged institutional structures and incorporated other agendas. Instead of completely dispensing with art-historical taxonomies, museum curators supplemented them by emphasizing the aesthetic apprehension of art rather than stressing its importance as evidence of historical change. The objects on display, although still arranged according to time and place of origin, thereby underwent an important revision. Now they represented aesthetic values, distilled out of the material remains of the past, that ultimately transcended historical evolution. As timeless manifestations of beauty they asserted to their beholders the assumption that central elements of human existence would never change.

During the earlier nineteenth century, evolutionary concepts of culture and history could comfort an aspiring yet unsuccessful middle class, in the face of relative political and social instability, with the idea of historical progress. But after 1871, the installation of a powerful national state continually diminished the prospects of constitutional reform. The expectation that essential shortcomings in Germany's political structures would endure found its equivalent in the rise of an aestheticism that reconciled its adherents to their role in the established order of society. At the same time this aestheticism allowed for close cooperation between museum managers and state authorities, since an institution promoting the timeless significance of received values obviously must have seemed appropriate to a traditional elite concerned about signs of social change.

However, the new paradigm of the art museum as propagator of aesthetic evaluation has survived the historical conditions of its formation in imperial Germany and other industrial societies of the period. Its continuing persistence is related to underlying processes of social transformation that reached far beyond the political agenda of museum curators or political authorities. The replacement of the previously limited art museum public, comprised of an educated elite, by a larger and less clearly defined urban middle-class audience was among the foremost of these transformations.[36] The development of curatorial art history as described in this essay was part of the museum's answer to this challenge. It demonstrates the continuity of institutional structures that remain virtually intact today, although the parameters of both museum administration and art-historical scholarship have changed dramatically in the meantime. The validity of academic historicism and its belief in the great narratives of general evolution have been shaken considerably by current deconstructionism. At the same time traditional connoisseurship has regressed into less prestigious parts of the commodities market, as museums collecting the paintings or sculptures of old masters have virtually disappeared from the sales rooms in postwar and contemporary Germany. Instead, museums have largely concentrated their efforts on the market for modern art, to which the connoisseurial attitude cannot be directly extended. While issues of authenticity and precise identification are of considerably reduced importance in this field, the aesthetic judgment required from connoisseurs such as Bode or Friedländer remains a central criterion of museum curators in their decisions regarding inclusion or exclusion. The unwillingness of today's museum curators to enter into an intensive exchange with academic discourses on culture and history about the way in which the art museum should address issues of cultural tradition for a contemporary audience is a reflection of the discursive configuration discussed here; so also is the consistency with which academic "historians" underrate the institutional constraints and discursive characteristics of the institution, when they aim their criticisms against the museum.

Notes

CHAPTER 1: INTRODUCTION

1. See Mary Warnock, *Memory* (London, 1987), p. 12 and passim.

2. Mieke Bal, *Double Exposures: The Subject of Cultural Analysis* (London, 1996), p. 3.

3. Daniel Sherman and Irit Rogoff, "Introduction: Frameworks for a Critical Analysis," in *Museum/Culture: Histories, Discourses, Spectacles* (Minneapolis, 1994), p. xiii. See also Eilean Hooper-Greenhill, *Museums and the Shaping of Knowledge* (London, 1992).

4. These discussions draw on the work of Michel Foucault and Pierre Bourdieu, as well as Jürgen Habermas, *The Structural Transformation of the Public Sphere* (Cambridge, Mass., 1989). See Tony Bennett, *The Birth of the Museum: History, Theory, Politics* (London, 1995); Susan Pearce, ed., *Museum Studies in Material Culture* (London, 1989).

5. On natural history and ethnography museums, see Ivan Karp and Steven D. Lavine, eds., *Exhibiting Cultures: The Poetics and Politics of Their Display* (Washington, D.C., 1991); George Stocking, ed., *Objects and Others: Essays on Museums and Material Culture* (Madison, Wis., 1985); Donna Harraway, "Teddy Bear Patriarchy: Taxidermy in the Garden of Eden, New York City, 1908–1936," in *Primate Visions* (New York, 1989); James Clifford, *The Predicament of Culture* (Cambridge, Mass., 1988); Annie Coombes, *Reinventing Africa: Museums, Material Culture, and Popular Imagination in Late Victorian and Edwardian England* (New Haven, Conn., 1994); David Jenkins, "Object Lessons and Ethnographic Displays," *Comparative Studies in Society and History* 36, no. 2 (1994). On the formation of national identity through museums, see Flora Kaplan, ed., *Museums and the Making of "Ourselves"* (London, 1994).

6. Christoph Asendorf discusses Honoré de Balzac's depiction of "the central fantasy of the collector, namely, the achievement of a state beyond time," in *Batteries of Life* (Berkeley, Calif., 1993), p. 53; see also Kevin Walsh, *The Representation of the Past* (London, 1992), pp. 7–38.

7. James Clifford, "On Art and Collecting," in *The Predicament of Culture* (Cambridge, Mass., 1985), p. 231.

8. Cited in David Farrell Krell, *Of Memory, Reminiscence, and Writing: On the Verge* (Bloomington, Ind., 1990), p. 76.

9. See Stephen Bann, *The Clothing of Clio* (Cambridge, 1984), and *Romanticism and the Rise of History* (New York, 1995).

10. On history in museums, see Thomas Schlereth, *Cultural History and Material Culture: Everyday Life, Landscapes, and Museums* (Ann Arbor, Mich., 1990); and Gaynor Kavanagh, ed., *Making Histories in Museums* (London, 1996). On heritage museums, see David Lowenthal, *The Heritage Crusade and the Spoils of History* (London, 1997); "Fabricating History," *History and Memory* 10, no. 1 (1998): 5–24; and *The Past Is a Foreign Country* (Cambridge, 1985). See also Walsh, *The Representation of the Past*.

11. Philip Fisher, "The Future's Past," *New Literary History* 6, no. 3 (spring 1975), pp. 587–606; p. 596.

12. For recent studies of collective memory theory, see the articles by Susan A. Crane, Alon Confino, and Daniel James, "AHR Forum: History and Memory," *American Historical Review* (December 1997): 1372–1412; Natalie Zemon Davis and Randolph Starn, eds., "Memory and Counter Memory," special issue of *Representations* 26 (spring 1989); James Fentress and Chris Wickham, *Social Memory* (Oxford, 1992); Patrick Hutton, *History as an Art of Memory* (Hanover, 1993). Iwona Irwin-Zarecka's *Frames of Remembrance: The Dynamics of Collective Memory* (New Brunswick, N.J., 1994) is designed to serve as a textbook and includes a useful annotated bibliography. Substantial catalogs of American, French, and British collective memory practices and some discussion of museums, respectively, include Micheal Kammen, *The Mystic Chords of Memory* (New York, 1991); Pierre Nora, ed., *Les lieux de mémoire* (Paris, 1984–92), revised and abridged in a translation, *Realms of Memory: Rethinking the French Past*, 3 vols. (New York, 1996–98); Lowenthal, *The Past Is a Foreign Country*; Raphael Samuel, *Theatres of Memory* (London, 1994). Anthropological approaches are presented in Fentress and Wickham, *Social Memory*; Thomas Butler, ed., *Memory: History, Culture, and the Mind* (Oxford, 1989); Paul Connerton, *How Societies Remember* (Cambridge, 1989); and the special issue "Memory and History," *History and Anthropology* 2, no. 2 (1986).

13. Maurice Halbwachs's essays on collective memory have been translated in two collections: *The Collective Memory* (New York, 1980) and *On Collective Memory*, edited by Lewis A. Coser (Chicago, 1992).

14. Nora, *Les lieux de mémoire*; see also Pierre Nora, "Between Memory and History: Les Lieux de Memoire," *Representations* 26 (spring 1989): 7–25.

15. I have argued that visitor expectations may be "distorted" when museums attempt to reorient visitors' experiences or when visitors' own memories of history or of previous museum visits are challenged; see "Memory, History, and Distortion in the Museum," *History and Theory*, theme issue 36: "Producing the Past" (1997): 44–63.

16. See "History and the Public: How Much Can We Handle? A Round Table About History After the *Enola Gay* Controversy," special issue of the *Journal of American History* 82, no. 3 (December 1995); Edward Linenthal and Tom Engelhardt, eds., *History Wars: The Enola Gay and Other Battles for the American Past* (New York, 1996); Mike Wallace, *Mickey Mouse History and Other Essays on American Memory*

(Philadelphia, 1996); "Remembering the Bomb: The 50th Anniversary in the United States and Japan," special issue of the *Bulletin of Concerned Asian Scholars* 27, no. 2 (1995); Crane, "Memory, History, and Distortion."

17. Ralph Rugoff, "The Nintendo Holocaust," in *Circus Americanus* (New York, 1997).

18. James Young, *The Texture of Memory: Holocaust Memorials and Meaning* (New Haven, Conn., 1995).

19. See Lawrence Weschler, *Mr. Wilson's Cabinet of Wonders* (New York, 1995).

20. Rudy Koshar, *Germany's Transient Pasts: Preservation and National Memory in the Twentieth Century* (Chapel Hill, N.C., 1998), p. 15.

21. Krzysztof Pomian, *Collectors and Curiosities* (Cambridge, 1990).

CHAPTER 2: ARCHI(VE)TEXTURES
OF MUSEOLOGY

1. See Jurij M. Lotman and B. A. Uspenskij, "Zum semiotischen Mechanismus der Kultur," in *Semiotica Sovietica*, vol. 2, edited by Karl Eimermacher (Aachen, 1986), p. 859.

2. Paula Findlen, "The Museum: Its Classical Etymology and Renaissance Genealogy," *Journal of the History of Collections* 1 (1989): 59–78 (abstract).

3. See Wolfgang Liebenwein, *Studiolo: Die Entstehung eines Raumtyps und seine Entwicklung bis um 1600* (Berlin, 1977).

4. See Giuseppe Olmi, *L'inventario del mondo: Catalogazione della natura e luoghi del sapere nella prima età moderna* (Bologna, 1992); and Helmut Zedelmaier, *Bibliotheca Universalis und Bibliotheca Selecta: Das Problem der Ordnung des gelehrten Wissens in der frühen Neuzeit* (Cologne, 1992), esp. on the works of Konrad Gessner (1545–48).

5. See Adrienne L. Kaeppler, "Museums of the World: Stages for the Study of Ethnohistory," in *Museum Studies in Material Culture*, edited by Susan M. Pearce (London, 1988), p. 83.

6. Steven Mullaney, "Strange Things, Gross Terms, Curious Customs: The Rehearsal of Cultures in the Late Renaissance," *Representations*, no. 3 (summer 1983): 53.

7. Niklas Luhmann, *Die Kunst der Gesellschaft* (Frankfurt am Main, 1995), pp. 489 f.

8. Ludewig Catel, *Museum: Begründet, entworfen und dargestellt nach seiner Urform* (Berlin, 1816) (with thanks to Susanne Holl for providing this reference).

9. Ibid., pp. 3 f.   10. Ibid., pp. 9 f.

11. Ibid., p. 12.   12. Ibid., p. 17.

13. See Uwe Hebekus, "Topik/Inventio," in *Einführung in die Literaturwissenschaft*, edited by Miltos Pechlivanos et al. (Stuttgart, 1995), p. 84.

14. See Johann Gustav Droysen, *Historik: Vorlesungen über Enzyklopädie und Methodologie der Geschichte*, edited by Rudolf Hübner (Munich, 1937), p. 42.

15. See Michael Fehr, "Müllhalde oder Museum: Endstationen in der Industriegesellschaft," in *Geschichte — Bild — Museum: Zur Darstellung von Geschichte im Museum*, edited by Michael Fehr and Stefan Grohé (Cologne, 1989), pp. 182–99.

16. See Thomas Ketelsen, *Künstlerviten, Inventare, Kataloge: Drei Studien zur Geschichte der kunsthistorischen Praxis* (Ammersbek, 1988), chap. 3.

17. Irving Wohlfarth, "Walter Benjamin's Last Reflections," *Glyph: Johns Hopkins Textual Studies* 3 (1978): 189.

18. See Karen Lang, "Monumental Unease: Monuments and the Making of National Identity in Germany," in *Imagining Modern German Culture: 1889–1910*, edited by Françoise Forster-Hahn (Washington, D.C., 1997), p. 285, citing Ernst von Wildenbruch, *Deutschland, sei wach!* (Berlin, 1915), p. 114.

19. Steffi Röttgen, "Das Papyruskabinett von Mengs in der Bibliotheca Vaticana," *Münchener Jahrbuch der bildenden Kunst* 31 (1980): 189–246.

20. See Paul de Man, "The Rhetoric of Temporality," in *Blindness and Insight: Essays in the Rhetoric of Contemporary Criticism* (Minneapolis, 1985), pp. 206 f.

21. Carolyn Springer, *The Marble Wilderness: Ruins and Representaton in Italian Romanticism, 1775–1850* (Cambridge, 1987), pp. 26 f.

22. Germanisches Nationalmuseum, *Die Aufgaben und die Mittel des germanischen Museums* (Nuremberg, 1872), p. 10.

23. Archives of the Jewish Museum, Prague, War Museum Fund, box 1943–45 (ZM i.c. 18).

24. For a thoughtful account of a visit to this museum today, see Stephen Greenblatt, "Resonance and Wonder," in *Literary Theory Today*, edited by Peter Collier and Helga Geyer-Ryan (Oxford, 1992), pp. 74–90.

25. See Hana Volavková, *Schicksal des jüdischen Museums in Prag* (Prague, 1965), p. 220.

26. Raul Hilberg, *Die Vernichtung der europäischen Juden*, vol. 2 (Frankfurt am Main, 1994), p. 1034.

27. Jean-Claude Pressac, *Die Krematorien von Auschwitz: Die Technik des Massenmordes* (Munich, 1994).

28. Hilberg, *Die Vernichtung der europäischen Juden*, 2:1046, citing Filip Müller, *Eyewitness Auschwitz: Three Years in the Gas Chambers* (New York, 1979), pp. 125 ff., and the Nuremberg war crimes trial affidavit of Rudolf Höß, March 14, 1946, NO-1210.

29. See Susan Crane, "Memory, Distortion, and History in the Museum," in "Producing the Past: Making Histories Inside and Outside the Academy," theme issue of *History and Theory*, 36 (1997): 44–63.

30. Walter Benjamin, "Theses on the Philosophy of History," in *Illuminations: Essays, and Reflections*, edited by Hannah Arendt (New York, 1969), p. 255.

31. Lily Díaz, "A Simultaneous View of History: The Creation of a Hypermedia Database," *Leonardo* 28, no. 4 (1995): 257.

32. Niklas Luhmann, "Gleichzeitigkeit und Synchronisation," in *Soziologische Aufklärung*, vol. 5: *Konstruktivistische Perspektiven* (Opladen, 1990), p. 109 and n. 34.

33. See Wolfgang Struck, "Geschichte als Bild und als Text: Historiographische Spurensicherung und Sinnerfahrung im 19. Jahrhundert," in *Zeichen zwischen Klartext und Arabeske*, edited by Susi Kotzinger and Gabriele Rippl (Amsterdam, 1994), pp. 349–61.

34. See David Crowther, "Archaeology, Material Culture, and Museums," in Pearce, *Museum Studies in Material Culture*, pp. 35–46.

35. Thomas A. Sebeok, "Pandora's Box: How and Why to Communicate 10,000 Years into the Future," in *On Signs*, edited by Marshall Blonsky (Baltimore, 1985), pp. 448–66.

36. See the exibition catalog of the Berlin Jewish Museum project *Daniel Libeskind: Between the Lines*, Joods Historisch Museum Amsterdam (Amsterdam, 1991); and Daniel Libeskind, *Kein Ort an dieser Stelle: Schriften zur Architektur—Visionen für Berlin*, edited by Angelika Stepken (Berlin, 1995).

37. There already exists a "Documentary Center of the Everyday Culture of the GDR" in Eisenhüttenstadt, eastern Germany. See Wolfgang Ernst and Katharina Flügel, eds., *Musealisierung der DDR? 40 Jahre als kulturgeschichtliche Herausforderung* (Bonn, 1992).

38. See Hans Ulrich Reck, *Erinnerung und Macht: Mediendispositive im Zeitalter des Techno-Imaginären* (Vienna, 1997).

39. Friedrich Kittler, "Museums on the Digital Frontier," in *The Ends of the Museum*, edited by Thomas Keenan (Barcelona, 1996), p. 74.

40. Johann Daniel Major (1634–93), professor of medicine, physician, natural scientist, curator of the botanical gardens and local historian in Kiel, defined museology as a specific discipline, in *Unvorgreifliches Bedencken von Kunst- und Naturalienkammern* (Kiel, 1674).

41. Horst Bredekamp, *Antikensehnsucht und Maschinenglauben: Die Geschichte der Kunstkammer und die Zukunft der Kunstgeschichte* (Berlin, 1993), pp. 100 f.

42. See http://neal.ctstateu.edu/history/world_history/archives/ archives.html.

43. See the CD-ROM *Eyewitness Encyclopedia of Science*, Dorling Kindersley Multimedia (New York, 1995).

44. Paul Otlet, *Traité de documentation: Le livre sur le livre* (Brussels, 1934).

45. A joint project of the Department of Art and Archaeology and the Interactive Computer Graphics Laboratory, Princeton University (M. Aronberg Levin, K. Perry, and Kirk D. Alexander), as described in a handout distributed at the International Congress of Art Historians at the Berlin International Congress Center in 1992.

46. Jean Davallon, "Le musèe est-il vraiment un média?" *Publics & Musèes*, no. 2 (December 1992): 99f.

47. Friedrich A. Kittler and Norbert Bolz, eds., *Computer als Medium* (Munich, 1993).

48. See Wolfgang Ernst, "Das imaginäre Dispositiv von Museum und Historie," in *Kult und Kultur des Ausstellens: Beiträge zur Praxis, Theorie und Didaktik des Mu-*

seums, edited by M. Erber-Groiß, S. Heinisch, H. C. Ehalt, and H. Konrad (Vienna, 1992) pp. 46–54.

49. H. G. Wells, *World Brain* (London, 1938), p. 49; quoted by Uwe Jochum, "Bibliotheksutopien," *Verband der Bibliotheken des Landes Nordrhein-Westfalen: Mitteilungsblatt* 44 (1994): 282.

50. See, e.g., René Ginouvès and Anne-Marie Guimer-Sorbets, *La constitution des donnés en archéologie classique: Recherches et expériences en vue de la préparation de bases de donnés* (Paris, 1978).

51. L. Bonfante, *Etruscan Life and Afterlife: A Handbook of Etruscan Studies* (Warminster, 1986), p. 4 (emphasis added).

52. Crowther, "Archaeology, Material Culture, and Museums," pp. 40ff.

53. Helmut Trotnow, "Fortführung und Neugestaltung: Die Konzeption des neu geplanten Museums zur Geschichte der deutsch-sowjetischen Beziehungen," *DHM Magazin*, no. 9 (summer 1993): 43.

54. Reinhard Rürup (a historian), "Karlshorst: Ort der Erinnerung und Zeichen für eine bessere Zukunft," ibid., p. 3.

55. Christoph Stölzl, "Zur Situation des Deutschen Historischen Museums in Berlin" (interview), in *Historische Faszination: Geschichtskultur heute*, edited by Klaus Füssmann, Heinrich Theodor Grütter, and Jörn Rüsen (Cologne, 1994), pp. 145–58.

56. See Gotthold Ephraim Lessing, *Laocoön: An Essay on the Limits of Painting and Poetry* [1766], translated by E. A. McCormick (Baltimore, 1984); and D. P. Dymond, *Archaeology and History: A Plea for Reconciliation* (London, 1974).

CHAPTER 3: A MUSEUM AND ITS MEMORY

1. Stephen Bann, *The Clothing of Clio: A Study of the Representation of History in Nineteenth-Century Britain and France* (Oxford, 1984).

2. Michael Fehr, "Aufklärung oder Verklärung," in *Geschichte sehen: Beiträge zur Ästhetik historischer Museen*, edited by Jörn Rüsen, Wolfgang Ernst, and Theodor Grütter (Pfaffenweiler, 1988), pp. 110–23.

3. Herbert Marcuse, "On the Affirmative Character of Culture" (1937), in *Kultur: Kultur und Gesellschaft*, vol. 1 (Frankfurt, 1965).

4. Translation by David Ward.

5. Hans Sedlmayer, "Peter Bruegel: Der Sturz der Blinden: Paradigma einer Strukturanalyse," in *Hefte des kunsthistorischen Seminars der Universität München*, vol. 1, edited by Hans Sedlmayer (Munich, 1957), p. 34.

6. E. B. Bloch, *Erbschaft dieser Zeit* (Frankfurt, 1992), p. 113.

7. Theodor Adorno, "Introduction to the Sociology of Music," in *Einleitung in die Musiksoziologie* (Reinbek, 1968).

8. Quoted in the encapsulation of Sonnabend's *Obliscence: Theories of Forgetting and the Problem of Matter*, reproduced in this volume, p. 85.

9. Hans Vaihinger, *Philosophie des Als-Ob* (Leipzig, 1911), p. 11 (translation by the author).

10. See below, p. 86.

11. Compare Max Imdahl, *Giotto* (Munich, 1981), p. 123.

12. See also Michael Fehr, ed., *Allan Wexler—Structures for Reflection* (Hagen, 1993).

13. See Karl Ernst Osthaus–Museum Hagen, *herman de vries, natural relations—eine skizze* (Nuremberg, 1989).

14. See Karl Ernst Osthaus–Museum Hagen, *Das Kabinett des Konservators von Johan van Geluwe* (Hagen, 1996).

15. See Michael Fehr and Barbara Schellewald, *Sigrid Sigurdsson's Vor der Stille—Ein kollektives Gedächtnis* (Cologne, 1995).

16. Ernst Bloch, "Der Faschismus als Erscheinungsform der Ungleichzeitigkeit," in *Theorien über den Faschismus*, edited by Ernst Nolte (Cologne, 1976), p. 182.

17. This and the following four paragraphs were translated by David Ward.

18. See Pierre Nora, *Les lieux de mémoire*, vol. 1 (Paris, 1984), p. 92.

19. Jens Kuhlenkampf, "Notiz über die Begriffe 'Monument' und 'Lebenswelt'," in *Kultur und Lebenswelt als Monument*, edited by Aleida Assman and Dietrich Harth (Frankfurt, 1991), pp. 26–33.

20. Documents in the Ernst Fuhrmann Archive at the Karl Ernst Osthaus–Museum prove that when already based in New York, he tried to obtain photographic material from the *Fotozentrale* of the Deutsches Museum der Kunst im Handel und Gewerbe.

21. Compare Kim Levin, "When Systems Collapse, Freak Events Such As These Rise Up Through the Cracks," *Village Voice*, January 19, 1993.

CHAPTER 4: CURIOUS CABINETS
AND IMAGINARY MUSEUMS

1. The museum first came to my attention through a press release in 1989. I have visited the museum on several occasions over the past decade. It is also worth mentioning that I'm not the only one who sought refuge in Borges when trying to describe this museum: see Lawrence Weschler, "Inhaling the Spore: Field Trip to a Museum of (Un)Natural History," *Harper's*, September 1994, pp. 47–58; and *Mr. Wilson's Cabinet of Wonder* (New York, 1995). See also Mario Biagioli, "Confabulating Jurassic Science," in *Technoscientific Imaginaries: Conversations, Profiles, and Memoirs*, edited by George Marcus (Chicago, 1995); Ralph Rugoff, "Beyond Belief: The Museum as Metaphor," in *Visual Display: Culture Beyond Appearances*, edited by Lynne Cooke and Peter Wollen (Seattle, 1995); Frederick Rose, "Next Thing You Know, They'll Show Us a Slithy Tove," *Wall Street Journal*, July 19, 1989, p. 1; Maria Porges, "A Fictional Museum of Imaginary Truths," *Artweek*, October 14, 1989, p. 1; David Whar-

ton, "Weird Science," *Los Angeles Times*, December 31, 1989, Calendar p. 90; Edward Ball and Fred Dewey, "The Riddle of History: Facts and Pseudo-Facts Converge in the New Subversive Anti-Museum," *New Statesman and Society*, March 2, 1990, pp. 39–40; Steve Root, "Not Necessarily the Smithsonian," *Los Angeles Magazine*, May 1990, pp. 62–63; Elizabeth A. Brown, "Light, Sound, and Satire Fill Two Off-beat L.A. Museums," *Christian Science Monitor*, June 24, 1991, p. 10; Ralph Rugoff, "Planned Obliscence," *LA Weekly*, June 21–27, 1991, p. 39.

2. Quoted in Ian Haywood, *The Making of History: A Study of the Literary Forgeries of James MacPherson and Thomas Chatterton in Relation to 18th-Century Ideas of History and Fiction* (Rutherford, N.C., 1986).

3. See Hal Foster, *Anti-Aesthetic: Essays in Postmodern Culture* (Port Townsend, Wash., 1983); and Donald Preziosi, "The Question of Art History," *Critical Inquiry*, 18, no. 2 (winter 1992): 363–86. Theory of exhibition and museum representation has developed remarkably in the last ten years; see particularly Susan Stewart, *On Longing: Narratives of the Miniature, the Gigantic, the Souvenir, and the Collection* (Baltimore, 1984); Stewart, "Death and Life, in That Order, in the Works of Charles Wilson Peale," in *The Cultures of Collecting*, edited by John Elsner and Roger Cardinal (Cambridge, Mass., 1994); and her contribution as well as other essays in Ivan Karp and Steven D. Lavine, eds., *Exhibiting Cultures: The Poetics and Politics of Their Display* (Washington, D.C., 1991). This collection, along with George Stocking, ed., *Objects and Others: Essays on Museums and Material Culture* (Madison, Wis., 1985), are the key texts on reconsiderations of museum practices from the anthropological viewpoint.

4. On the history of curiosity cabinets, see O. R. Impey and A. G. MacGregor, eds., *The Origins of Museums* (Oxford, 1985); and Lorraine Daston and Katherine Park, *Wonders and the Order of Nature* (New York, 1998). On Italian collections, see Krzysztof Pomian, *Collectors and Curiosities* (Cambridge, 1990); and Paula Findlen, *Possessing Nature: Museums, Collecting, and Scientific Culture* (Berkeley, Calif., 1994). On British collecting, see Eilean Hooper-Greenhill, *Museums and the Shaping of Knowledge* (London, 1992). For an inventory of cabinets, see Barbara Jean Balsinger, "The Kunst- und Wunderkammern: A Catalogue Raisonné of Collecting in Germany, France, and England, 1565–1750" (Ph.D. thesis, University of Pittsburgh, 1970); see also Julius von Schlosser, *Die Kunst- und Wunderkammern der Spätrenaissance* (Leipzig, 1908). For details on German collections, see Gudrun Calov, *Museen und Sammler des 19. Jahrhunderts in Deutschland*, a special issue of *Museumskunde*, vol. 38 (1969).

5. Edward Alexander, *Museums in Motion: An Introduction to the History and Functions of Museums* (Nashville, Tenn., 1979).

6. Johann Heinrich Zedler, *Grosses vollständiges Universal-Lexikon aller Wissenschaften und Kunste*, 64 vols. (Halle and Leipzig, 1732–50), 7:557–62.

7. Roger Chartier, *The Cultural Uses of Print in Early Modern France* (Princeton, N.J., 1987), p. 201.

8. David Murray, *Museums: Their History and Their Use* (Glasgow, 1904), pp. 35 ff.; also Alma Wittlin, *The Museum: Its History and Its Tasks* (London, 1948), pp. 3–5.

9. Zedler, *Universal-Lexikon*, 24:173.

10. Pomian, *Collectors and Curiosities*, p. 56.

11. Ibid., p. 59.

12. Ibid., p. 125. From *La Science des medailles antiques et modernes, par le P. Joubert, avec des remarques historiques et critiques de M. de La Bastie*, vol. 1 (Paris, 1739), p. 33.

13. Pomian's thesis is that "it is the social hierarchy which necessarily leads to the birth of collections, those sets of objects kept out of the economic circuit, afforded special protection and put on display" (*Collectors and Curiosities*, p. 32). In the case of Diderot and the Encyclopedists, he argues that they attacked "curiosité" as "a 'desire to acquire' not only the sort of object with which the enthusiast filled his rooms but also, if not above all, a social position enabling one to exert a decisive influence on the lives of artists and on their art itself," the producers of the collectible objects (ibid., p. 137).

14. Paula Findlen, "Jokes of Nature and Jokes of Knowledge: The Playfulness of Scientific Discourse in Early Modern Europe," *Renaissance Quarterly* 43 (1990): 303.

15. Murray, *Museums*, p. 194.

16. Ibid., p. 204.

17. Walter Benjamin, *Illuminations* (New York, 1969), p. 244.

18. Murray cites the exasperation of a French visitor to the British Museum in 1810, who reported that "We had not time allowed to examine anything; our conductor pushed on without minding questions, or unable to answer them, but treating the company with double entendres or witticisms on various subjects of natural history, in a style of vulgarity and impudence which I should not have expected to have met in this place and in this country" (*Museums*, p. 212 n). Given that tickets to the museum were much sought after and the number of visitors restricted, having to rush through the collection must have been frustrating; but what is particularly interesting here is that the visitor appears to have heard some of the stories about curious objects without being amused by them.

19. Arthur MacGregor, "Collectors and Collections of Rarities in the Sixteenth and Seventeenth Centuries," in *Tradescant's Rarities: Essays on the Foundation of the Ashmolean Museum, 1683* (Oxford, 1983), p. 74.

20. Ibid., p. 78. 21. Ibid., p. 82.

22. Ibid., p. 88. 23. Ibid., pp. 91–92.

24. Ibid., p. 93.

25. My point supplements, rather than counters, Svetlana Alpers's argument that early modern collecting focused on objects "judged to be of visual interest" ("The Museum as a Way of Seeing," in Karp and Lavine, *Exhibiting Cultures*, p. 26) rather than judged to have interesting stories attached to them. Art-historical objects underwent similar reevaluations in the historical transition from cabinet to museum;

while the history of art museums is necessarily integrated into that of the modern museum as a whole, disciplinary distinctions have tended to segregate types of museums (natural-historical, art-historical, ethnographic, historical) in ways that overlook potential similarities of development.

26. On the nature of antiquarian collecting, see Arnaldo Momigliano, "The Rise of Antiquarian Research," in *Classical Foundations of Modern Historiography* (Berkeley, Calif., 1990); and Stephen Bann, *The Clothing of Clio* (Cambridge, 1984) and *Romanticism and the Rise of History* (New York, 1995).

27. In much the same way, the Museum of Jurassic Technology's pamphlet on "Obliscence" comes equipped with footnotes, publication data, and Library of Congress Cataloging-in-Publication Data; see below, pp. 81–90. For a discussion of Macpherson's "cheats," see Haywood, *The Making of History*.

28. See Eva Schulz, "Notes on the History of Collecting and Museums," *Journal of the History of Collections* 2, no. 2 (1990): 205–18.

29. I discuss this development in *Collecting and Historical Consciousness in Early-Nineteenth-Century Germany* (Ithaca, N.Y., forthcoming).

30. Gustav Klemm, *Zur Geschichte der Sammlungen für Wissenschaft und Kunst in Deutschland* (Berbst, 1837), p. 152.

31. Foucault wrote, "I am concerned here with observing how a culture experiences the propinquity of things, how it establishes the tabula of their relationships and the order by which they must be considered"; *The Order of Things* (New York, 1970), p. xxiv. An archaeology of order, then, will concentrate on the language in which narratives about natural history are constructed and the process by which the human sciences develop their control over the discourses of natural history and science.

32. This interpretive style lives on in many modern histories of the museum. To cite one example, Edward Alexander writes of Sir Hans Sloane, one of the founding fathers of the British Museum, that "Not only did Sloane collect widely and well. He also *understood the need* of a museum to put its holdings in order and provide a proper record for each specimen or object" (my emphasis). Indeed, Sloane used very similar words: "The putting into some kind of Order my Curiosities . . . was necessary in Order to their Preservation and Uses." But Alexander's presumption of the "need" that Sloane "understood" implies a retroactive participation in modern collecting practices, rather than simply stating that Sloane in fact was developing new strategies for his collecting in opposition to a larger trend, the assembly of curiosities. See Edward Alexander, *Museum Masters: Their Museums and Their Influence* (Nashville, Tenn., 1983), p. 29.

33. Klemm, *Zur Geschichte der Sammlungen*, p. 146.

34. Ibid., pp. 238–39.

35. E. H. Toelken, *Erklärendes Verzeichniss der antiken Denkmäler im Antiquarium des königlichen Museums zu Berlin* (Berlin, 1835), p. xxi.

36. Calov, *Museen und Sammler*, p. 54.

37. Ibid., p. 59.

38. See Ekkehard Mai, "'Wallrafs Chaos' (Goethe)—Städels Stiftung" in *Sammler, Stifter und Museen: Kunstförderung im 19. Jahrhundert*, edited by Mai and Peter Paret (Cologne, 1993), pp. 63–80.

39. Reinhard Fuchs, "Zur Geschichte der Sammlungen des rheinischen Landesmuseums Bonn," in *Rheinisches Landesmuseum Bonn: 150 Jahre Sammlungen, 1820–1970* (Düsseldorf, 1971), p. 6.

40. Ibid., p. 4.

41. Ibid., p. 16.

42. Ibid., p. 17.

43. August W. Schlegel, "Kunst- und Antiquitäten-Sammlung des Herrn Canonicus Pick in Bonn," in *Sämmtliche Werke*, edited by Edward Böcking, vol. 9 (Leipzig, 1846), pp. 356–59.

44. Leopold von Ledebur, *Leitfaden für die königliche Kunstkammer und das Ethnographische Cabinet zu Berlin* (Berlin, 1844), p. 102.

45. Michael Fehr, "Das Museum—Ort des Vergessens," in *Zeitphänomenon Musealisierung*, edited by Wolfgang Zacharias (Essen, 1990), p. 221.

CHAPTER 6: HISTORY AND ANTI-HISTORY

I am grateful to all the curators, gallery owners, and critics who discussed the Japanese photography scene with me in the summer of 1995 and since. I particularly thank Masuda Rei and Okatsuka Akiko for their time and insight, and Peter C. Bunnell of Princeton University for his early and generous guidance.

Throughout this essay, I follow the standard practice of placing Japanese surnames before given names.

1. The Meiji period extended from 1868 to 1912.

2. I am indebted to Raphael Samuel's book, *Theatres of Memory*, for the term "retrochic" and for his conception of history as "a social form of knowledge; the work, in any given instance, of a thousand different hands . . . the ensemble of activities and practices in which ideas of history are embedded or a dialectic of past-present relations is rehearsed." *Theatres of Memory*, vol. 1: *Past and Present in Contemporary Culture* (London, 1994), p. 8.

3. Abigail Solomon-Godeau analyzes the distinction between photography as art and photography as document through the analogy of two axes, "one axis—supposed to consist of subjectivity, art, and beauty (the axis of the icon)—and another axis—composed of science, truth, objectivity, and technology (the axis of the index)." Abigail Solomon-Godeau, *Photography at the Dock: Essays in Photographic History, Institutions, and Practices* (Minneapolis, 1991), p. xxii.

4. See Kosaku Yoshino's discussion of cultural nationalism in *Cultural Nationalism in Contemporary Japan: A Sociological Inquiry* (New York, 1992).

5. Here as elsewhere I follow exactly the museums' own translation and romanization, no matter how awkward.

6. This is the term used by Nakamura Hiromi in "Exhibition Notes: The Beat of -ism, The 1st Tokyo International Photo-Biennale," in *-ism '95: The 1st Tokyo International Photo-Biennale* (Tokyo, 1995), p. 13.

7. Nakamura, "Exhibition Notes: The Beat of -ism," p. 13.

8. Osamu James Nakagawa, "Artist's Statement," in *-ism '95: The 1st Tokyo International Photo-Biennale*, p. 59.

9. Among U.S. publications featuring Nakagawa's work is *Aperture*, no. 136 (*Metamorphoses: Photography in the Electronic Age*) (summer 1994): 26–31.

10. Nakagawa, "Artist's Statement," pp. 58–59.

11. Roland Barthes, *Camera Lucida: Reflections on Photography*, translated by Richard Howard (New York, 1981), p. 15.

12. Nakamura, "Exhibition Notes," p. 13.

13. Kim Seung-Kon, "The Role of the Tokyo International Photo-Biennale," in *-ism '95: The 1st Tokyo International Photo-Biennale*, p. 18.

14. Ibid.

15. Anne Wilkes Tucker, untitled, in *-ism '95: The 1st Tokyo International Photo-Biennale*, p. 17.

16. The message from juror Jean-Luc Monterosso, director of the Maison Européenne de la Photographie and artistic director of *Mois de la Photo à Paris*, is so brief and so polite that no conclusions can be drawn from it.

17. Leon Borensztein, "Artist's Statement," in *-ism '95: The 1st Tokyo International Photo-Biennale*, p. 37.

18. For a discussion of other versions of Yamamoto Masao's *Kū no Hako*, see my "Global Culture in Question: Japanese Photography in Contemporary America," in *Japan outside Japan*, edited by Harumi Befu and Sylvie Guichard-Anguis (London, forthcoming).

19. Ampo Fumiko, "Artist's Statement," in *-ism '95: The 1st Tokyo International Photo-Biennale*, p. 89.

20. Ampo was born in Yokohama in 1968; Yoshimoto in 1964.

21. John Whittier Treat has suggested that the antipolitical pose of Yoshimoto Banana should not be taken at face value. See his "Yoshimoto Banana Writes Home: *Shōjo* Culture and the Nostalgic Subject," *Journal of Japanese Studies* 19, no. 2 (summer 1993): 353–87.

22. Iizawa Kōhtarō, "Cropping and Repetition—Modernism in Photography," *Objects, Faces, and Anti-Narratives—Rethinking Modernism* (Tokyo, 1995), p. 113. Iizawa's talents are better represented elsewhere. See, for instance, his essays in *Japanese Contemporary Photography: Twelve Viewpoints* (Tokyo, 1990); or in Robert Stearns, *Photography and Beyond in Japan: Space, Time, and Memory* (Tokyo, 1995). In all these publications as well as in the magazine *déjà-vu*, his given name is romanized as Kōhtarō rather than the more standard Kōtarō.

23. Kasahara Michiko, "Objects, Faces, and Anti-Narratives," in *Objects, Faces, and Anti-Narratives—Rethinking Modernism*, p. 117.

24. "Squabbling Delays War Ceremony," *Japan Times*, July 5, 1995, p. 1. Initially the ceremony was scheduled for August 15 in Tokyo's Yoyogi National Stadium with novelist Shiba Ryotaro giving the main memorial speech.

25. Sheryl WuDunn, "Japanese Apology Is Met with Praise and Disagreement," *New York Times*, August 16, 1995, p. 1.

26. For discussions of the resistance to remembering the war, see Norma Field, *In the Realm of the Dying Emperor* (New York, 1991); Ian Buruma, *The Wages of Guilt: Memories of War in Germany and Japan* (New York, 1994); and Ienaga Saburo, *The Pacific War, 1931–1945* (New York, 1978).

27. Works by some of the artists in this group, Hosoe Eikoh, Tōmatsu Shōmei, and Moriyama Daidō, can be seen in *Black Sun: The Eyes of Four*, a special issue of *Aperture* (no. 102, spring 1986), edited by Mark Holborn.

28. The idea of the canon has been widely discussed by literary theorists. An excellent introduction to this issue is John Guillory, "Canon," in *Critical Terms for Literary Study*, edited by Frank Lentricchia and Thomas McLaughlin, 2d ed. (Chicago, 1995), pp. 233–49. For a discussion of Asian canons, see the updated edition of Wm. Theodore de Bary and Irene Bloom, eds., *Eastern Canons: Approaches to the Asian Classics* (New York, 1990).

29. I have discussed the resistance to photography at the National Museum of Modern Art, Tokyo, in "Raw Photographs and Cooked History: Photography's Ambiguous Place in Tokyo's Museum of Modern Art," *East Asian History*, no. 12 (December 1996, published July 1998): 121–34.

30. Masuda Rei, "Tokyo Kokuritsu kindai bijutsukan ni okeru shashinten 1953–1974: kakō no tenrankai ga shisasuru koto" [Photography and the National Museum of Modern Art, Tokyo, 1953–1974: A review of past exhibitions], in *Tokyo kokuritsu kindai bijutsukan to shashin 1953–1995* [Photography and the National Museum of Modern Art, Tokyo, 1953–1995] (Tokyo, 1995), p. 13 (my translation).

31. During the summer of 1995, Tokyo galleries displayed work by a range of photographers including James Welling, David Stetson, Jacques-Henri Lartigue, and Okumura Mitsuya, none of whom is overtly concerned with historical themes. Painting galleries tended to be equally ahistorical with the exception of the Ota Gallery, which held deliberately political exhibitions of Shimada Yoshiko's controversial works on the emperor and wartime "comfort women" as well as antiwar collages by Kusama Yayoi. Outside Tokyo, the nearby Yokohama Museum of Art held an exhibition titled *Photography in the 1940s*. I have discussed the delicate problem of evoking this decade through photographs in "Photography, National Identity, and the 'Cataract of Times': The Place of the Curator and the Case of Japan," *American Historical Review* 103, no. 5 (December 1998): 1474–501.

32. Samuel, *Theatres of Memory*, 1:27.

33. *Shitamachi* literally means "downtown" and refers to those congested, lively areas of old Tokyo where commoners as opposed to samurai lived during the Edo period (1600–1868).

34. See Kuwabara Kineo, *Manshū shōwa jūgo nen* [Manchuria in the fifteenth year of Showa] (Tokyo, 1974). In the Western calendar, Showa 15 is 1940.

35. John Berger, "Understanding a Photograph," in *Classic Essays on Photography*, edited by Alan Trachtenberg (New Haven, Conn., 1980), p. 293.

36. Iizawa Kōhtarō, "Tokyo Shashin: Kuwabara Kineo to Gochō Shigeo" in Gallery One's brochure on the show. In the brochure's résumé of Kuwabara's career, his work in Manchuria is not mentioned. Despite the fact that Gallery One, part of the Park Tower Art Program, is private, it may still be subject to codes of discretion because of corporate sponsorship. In this case the corporate sponsor was the Tokyo Gas Urban Development Company, which claims to support cultural and artistic development to promote a "comfortable" or "pleasant" (*kaiteki na*) urban life.

37. Sekiji Kazuko, "Looking at Tokyo, City of Photographs," *Tokyo/City of Photographs* (Tokyo, 1995), p. 236.

38. Ibid., "Foreword" (unpaginated).

39. Okatsuka Akiko, *The Founding and Development of Modern Photography in Japan* (Tokyo, 1995), p. 9.

40. Ibid, p. 173.

41. Ibid., p. 9.

42. Private conversation, July 7, 1995. Nakajima Tokuhiro, chief curator at the Hyōgo Prefectural Museum of Modern Art, Kobe, has also worked to recover these images. See Nakajima, "Background of the Wandering Jews," *Pilotis* (Hyōgo Prefectural Museum of Modern Art News) no. 77 (July 1990).

43. Okatsuka, *The Founding and Development of Modern Photography in Japan*, p. 21.

44. Siegfried Kracauer, "Photography," *Critical Inquiry* 19, no. 3 (spring 1993): 424.

45. Review media, it should be said, play a smaller role in such debates than they do in the United States and Europe.

46. The work of these museum curators is much less controversial than that of the small but obstreperous band of artists who directly attack the taboos surrounding images of the war and of the emperor himself. Compared with artist Shimada Yoshiko's work on the so-called comfort women or Oura Nobuyuki's *Embracing Perspectives* series (1982–85), which focuses on Emperor Hirohito, exhibitions insisting on the historicity of photographic images may appear relatively innocuous. See Nancy Shalala, "Censorship Silences Japanese Artists," *Asian Art News*, September–October 1994, pp. 62–67; Nancy Shalala, "Hidden Terrors Put Gag on Art World," *Japan Times*, July 10, 1994, p. 10; and E. Patricia Tsurumi, "Censored in Japan: Taboo Art," *Bulletin of Concerned Asian Scholars* 26, no. 3 (1994): 66–70.

CHAPTER 7: REALIZING MEMORY,
TRANSFORMING HISTORY

Sources of epigraphs are as follows: Jacques Lacan, *The Language of the Self*, translated and edited by Anthony Wilden (Baltimore, 1968), p. 63; Jimmie Durham,

"Cowboys and . . . : Notes on Art, Literature, and American Indians in the Modern American Mind," in *State of Native America*, edited by M. Annette Jaimes (Boston, 1992), p. 437; and Michel de Certeau, *Heterologies: Discourse on the Other*, translated by Brian Massumi (Minneapolis, 1986), p. 4.

1. See Michael Baxandall, "Exhibiting Intention: Some Preconditions of the Visual Display of Culturally Purposeful Objects," in *Exhibiting Cultures: The Poetics and Politics of Museum Display*, edited by Ivan Karp and Steven D. Lavine (Washington, D.C., 1990), pp. 32–41; Leah Dilworth, "Object Lessons," *American Quarterly* 45, no. 2 (1993): 257–80; David Jenkins, "Object Lessons and Ethnographic Displays: Museum Exhibitions and the Making of American Anthropology," *Society for Comparative Study of Society and History* 36, no. 2 (1994): 242–70.

2. Perhaps the best-known example is Benjamin Lee Whorf's contrast between the construction of time in Hopi and that in "Standard Average European" in his classic essay "The Relation of Habitual Thought and Behavior to Language," in *Language, Thought, and Reality*, edited by John B. Carroll (Cambridge, Mass., 1956): Hopi verbs have no "tenses like ours, but have validity-forms ('assertions'), aspects, and clause-linkage forms (modes), that yield even greater precision of speech. The validity forms denote that the speaker (not the subject) reports the situation (answering to our past and present) or that he expects it (answering our future). . . . The expective expresses anticipation existing EARLIER than objective fact, and coinciding with objective fact LATER than the status quo of the speaker, thus status quo, including all the subsummation of the past therein, being *expressed by the reportive*. Our notion of 'future' seems to represent at once the earlier (anticipation) and the later (afterwards, what will be), as Hopi shows. This paradox may hint of how elusive the mystery of real time is, and how artificially it is expressed by a linear relation of past-present-future" (p. 144).

3. At contact there were at least five hundred indigenous Nations in North America, groups with a very wide range of cultural and communicative strategies. Within surviving groups, personal adaptation of those traditions now spans a very great range of knowledge and behaviors. Tribal differences are not the focus of this article; my goal is to work toward developing a method that is precise enough to recognize and articulate both inter- and intracultural differences, not to obliterate them through unnecessary generalizations.

4. James Clifford has been an astute observer of contemporary American Indians, museum exhibition practices, and intercultural communication. See his *The Predicament of Culture: Twentieth-Century Ethnography* (Cambridge, Mass., 1988); "Four Northwest Coast Museums: Travel Reflections," in Karp and Lavine, *Exhibiting Cultures*, pp. 212–54; and *Routes: Travel and Translation in the Late Twentieth Century* (Cambridge, Mass., 1997). Clifford's descriptions and conclusions may seem similar to those presented here; however, mine are presented in a manner less ironic and also perhaps more systematic. My experience has been that irony may preclude levels of reflexivity regarding cultural standpoints, ultimately rendering a paradoxical

relationality of their fundamental differences more opaque. See Diana Drake Wilson, "Western Heritage and Its *Autres*: Cowboys and Indians, Facts and Fictions," in *Semiotics of the Media: State of the Art, Projects, and Perspectives*, edited by Winifred Noth (Berlin, 1994).

5. In *The Book of Memory: A Study of Memory in Medieval Culture* (Cambridge, 1990), Mary Carruthers describes the concerns and assumptions about memory of medieval poets and readers. Some of these memory and religious practices are strikingly parallel to those of American Indian traditional and contemporary ones: medieval "memorial" culture made "present the voices of what is past, not to entomb either the past or the present, but to give them life together in a place common to both in memory" (p. 260). Such parallelisms between American Indian traditions and those of a European past do not, in my opinion, represent parallelisms between evolutionary stages of cognitive and cultural development, but are the results of a finite range of possibilities for the organization of knowledge and knowing that are humanly chosen in historical circumstances with an awareness of their public and personal consequences.

6. Richard Terdiman, "Deconstructing Memory: Representing the Past and Theorizing Culture in France Since the Revolution," *Diacritics* 15, no. 4 (1985): 20–21.

7. See Diana Drake Wilson, "Understanding Misunderstanding: American Indians in Euro-American Museums" (Ph.D. diss., University of California, Los Angeles).

8. The words *contiguity* and *similarity* are used in two different traditions with a very critical distinction between them. In the philosophical tradition the meaning of *contiguity* and *similarity* derived from a set of laws of the associations of ideas proposed by the British empiricist philosophers David Hume (1748) and John Stuart Mill (1843). These are very different from the three laws of sympathetic magic — contagion, similarity, and opposites — as described by E. B. Tylor in *Primitive Culture* and elaborated by Frazer in *The Golden Bough* and Marcel Mauss in *A General Theory of Magic*. One of these fundamental differences, recognized by Tylor, Frazer, and Mauss, is that "the laws of association are limited to the domain of thought; they [are believed to] operate only within the head. The laws of magic project these laws into the real world; that is, the physical world is held to be organized along principles similar to the laws of thought." Paul Rozin and Carol Nemeroff, "The Laws of Sympathetic Magic: A Psychological Analysis of Similarity and Contagion," in *Cultural Psychology: Essays in Comparative Human Development*, edited by James W. Stigler, Richard A. Shweder, and Gilbert Herdt (Cambridge, 1990), p. 297.

9. Roman Jakobson, *On Language*, edited by Linda Waugh and Monique Monwille-Burston (Cambridge, Mass., 1990), p. 133.

10. Rozin and Nemeroff, "The Laws of Sympathetic Magic," p. 223.

11. Ibid., p. 226.

12. American Indian English(es) are founded on a rich diversity of indigenous languages and conditions of relevance. For a brief discussion of how American Indian English, or "Red English," has entered into print, see Anthony Mattina, "North Ameri-

can Indian Mythography," in *Recovering the Word: Essays on Native American Literature*, edited by Brain Swann and Arnold Krupat (Berkeley, Calif., 1987), pp. 129–48.

13. Terdiman, "Deconstructing Memory," pp. 20–21.

14. One of the defining circumstances of capitalist relations may be the migration
of material memory from person to tool *only*, and the repression of the "migration"
from material to person: "In most noncapitalist societies . . . production as . . . a distinct realm is not recognizable as such but rather is subsumed by broader social institutions that prefigure and transcend it. . . . [T]he relationship of production to other
social domains is the reverse of that in capitalism. . . . It becomes an effect rather than
a cause. In social contexts such as these, conceptual categories that direct our attention to production arbitrarily separate it from the social context in which it is embedded. By distinguishing it conceptually, they imply that there is insight to be gained
by doing so. While this is the case in capitalist societies, granting conceptual recognition to production in societies where it has no autonomy or independent agency
reifies production and forces noncapitalist societies into a capitalist mold." David Nu-
gent, "Property Relations, Production Relations, and Inequality: Anthropology, Political Economy, and the Blackfeet," *American Ethonologist* 21, no. 2 (1993): 336 (my
emphasis).

15. Roland Barthes, "To Write an Intransitive Verb," in *The Structuralists from
Marx to Levi-Strauss*, edited by Richard and Fernande DeGeorge (Garden City, N.Y.,
1972), pp. 164–65; quoted in Gregory Ulmer, *Applied Grammatology: Post(e)-Peda-
gogy from Jacques Derrida to Joseph Beuys* (Baltimore, 1985), p. 231.

16. Jacques Derrida, *Speech and Phenomena*, translated by David B. Allison
(Evanston, Ill., 1973), p. 137.

17. Terdiman, "Deconstructing Memory," pp. 20–21.

18. Dennis Tedlock, *Days from a Dream Almanac* (Urbana, Ill., 1990), p. 91.

19. See especially Thomas J. Csordas, "Embodiment as a Paradigm for Anthropology," *Ethos* 18 (1990): 5–47; "The Body as Representation and Being in the World,"
in *Embodiment and Experience: The Existential Ground of Culture and Self* (London,
1994), pp. 1–23; and "Words from the Holy People: A Case Study in Navajo Phenomenology," ibid., pp. 269–89.

20. Terdiman, "Deconstructing Memory," pp. 22–23; the quotation is from M. M.
Bakhtin, *The Dialogical Imagination: Four Essays by M. M. Bakhtin*, translated by
Caryl Emerson and Michael Holquist (Austin, Tex., 1981), p. 293.

CHAPTER 8: GLOBAL CULTURE,
MODERN HERITAGE

Portions of this research were conducted at the Palace Museum in Beijing during
the summer of 1995 under the auspices of a Keefer Junior Faculty Development
Grant from Beloit College. Qing Hua University generously provided a place for me
and my family to live during this period. I also wish to thank Susan Crane, Karen-

Mary Davalos, Nina Dorrance, Kris Hardin, James Robertson, Linda Sturtz, and two anonymous reviewers for their careful readings and insightful comments on various versions of this paper.

1. Cited in *China: A Literary Companion*, edited by A. C. Grayling and Susan Whitfield (London, 1994), p. 26.

2. Gu Gong Bowuyuan, *Zijin Cheng* [Forbidden City], (Beijing, 1970–)

3. For further discussion of museums as sites of ritual practice, see, for example, Carol Duncan, *Civilizing Rituals* (New York, 1995); and Donald Horne, *The Great Museum: Re-Presentations of History* (London, 1994).

4. As Rubie Watson writes in the introduction to *Memory, History, and Opposition Under State Socialism* (Santa Fe, N.M., 1994), "they 'remember' because they share with others sets of images that have been passed down to them through the media of memory—through paintings, architecture, monuments, ritual, storytelling, poetry, music, photos, and film" (p. 8).

5. Jeffrey Meyer, *The Dragons of Tiananmen: Beijing as a Sacred City* (Columbia, S.C., 1991), pp. 190–91.

6. Ibid.

7. Frank Dorn, *The Forbidden City: The Biography of a Palace* (New York, 1970), p. 300.

8. Various monuments to the Communist Revolution have been erected outside of the Forbidden City. For further discussion of these monuments and their meaning for the Forbidden City, see Rubie Watson, "Palaces, Museums, and Squares: Chinese National Spaces," *Museum Anthropology* 19, no. 2 (1995): 7–19.

9. I have found little published information regarding the actual demographics of visitors to the Palace Museum. My brief discussion here is based on observations within the museum, as well as casual conversations with others visiting Beijing. The broader questions raised in this essay arise out of the ways in which the museum "guides" visitors into taking particular paths that generate particular perspectives, rather than out of the individual experiences of visitors to the museum.

10. This map constitutes a modified version of similar maps and narrative descriptions from local guidebooks that I purchased at curio stands, gift shops, and book stores in Beijing.

11. Visitors can also enter through the northernmost Shenwu Gate and wind their way through the various courtyards into the open spaces of the Outer Court. The visual impact of the inverted path is less dramatic, but the constraints on where visitors can wander remain the same.

12. One exception is the imperial bridal chamber located in the western portion of the Kun Ning Palace, restored to look as it did at the time of the marriage of the Guang Xu emperor. Another exception is the Chu Xiu Palace, which has been restored to look as it did when it was inhabited by the Empress Dowager at the time of her fiftieth birthday.

13. Chen Yongfa, Ma Linying, and Zhang Hua, eds., *Zijin Cheng Bai Ti* [The Forbidden City: One hundred questions] (Beijing, 1992).

14. Horne, *The Great Museum*, p. 16.

15. Ibid., p. 8.

16. I have discussed this process in more detail in "Preserving the Palace: Museums and the Making of Nationalism(s) in Twentieth Century China," *Museum Anthropology* 19, no. 2 (1995): 20–30. See also Watson, *Memory, History, and Opposition*, pp. 1–20.

17. Chen, Ma, and Zhang, *Zijin Cheng Bai Ti*; Ke Zhengwen, *Gu Gong Zongtan* [Palace lectures] (Beijing, 1994).

18. Na Zhiliang, *Fu Jin-yi Wang Hua Guo Bao: Gu Gong Wushi Nian* [Reflections on past stories of national treasures in light of the present: Fifty years at the Palace Museum] (Hong Kong, 1984), p. 38.

19. Pierre Rycksman, "The Chinese Attitude Towards the Past," *Papers on Far Eastern History* 39 (1989): 1–16.

20. In a *New York Times Magazine* article, "Don't Mess with Our Cultural Patrimony!" (March 17, 1996, p. 33), Andrew Solomon hints at the awe that this collection can inspire: "[S]pread before you like a fool's supper is the greatest art of China: neolithic jades, Chou drinking vessels, Sung porcelains, Ch'ing treasure boxes and, most of all, an astonishing collection of T'ang and Sung painting and calligraphy. This work, accumulated by emperors over more than 11 centuries of dynastic rule, is still called the Imperial Collection. No Western museum has such a concentration of great work, but then no Western country has a history as immense as China's."

21. It should come as no surprise that the National Palace Museum in Taiwan emphasizes in its exhibitions and public relations material the heroic efforts to preserve and transport the imperial collections throughout the Japanese invasion of China and, later, during the Civil War.

22. For an interesting account of similar transformations occurring on Taiwan, see Marshall Johnson, "Making Time: Historic Preservation and the Space of Nationality," *Positions* 2, no. 2 (1994): 177–249.

23. Gu Gong Bowuyuan, *Jian Yuan Liushi Zhou Nian Ji Nian 1925–1985* [Commemorating the sixtieth anniversary of the founding of the museum], special issue of *Gu Gong Bowuyuan* 29, no. 3 (1985).

24. My reference to cost here is largely speculative—based on the obvious requirements of maintaining a wooden structure more than five hundred years old. I have been unable to locate published information regarding the annual operating costs or budget of the museum, nor was I able to elicit this information from museum staff members with whom I worked on various aspects of this project.

25. Zhang Langlang, "My Home Is next to Tianmen Square," in *New Ghosts, Old Dreams: Chinese Rebel Voices*, edited by Geremie Barme and Linda Jarvin (New York, 1992), p. 111.

26. For more detailed histories and other interpretations of the symbolic signifi-

cance of Tianmen Square and the revolutionary monuments built there, see Wu Hong, "Tianmen Square: A Political History of Monuments," *Representations* 34 (1991): 84–117; Rudolf Wagner, "Reading the Chairman Mao Memorial Hall in Peking," in *Pilgrims and Sacred Sites in China*, edited by Susan Naquin and Chun-fang Yu (Berkeley, Calif., 1992), pp. 378–423; and Watson, *Memory, History, and Opposition*, pp. 1–20.

27. Liu Yiran, "Rocking Tianmen," in Barme and Jarvin, *New Ghosts, Old Dreams*, p. 15, (my emphasis).

28. Ibid., pp. 20–21 (my emphasis).

29. David Lowenthal, "Identity, Heritage, and History," in *Commemorations: The Politics of National Identity*, edited by John R. Gillis (Princeton, N.J., 1994), p. 44.

CHAPTER 9: THE MODERN MUSES

1. This subject is discussed in greater detail in Paula Findlen, *Possessing Nature: Museums, Collecting, and Scientific Culture in Early Modern Italy* (Berkeley, Calif., 1994). The literature on collecting is sufficiently large by now that I will only indicate the most relevant works to this study: Oliver Impey and Arthur MacGregor, eds., *The Origins of Museums: The Cabinet of Curiosities in Sixteenth- and Seventeenth-Century Europe* (Oxford, 1985); Krzysztof Pomian, *Collectors and Curiosities: Paris and Venice, 1500–1800* (London, 1990); and Giuseppe Olmi, *L'inventario del mondo. Catalogazione della natura e luoghi del sapere nella prima età moderna* (Bologna, 1992).

2. Claudio Franzoni, "'Rimembranze d'infinite cose': Le collezioni rinascimentali di antichità," in *Memoria dell'antico nell'arte italiana*, edited by Salvatore Settis, vol. 1 (Turin, 1984), pp. 299–360.

3. In Frances Yates, *The Art of Memory* (Chicago, 1966), p. 46; Biblioteca Nazionale, Florence, *Cod. Magl.* II, 1, 13, f. 1; and Paolo Rossi, *Clavis universalis. Arti della memoria e logica combinatoria da Lullo e Leibniz* (Milan, 1960), p. 62.

4. On this subject, the classic works remain Yates, *The Art of Memory*; and Rossi, *Clavis universalis*. More recently, Lina Bolzoni has given a new interpretation of the *ars mnemonica* that encompasses a wider variety of sources and practices, and specifically connects mnemonics and collecting; see her *La stanza della memoria. Modelli letterari e iconografici nell'età della stampa* (Turin, 1995).

5. Walter Ong, "System, Space, and Intellect in Renaissance Symbolism," in *The Barbarian Within and Other Fugitive Essays and Studies* (New York, 1962), p. 73.

6. In Yates, *Art of Memory*, pp. 130–32.

7. Giulio Camillo Delminio, *L'idea del theatro dell'eccelent. M. Giulio Camillo* (Florence, 1550), p. 14.

8. Biblioteca Universitaria, Bologna (hereafter BUB), *Aldrovandi*, ms. 21, III, c. 428r. See Ulisse Aldrovandi, *Delle statue antiche romane che per tutta Roma in diversi luoghi e case si vedono*, in Lucio Mauro, *Le antichità della città di Roma* (Venice, 1556).

9. Ulisse Aldrovandi, "Avvertimenti del Dottore Aldrovandi" (1581), in *Trattati d'arte del Cinquecento*, edited by Paola Barocchi (Bari, 1961), p. 512.

10. For Aldrovandi's criticisms of the Lullian approach to memory, see Giuseppe Olmi, *Ulisse Aldrovandi. Scienza e natura nel secondo Cinquecento* (Trent, 1976), pp. 82–90. Olmi discusses Aldrovandi's ownership of memory treatises by Camillo and other writers on p. 78.

11. BUB, *Aldrovandi*, ms. 21, II, c. 268, in Olmi, *Ulisse Aldrovandi*, p. 83.

12. Richard J. Durling, "Conrad Gesner's *Liber amicorum* 1555–1565," *Gesnerus* 22 (1965): 134–57; and BUB, *Aldrovandi*, ms. 110. For Quiccheberg's account of Aldrovandi's museum, see Samuel Quiccheberg, *Inscriptiones vel tituli Theatri Amplissimi* (Munich, 1565), p. 18.

13. Quiccheberg, *Inscriptiones*, p. 15. On this text, see Werner Hüllen, "Reality, the Museum, and the Catalogue: A Semiotic Interpretation of Early German Texts of Museology," *Semiotica* 80 (1990): 267–68; and Harriet Hauger, "Samuel Quiccheberg: 'Inscriptiones vel Tituli Theatri Amplissimi': Über die Entstehung der Museen und das Sammeln," in *Universität und Bildung: Festschrift Laetitia Boehm zum 60. Geburtstag*, edited by Winfried Müller, Wolfgang J. Smolka, and Helmut Zedelmaier (Munich, 1991), pp. 129–39.

14. Hüllen, "Reality," p. 268.

15. Tommaso Campanella, *The City of the Sun: A Poetic Dialogue*, translated by Daniel J. Donno (Berkeley, Calif., 1981), p. 37.

16. Claude Clemens, *Musei sive bibliothecae tam privatae quam publicae extructio, cura, usus* (Leiden, 1635), sig.*4v. This subject is discussed in greater detail in Findlen, "The Museum: Its Classical Etymology and Renaissance Genealogy," *Journal of the History of Collections* 1 (1989): 59–78.

17. "Protesta di D. Teodoro Bondini a chi legge," in Lorenzo Legati, *Museo Cospiano* (Bologna, 1677), n.p.

18. In Luciano Canfora, *The Vanished Library: A Wonder of the Ancient World*, translated by Martin Ryle (Berkeley, Calif., 1989), p. 37. Canfora's book provides a marvelous introduction to the ambivalent legacy of Alexandria. For a longer view, see Steve Fuller and David Gorman, "Burning Libraries: Cultural Creation and the Problem of Historical Consciousness," *Annals of Scholarship* 4 (1987): 105–19.

19. Archivum Romanum Societatis Jesu, *Rom.* 138. *Historia* (1704–29), XVI, f. 182r (Filippo Bonanni, "Notizie circa la Galleria del Collegio Romano," January 10, 1716).

20. Marion Rothstein, "Etymology, Genealogy and the Immutability of Origins," *Renaissance Quarterly* 43 (1990): 333.

21. BUB, *Aldrovandi*, ms. 21, II, c. 12 (Bologna, n.d.)

22. The use of this imagery is discussed in greater detail in Findlen, *Possessing Nature*, pp. 352–65.

23. Ulisse Aldrovandi, *Discorso naturale*, in Sandra Tugnoli Pattaro, *Metodo e sistema delle scienze nel pensiero di Ulisse Aldrovandi* (Bologna, 1981), p. 181.

24. BUB, *Aldrovandi*, ms. 66, cc. 356r–v (Bologna, November 12, 1567).

25. Aldrovandi, "Avvertimenti," p. 512.

26. During his lifetime, Aldrovandi published only four volumes of his natural history, between 1599 and 1602. His difficulties financing his publications were typical of many Renaissance encyclopedists who found it easier to acquire objects from patrons for their museums than to extract money from them.

27. Aldrovandi, *Discorso naturale*, in Pattaro, *Metodo e sistema*, p. 181.

28. "Testamento di Ulisse Aldrovandi," in Giovanni Fantuzzi, *Memoria della vita di Ulisse Aldrovandi* (Bologna, 1774), p. 76.

29. For more on this story, see Cristiana Scappini and Maria Pia Torricelli, *Lo Studio Aldrovandi in Palazzo Pubblico (1617–1742)*, edited by Sandra Tugnoli Pattaro (Bologna, 1993).

30. Federico Borromeo, *Musaeum*, in Arlene Quint, *Cardinal Federico Borromeo as a Patron and a Critic of the Arts and His Musaeum of 1625* (New York, 1986), p. 259. The classic study of Renaissance portraiture remains John Pope-Hennessy, *The Portrait in the Renaissance* (London, 1966).

31. Franzoni, "Rimembranze d'infinite cose," p. 309; T. E. Mommsen, "Petrarch and the Decoration of the Sala Virorum Illustrium in Padua," *Art Bulletin* 34 (1952): 95–116; Luciano Cheles, *The Studiolo of Urbino: An Iconographic Interpretation* (University Park, Pa., 1986), pp. 22–23; and Scott Jay Schaeffer, "The Studiolo of Francesco I de' Medici in the Palazzo Vecchio in Florence," (Ph.D. diss., Bryn Mawr College, 1976), pp. 116–18.

32. Anton Francesco Doni, *Tre libri di lettere* (Venice, 1552), p. 81 (Como, July 20, 1543). See also the conference proceedings *Paolo Giovio: Il Rinascimento e la memoria* (Como, 1985); and Franzoni, "Rimembranze d'infinite cose," pp. 356–58.

33. See Niccolò Machiavelli, *Lettere*, edited by Franco Gaeta (Milan, 1961), pp. 301–6. This passage is discussed more fully in Findlen, "The Museum"; and Sebastiano de Grazia, *Machiavelli in Hell* (Princeton, N.J., 1989). For a broader view of the tradition initiated by Giovio, see Carlo Dionisotti, "La galleria degli uomini illustri," in *Cultura e società nel Rinascimento. Tra riforme e manierismi*, edited by Vittore Branca and Carlo Ossola (Florence, 1984), pp. 449–61. Giovio's activities are discussed in T. C. Price Zimmerman, *Paolo Giovio: The Historian and the Crisis of Sixteenth-Century Italy* (Princeton, N.J., 1995).

34. Gigliola Fragnito, *In museo e in villa. Saggi sul Rinascimento perduto* (Venice, 1988), pp. 65–108 and 159–214, passim.

35. Giovan Battista Olivi, *De reconditis et praecipuis collectaneis ab honestissimo, et solertiss[i]mo Francisco Calceolari Veronensi in musaeo adservatis* (Venice, 1584), sig. +3v; BUB, *Aldrovandi*, ms. 136, XIX, c. 156r (1592–93).

36. Dario Franchini et al., *La scienza a corte. Collezionismo eccletico, natura e immagine a Mantova fra Rinascimento e Manierismo* (Rome, 1979), p. 124; and Lucia Tongiorgi Tomasi, "Il 'nuovo' giardino dei semplici e la sua galleria," in *Livorno e Pisa. Due città e un territorio nella politica dei Medici* (Pisa, 1980), pp. 534–38.

37. Mario Fanti, "La villeggiatura di Ulisse Aldrovandi," *Strenna storica bolognese* 8 (1958): 35–36. The inscription under Francesco I's portrait underscored his role as an heir of Alexander, reading: "Magnos magna decere viros Francisce probasti virtute, effigie nomine et ingenio."

38. Filippo Baldinucci, *Notizie*, IV, in Edward L. Goldberg, *Patterns in Late Medici Art Patronage* (Princeton, N.J., 1983), p. 35.

39. Pierre Gassendi, *The Mirrour of True Nobility & Gentility: Being the Life of the Renowned Nicolaus Claudius Fabricius Lord of Peiresk, Senator of the Parliament at Aix*, translated by W. Rand (London, 1657), p. 41.

40. Franzoni, "Rimembranze d'infinite cose," p. 303.

41. Fantuzzi, *Memorie*, p. 84.

42. Giuseppe Gabrieli, "Il Carteggio Linceo della vecchia accademia di Federigo Cesi (1603–30)," *Memorie della R. Accademia Nazionale dei Lincei: Classe di scienze morali, storiche e filologiche*, ser. 6, vol. 7, fasc. 2–3 (1939), p. 348 (Federico Cesi to Francesco Stelluti, Rome, second half of April 1613). On Della Porta's museum, see Giorgio Fulco, "Per il 'museo' dei fratelli Della Porta," in *Il Rinascimento meriodionale. Raccolta di studi pubblicata in onore di Mario Santoro* (Naples, 1986), pp. 3–73.

43. Fulco, "Per il museo," pp. 23–24.

44. The image of Della Porta as a Muse was already in circulation. Contemporary poets referred to Giovan Vincenzo as the "Musa fallì" and to Giovan Battista as the "Musa gentil." Ibid., pp. 30, 64 n. 83.

45. Rossi published his work under the Greek pseudonym of Giario Nicio Eritreo.

46. Pontificia Università Gregoriana, Rome (hereafter PUG), *Kircher*, ms. 558 (IV), f. 142r ("Instrumentum Alfonsi Donnini supra donationem suo Galeria," May 7, 1651).

47. PUG, *Kircher*, ms. 565 (XI), f. 292r (Egidio Constantini to Kircher, Toscanella, July 7, 1657); ms. 566 (XII), f. 39 (Giovan Battista Müller to Kircher, Recenati, July 2, 1677); and R. J. W. Evans, *The Making of the Habsburg Monarchy, 1550–1700: An Interpretation* (Oxford, 1979), p. 434.

48. Pietro Scarabelli, *Museo o galeria adunata del sapere, e dallo studio del Sig. Canonico Manfredo Settala Nobile Milanese*, translated by Paolo Terzago (Tortona, 1666), p. 171. Since there are differences between the Latin catalog authored by Scarabelli and Terzago's Italian version of it, I have presented Terzago as the author of the latter.

49. *Il Museo del Cardinale Federico Borromeo*, translated by Luigi Grasselli, edited by Luca Beltrami (Milan, 1909), p. 45. For Borromeo's interest in mnemonics, see Bolzoni, *La stanza della memoria*, pp. 79–81.

50. BUB, *Aldrovandi*, ms. 6, I, c.11v (Bologna, September 19, 1577). I have discussed the subject of gift-giving in greater detail in Findlen, "The Economy of Scientific Exchange in Early Modern Italy," in *Patronage and Institutions: Science, Technology, and Medicine and the European Courts, 1500–1750*, edited by Bruce Moran (Woodbridge, England, 1990), pp. 5–24.

51. BUB, Cod. 9, no. 35 (Aldrovandi to Monsignor Alberto Bolognetti, Bologna, September 6, 1578), f. 1r.

52. Alessandro Tosi, ed., *Ulisse Aldrovandi e la Toscana. Carteggio e testimonianze documentarie* (Florence, 1989), p. 298 (Aldrovandi to Francesco I, Bologna, May 5, 1586). Aldrovandi's patronage relationship with Francesco I is discussed more fully in Findlen, *Possessing Nature*, pp. 353, 357–59.

53. Ludovico Frati, "La vita di Ulisse Aldrovandi scritta da lui medesimo," in *Intorno alla vita e alle opere di Ulisse Aldrovandi* (Imola, 1907), p. 28.

54. BUB, *Aldrovandi*, ms. 382, III, c. 253 (Imperato to Aldrovandi, Naples, July 10, 1573).

55. BUB, *Aldrovandi*, ms. 5, c. 19 (Aldrovandi to Jacobus Laurentius, June 1584).

56. Biblioteca Comunale degli Intronati, Siena, *Autografi Porri*, Filza 5, n. 85 (K XI, 53) (Rome, April 28, 1662). The second quote comes from John Fletcher, "Kircher and Duke August of Wolfenbüttel," in *Enciclopedismo in Roma barocca: Athanasius Kircher e il Museo del Collegio Romano tra Wunderkammer e museo scientifico*, edited by Mariastella Casciato, Maria Grazia Ianniello, and Maria Vitale (Venice, 1986), p. 289.

57. Gabrieli, "Il carteggio linceo," fasc. 2, p. 348.

58. Ibid., p. 347.

59. Ibid., fasc. 3, p. 1217 (Stelluti to Galileo, Acquasparta, August 2, 1632).

60. Borromeo, *Musaeum*, p. 43. For a more detailed discussion of Borromeo's art collection, see Pamela Jones, *Federico Borromeo and the Ambrosiana: Art and Patronage in Seventeenth-Century Milan* (Cambridge, 1993).

61. Jones, *Federico Borromeo*, p. 66.

62. Ibid., p. 68.

63. On this subject, see Giovanni Cipriani, *Gli obelischi egizi: Politica e cultura nella Roma barocca* (Florence, 1993); and Erik Iversen, *The Myth of Egypt and Its Hieroglyphs* (Copenhagen, 1961).

64. Luciano Berti, *Il Principe dello Studiolo* (Florence, 1967), p. 68.

65. PUG, *Kircher*, ms. 565 (XI), f. 292r (Cocumella, September 9, 1672). This passage is also discussed in Bolzoni, *La stanza della memoria*, p. 265.

CHAPTER 10: THE QUARREL OF THE ANCIENTS
AND MODERNS IN THE GERMAN MUSEUMS

1. For an excellent treatment of the "quarrel," see Joseph M. Levine, *The Battle of the Books: History and Literature in the Augustan Age* (Ithaca, N.Y., 1991).

2. See George Iggers, *The German Conception of History* (Middletown, Conn., 1968).

3. A more detailed presentation of this argument can be found in my book, *Down from Olympus: Archaeology and Philhellenism in Germany, 1750–1970* (Princeton, N.J., 1996).

4. See Steven Moyano, "Quality vs. History: Schinkel's Altes Museum and Prussian Arts Policy," *Art Bulletin* 72 (1990): 585–608.

5. Ibid., p. 601.

6. Even the proto-"historicist" philosopher J. G. Herder shared this view. See Robert E. Norton, *Herder's Aesthetics and the European Enlightenment* (Ithaca, N.Y., 1991), pp. 216–32.

7. Wolfgang Ehrhardt, *Das akademische Kunstmuseum der Universität Bonn unter der Direktion von Friedrich Gottlieb Welcker und Otto Jahn* (Opladen, 1982), p. 13.

8. Warburg's report on cast collections in Germany is dated May 26, 1909, and can be found in the Warburg Institute, London, Wuttke no. 72.

9. *Verzeichniss der in der Formerei der Königlichen Museen käuflichen Gipsabgüsse* (Berlin, 1893).

10. See Renate Petras, *Die Bauten des Berliner Museumsinsel* (Berlin, 1989), p. 157.

11. For an intriguing examination of these local *Vereine* and their contribution to historicism, see Susan Crane, "Collecting and Historical Consciousness: New Forms for Collective Memory in Early-Nineteenth-Century Germany" (Ph.D. diss., University of Chicago, 1992).

12. Like the princely "cabinets" on which they were probably modeled, local museums contained an assortment of natural and man-made objects, all of which were intended, however, not so much to appeal to the curiosity as to testify to the rich and long cultural heritage of the province.

13. For more on these reforms, see pp. 189–91.

14. Wolfgang Ehrhardt, *Das akademische Kunstmuseum*, p. 31.

15. Dorow quoted in Reinhold Fuchs, "Zur Geschichte der Sammlungen des Rheinischen Landesmuseums," in *Rheinisches Landesmuseum Bonn: 150 Jahre Sammlungen* (Düsseldorf, 1971), pp. 75–76.

16. For an excellent survey of one region's localist activities, see Celia Applegate, *A Nation of Provincials: The German Idea of Heimat* (Berkeley, Calif., 1990).

17. See Heinrich Härke, "All Quiet on the Western Front? Paradigms, Methods, and Approaches in West German Archaeology," in *Archaeological Theory in Europe: The Last Three Decades*, edited by Ian Hodder (New York, 1991), pp. 187–222.

18. On Müller, see Josine Blok, "Quest for a Scientific Mythology: F. Creuzer and K. O. Müller on History and Myth," *History and Theory*, suppl. vol. 33 (1994): 26–52. On Lepsius, see Elke Freier and Walter F. Reineke, eds., *Karl Richard Lepsius (1810–1884)*, Schriften zur Geschichte und Kultur des alten Orients, vol. 20 (Berlin, 1988).

19. Bunsen's "Egyptology" was ultimately much different from that of Lepsius; his *Aegyptens Stelle in der Weltgeschichte*, 5 vols. (Hamburg, 1845–57) aimed at the creation of a "world-historical" chronology that would integrate biblical texts and classical historiography. Lepsius, on the other hand, wanted to write the history of Egypt, using Egyptian as well as classical texts. See Suzanne Marchand, "The End of Egyptomania," in *Ägyptomanie: Europäische Ägyptenimagination von der Antike bis heute*, edited by Wilfried Seipel (forthcoming).

20. Founded in 1828, this collection was composed largely of artifacts from the private collection of General Heinrich von Minutoli.

21. Adolf Erman, *Mein Werden und mein Wirken: Erinnerungen eines alten Berliner Gelehrten* (Leipzig, 1929), p. 122.

22. See Mommsen's speech before the Reichstag on March 16, 1876, reprinted as "Über die Königlichen Museen," in *Reden und Aufsätze* (Berlin, 1905), p. 233.

23. In 1872, Heinrich von Treitschke attacked the dilletantry of General Director Guido von Usedom in the pages of the *Preußische Jahrbücher*. See Ludwig Pallat, *Richard Schöne* (Berlin, 1959), p. 110.

24. See Marchand, *Down from Olympus*, chap. 6.

25. On Elgin's difficulties, see William St. Clair, *Lord Elgin and the Marbles* (London, 1967).

26. See Marchand, "The Excavations at Olympia: An Episode in German-Greek Cultural Relations," in *Greek Society in the Making, 1863–1913: Realities, Symbols, and Visions*, edited by Philip Carabott (Aldershot, Hampshire, 1997), pp. 73–85.

27. Count Radolin to Foreign Ministry, July 17, 1894, Potsdam, Zentrales Staatsarchiv, Auswärtiges Amt (Rechtasabteilung) 37718, pp. 2–4.

28. See Marchand, *Down from Olympus*, chap. 6.

29. Karl Scheffler, *Berliner Museumskrieg* (Berlin, 1921), pp. 44–46.

30. Ibid., p. 76.

31. Petras, *Die Bauten der Berliner Museumsinsel*, p. 138.

32. Richard Schöne, "Zur Erinnerung" (1896), in *Der Entdecker von Pergamon: Carl Humann*, edited by Carl Schuchhardt and Theodor Wiegand (Berlin, 1931), p. 10.

33. Bode to Education Ministry, March 28, 1911, Staatliches Museumsarchiv, Berlin, Islamisches Museum, 15. Bode did not mention classical antiquities; presumably, he thought the state support of these museum departments adequate, or even excessive.

34. See Martin Sonnabend, *George Swarzenski und das Liebieghaus (Zur Gründung des Liebieghauses)* (Frankfurt, 1990), pp. 24–35.

35. On Bode's plans for the Museums Island, see also Thomas Gaehtgens, *Der Berliner Museumsinsel im Deutschen Kaiserreich* (Berlin, 1987), pp. 102–11.

36. There is a large literature on school reform. For one excellent treatment of the nineteenth-century battles, see James Albisetti, *Secondary School Reform in Imperial Germany* (Princeton, N.J., 1983).

37. Wolf Schierbrand, ed. and trans., *The Kaiser's Speeches: Forming a Character Portrait of Emperor William II* (New York, 1903) pp. 212–17 (quotation, p. 214).

38. See Kaiser Wilhelm II, *Erinnerungen an Corfu* (Berlin, 1924).

39. Ulrich von Wilamowitz-Moellendorff, "Philologie und Schulreform," in *Reden und Vorträge*, 3d ed. (Berlin, 1913), p. 115.

40. See Marchand, *Down from Olympus*, chap. 4.

41. See Marchand, "The Excavations at Olympia."

42. Königliche Akademie der Wissenschaften to Bosse, February 13, 1897, Potsdam, Zentrales Staatsarchiv, Auswärtiges Amt (Rechtsabteilung) 37691, pp. 11–14.

43. This analogy is not accidental—Ratzel apparently drew heavily on the work of his zoologist colleague at the University of Leipzig, Moriz Wagner.

44. Ratzel, *Anthropo-Geographie* (Leipzig, 1882), pp. 31–32.

45. On Schmidt, see Ernest Brandewie, *When Giants Walked the Earth: The Life and Times of Wilhelm Schmidt, SVD* (Fribourg, 1990); and Suzanne Marchand, "Priests Among the Pygmies: The Counter Reformation in Austrian Ethnology," in *Worldly Provincials: German Anthropology in the Age of Empire*, edited by Matti Bunzl and Glenn Penny (forthcoming).

46. Sven Hedin, *Fünfzig Jahre Deutschland* (Leipzig, 1938), pp. 25–27, 39; Erich von Drygalski, *Ferd. Frhr. v. Richthofen* (Leipzig, 1905).

47. Ferdinand Freiherr von Richthofen, *Führer für Forschungsreisende* (Berlin, 1886).

48. Hedin, *Fünfzig Jahre Deutschland*, p. 42.

49. My information on Penck comes from Gerhard Engelmann, *Ferdinand von Richthofen 1833–1905; Albrecht Penck 1858–1945: Zwei markante Geographen Berlins*, Erdkundliches Wissen, no. 91 (Stuttgart, 1988), pp. 25–35.

50. Albrecht Penck, "Der Krieg und das Studium der Geographie," *Zeitschrift der Gesellschaft für Erdkunde zu Berlin* 64, nos. 3–4 (1916): 45.

51. This statistic was provided by the director of one such state-funded museum, Karl Schumacher, in "Das Römisch-Germanische Central-Museum von 1901–1926," in *Festschrift zur Feier des 75-jährigen Bestehens des Römisch-Germanischen Centralmuseums zu Mainz 1927* (Mainz, 1927), p. 64.

52. Hedin, *Fünfzig Jahre Deutschland*, p. 92.

53. On Kossinna, see Ulrich Veit, "Gustav Kossinna und V. Gordon Childe: Ansätze zu einer theoretischen Grundlegung der Vorgeschichte," *Saeculum* 35 (1984): 326–64; and Günther Smolla, "Gustaf Kossinna nach 50 Jahren: Kein Nachruf," *Acta Praehistorica et Archaeologica* 16–17 (1984–85): 9–14; on Strzygowski, see Suzanne Marchand, "The Rhetoric of Artifacts and the Decline of Classical Humanism: The Case of Josef Strzygowski," *History and Theory*, suppl. vol. 33 (1994): 106–30.

54. On Morelli, see Carlo Ginzburg, "Clues: Roots of an Evidential Paradigm," in *Clues, Myths, and the Historical Method*, translated by John and Anne Tedeschi (Baltimore, 1989); on Riegl, see Margaret Rose Olin, *Forms of Representation in Alois Riegl's Theory of Art* (University Park, Pa., 1992).

55. Alain Schnapp, in *La conquète du passé: Aux origines de l'archéologie* (Paris, 1993), argues, rightly, that antecedents of the study of local antiquities are to be found in late Renaissance Scandinavia and England (pp. 139–42, 160–67). The study of local artifacts as a mass phenomenon in the German-speaking lands, however, really begins only in the wake of the Napoleonic Wars.

56. Schliemann to Justizrat Plat, January 27, 1872, in *Heinrich Schliemann: Briefwechsel*, vol. 1 (*1842–1875*), edited by Ernst Meyer (Berlin, 1953), pp. 200–201.

57. Moriz Hoernes, "Grundlinien einer Systematik der prähistorischen Archäologie," in *Zeitschrift für Ethnographie* 25 (1893): 53.

58. See Frobenius, *Auf den Trümmern des klassischen Atlantis, 1910 bis 1912*, vol. 1 of *Und Afrika sprach* (Berlin, 1912), esp. pp. 364–75.

59. Frobenius, *Im Schatten des Kongostaates* (Berlin, 1907), p. 10.

60. On Dahn, see Herbert Meyer, *Felix Dahn* (Leipzig, 1913).

61. See Marchand, *Down from Olympus*, chap. 4.

62. Sonnabend, *Georg Swarzenki*, pp. 18–20, 34–40.

63. Heinrich Schäfer, "Einleitung," in Schäfer and Walter Andrae, *Die Kunst des alten Orients*, Propyläen-Kunstgeschichte, vol. 2 (Berlin, 1925), pp. 11–19.

64. Wilhelm von Bode, *Mein Leben*, vol. 1 (Berlin, 1930), pp. 57–63.

65. Renate Sanatani, *Rabindranath Tagore und das deutsche Theater der zwanziger Jahre* (Frankfurt, 1983), p. 45.

66. Frobenius, *Das unbekannte Afrika: Aufhellung der Schicksale eines Erdteils* (Munich, 1923), p. xii.

CHAPTER 11: THE MUSEUM'S DISCOURSE ON ART

1. Max J. Friedländer, *Von Kunst und Kennerschaft* (Leipzig, 1992), pp. 91–92.

2. For a general account of competitive nationalism and its transformations during the *Kaiserreich*, see Thomas Nipperdey, *Deutsche Geschichte 1866–1918*, vol. 2 (Munich, 1993), pp. 595–608; Hans-Ulrich Wehler, *Von der deutschen "Doppelrevolution" bis zum Beginn des ersten Weltkrieges*, Deutsche Gesellschaftsgeschichte, vol. 3 (Munich, 1995), pp. 938–60; Hermann Glaser, *Bildungsbürgertum und Nationalismus: Politik und Kultur im wilhelminischen Deutschland*, Deutsche Geschichte der neuesten Zeit (Munich, 1993). An early source for the broad implications of the topos of German "belatedness" is Georg Brandes, *Berlin som tysk Rigshovestad* (Copenhagen, 1885) (*Berlin als deutsche Reichshauptstadt: Erinnerungen aus den Jahren 1877 bis 1883*, edited by Erik M. Christensen and Hans-Dietrich Loock [Berlin, 1989]).

3. For the museum policy of the Prussian state in the late nineteenth century, see Ludwig Pallat, *Richard Schöne, Generaldirektor der Königlichen Museen zu Berlin: Ein Beitrag zur Geschichte der preussischen Kunstverwaltung 1872–1905*, edited by Paul Ortwin Rave (Berlin, 1959); Stephan Waetzoldt, "Museumspolitik—Richard Schöne und Wilhelm von Bode," in *Kunstverwaltung, Bau- und Denkmalpolitik im Kaiserreich*, edited by Waetzoldt and Ekkehard Mai, Kunst, Kultur und Politik im Deutschen Kaiserreich, vol. 1 (Berlin, 1981), pp. 481–90; Thomas W. Gaehtgens, *Die Berliner Museumsinsel im Deutschen Kaiserreich: Beiträge zur Kulturpolitik der Museen in der wilhelminischen Epoche* (Berlin, 1992).

4. On Bode, see Edward P. Alexander, *Museum Masters: Their Museums and*

Their Influence (Nashville, Tenn., 1983), pp. 205–38; Werner Beyrodt, "Wilhelm von Bode," in *Altmeister moderner Kunstgeschichte,* edited by Heinrich Dilly (Berlin, 1990), pp. 19–34; Sigrid Otto, "Wilhelm von Bode: Journal eines tätigen Lebens, in *Wilhelm von Bode: Museumsdirektor und Mäzen* (exhibition catalog) (Berlin, 1995), pp. 23–50; Peter-Klaus Schuster, "Bode als Problem," in *Wilhelm von Bode als Zeitgenosse der Kunst* (exhibition catalog) (Berlin, 1995), pp. 1–31.

5. On the institutionalization of art history in Germany, see Heinrich Dilly, *Kunstgeschichte als Institution* (Frankfurt/Main, 1979); Werner Beyrodt, "Kunstgeschichte als Universitätsfach," in *Kunst und Kunsttheorie 1400–1900,* edited by Peter Ganz et al. (Wiesbaden, 1991), pp. 313–33.

6. For an analysis of the role of family dynasties in the academic professions of imperial Germany, see Fritz K. Ringer, *The Decline of the German Mandarins: The German Academic Community, 1890–1933* (Cambridge. Mass., 1969).

7. On Grimm, see Wilhelm Waetzold, *Deutsche Kunsthistoriker,* vol. 2 (Berlin, 1986), pp. 214–38; Peter H. Feist, "Hundert Jahre nach Herman Grimm, dreißig Jahre seit der Befreiung vom Faschismus: Die Entwicklung der Kunstwissenschaft an der Berliner Universität 1875–1975," in *Künstlerisches und kunstwissenschaftliches Erbe als Gegenwartsaufgabe,* Referate der Arbeitstagung vom 16.–18.8.1975 (Berlin, 1975), pp. 1–38; Udo Kultermann, *Geschichte der Kunstgeschichte: Der Weg einer Wissenschaft* (Munich, 1990), pp. 122–24.

8. Herman Grimm, "Das Universitätsstudium der neueren Kunstgeschichte," *Deutsche Rundschau* 66 (1891): 390–413.

9. Ibid., p. 405.

10. For a museum of reproductions in Paris, see Albert Boime, "Le musée des copies," *Gazette des Beaux-Arts* 106 (1964): 237–47; and Paul Duro, "Le musée des copies de Charles Blanc à l'aube de la IIIe république," *Bulletin de la Société de l'Histoire de l'Art Français* (1985): 283–313. A similar attempt in Berlin proved to be abortive; see Robert Bussler, *Der Rafael-Saal: Verzeichniss der im Königlichen Orangeriehause zu SansSouci auf allerhöchsten Befehl aufgestellten Copien nach Gemälden von Rafael Sanzio* (Berlin, 1858); and Götz Eckhardt, *Die Orangerie im Park von Sanssouci* (Potsdam, 1988), pp. 10–12, 21–32. On the practice of collecting casts, see also Suzanne Marchand's essay in this volume.

11. On the collection in Berlin, see Gertrud Platz-Horster, "Zur Geschichte der Sammlung von Gipsabgüssen in Berlin," in *Berlin und die Antike* (exhibition catalog), vol. 2 (Berlin, 1979), pp. 273–92; Viola Vahrson, "Die Krise der historischen Kunstbetrachtung: Die Berliner Abgußsammlung zwischen Enzyklopädie und Aura," in *Museumsinszenierungen: Zur Geschichte der Institution des Kunstmuseums: Die Berliner Museumslandschaft 1830–1990,* edited by Alexis Joachimides et al. (Berlin, 1995), pp. 81–92. On the building program see also Pallat *Richard Schöne,* pp. 119–25, 209–10, 298. For a similar development in the United States, see Walter Muir Whitehill, *Museum of Fine Arts, Boston: A Centennial History* (Cambridge, Mass., 1970).

12. W. Koopmann, "Prof. Herman Grimm contra Galeriedirector Bode," *Die Gegenwart* 39, no. 13 (1891): 198–202. The identity of the author of the piece remains obscure, since he does not otherwise appear in contemporary records, and the name may well have been a pseudonym of someone in Bode's entourage, or even of the director himself.

13. Ibid., p. 199.

14. Wilhelm von Bode, *Mein Leben*, 2 vols. (Berlin, 1930), 1:151–52.

15. Emperor Friedrich III, memorandum of February 1888, in Zentralarchiv der Staatlichen Museen zu Berlin Preußischer Kulturbesitz, Nachlaß Bode, no. 140. For a discusssion of the Berlin museum in light of this document, see Alexis Joachimides, "Die Schule des Geschmacks: Das Kaiser-Friedrich-Museum als Reformprojekt," in Joachimides et al. *Museumsinszenierungen*, pp. 142–56; for a general account of the political support that the *Kunstgewerbe* movement attracted at this time, see Karl Heinz Kaufhold, "Fragen der Gewerbepolitik und Gewerbeförderung," in *Kunstpolitik und Kunstförderung im Kaiserreich*, edited by Ekkehard Mai, Stephan Waetzold, and Hans Pohl, Kunst, Kultur und Politik im Deutschen Kaiserreich, vol. 2 (Berlin, 1982), pp. 95–109.

16. On the political origins of *Kulturgeschichte*, see Thomas Nipperdey, "Kulturgeschichte, Sozialgeschichte, historische Anthropologie," *Vierteljahrsschrift für Sozial- und Wirtschaftsgeschichte* 55 (1968): 145–64; Bernward Deneke, "Die Museen und die Entwicklung der Kulturgeschichte," in *Das kunst- und kulturgeschichtliche Museum im 19. Jahrhundert: Vorträge des Symposiums im Germanischen Nationalmuseum Nürnberg*, edited by Deneke and Rainer Kahsnitz (Munich, 1977), pp. 118–32.

17. For the history of the discipline in general, see Dilly, *Kunstgeschichte als Institution*; Michael Podro, *The Critical Historians of Art* (New Haven, Conn., 1982); Germain Bazin, *Histoire de l'histoire de l'art de Vasari à nos jours* (Paris, 1986).

18. For a contemporary account of their style of lecturing, see the autobiography of Werner Weisbach: *Und alles ist zerstorben* (Vienna, 1937), pp. 126–29 (Grimm), 132–33 (Wölfflin).

19. Heinrich Wölfflin, "Prolegomena zu einer Psychologie der Architektur" (Ph.D. diss., University of Munich, 1886), reprinted in his *Kleine Schriften*, edited by Joseph Gantner (Basel, 1946), pp. 13–47; his main source of inspiration was Robert Vischer, *Über das optische Formgefühl* (Stuttgart, 1873).

20. Adolf von Hildebrand, *Das Problem der Form in der bildenden Kunst* (Straßburg, 1893), reprinted in his *Gesammelte Schriften zur Kunst*, edited by Henning Bock (Cologne, 1969), pp. 41–350.

21. Heinrich Wölfflin, *Kunstgeschichtliche Grundbegriffe: Das Problem der Stilentwicklung in der neueren Kunst* (Munich, 1915). On Wölfflin, see Joan G. Hart, "Heinrich Wölfflin: An Intellectual Biography" (Ph.D. diss., University of California, Berkeley, 1981); Meinhold Lurz, *Heinrich Wölfflin: Biographie einer Kunsttheorie* (Worms, 1981); and Nikolaus Meier: "Heinrich Wölfflin 1864–1945," in *Altmeister moderner Kunstgeschichte*, edited by Heinrich Dilly (Berlin, 1990), pp. 63–79.

22. For a comparison between Wölfflin's ideas and those of contemporary aestheticism, see Edgar Wind, *Art and Anarchy* (London, 1963), pp. 16–31; and Kultermann, *Geschichte der Kunstgeschichte*, pp. 315–20.

23. For a particularly critical evaluation of Bode's personality, see Weisbach, *Und alles ist zerstorben*, p. 211.

24. For the *Giovannino*, see ibid., p. 133; Bode's attribution is not accepted today, although evidence is lacking, since the piece disappeared in 1945.

25. Ludwig Justi, untitled memoirs, vol. 2, pp. 132–33, unedited manuscript (c. 1933–36) in the Zentralarchiv der Staatlichen Museen zu Berlin Preußischer Kulturbesitz, to be published by Kurt Winkler and Thomas Gaehtgens.

26. Max J. Friedländer, *Der Kunstkenner* (Berlin, 1920), reprinted and enlarged in his *Kunst und Kennerschaft*; on Friedländer, see Jacob Rosenberg, "Friedländer and the Berlin Museum," *Burlington Magazine* 99 (1957): 83–85; Hugo Perls, "Erinnerung an Friedländer," in Max J. Friedländer, *Über die Malerei* (Munich, 1963), pp. 8–23; Julius S. Held, "Evocation de Max J. Friedländer," *Revue de l'Art* 42 (1978): 37–40.

27. On Morelli, see Wind, *Art and Anarchy*, pp. 32–51; Richard Wollheim, "Giovanni Morelli and the Origins of Scientific Connoisseurship," in *On Art and the Mind: Essays and Lectures* (London, 1973), pp. 177–201; Henri Zerner, "Giovanni Morelli et la science de l'art," *Revue de l'art* 40–41 (1978): 209–15; Jaynie Anderson, "Giovanni Morelli et sa définition de la 'scienza dell'arte,'" ibid., vol. 75 (1987): 49–55.

28. Friedländer, *Kunst und Kennerschaft*, pp. 90–91.

29. For an account of this acquisition, see Bode, *Mein Leben*, 2:232–34.

30. The painting is still in the Berlin Gemäldegalerie today (inventory no. 1718) under the same attribution, nowadays dated slightly earlier than 1475; see *Gemäldegalerie Staatliche Museen Preußischer Kulturbesitz: Katalog der ausgestellten Gemälde des 13.–18. Jahrhunderts* (Berlin-Dahlem, 1975), pp. 177–78.

31. For Riegl, see Margaret Iversen, "Style as Structure: Alois Riegls Historiography," *Art History* 2 (1979): 62–72; Podro, *The Critical Historians of Art*, pp. 71–97; Wolfgang Kemp, "Alois Riegl 1858–1905," in *Altmeister moderner Kunstgeschichte*, edited by Heinrich Dilly (Berlin, 1990), pp. 37–60.

32. Heinrich Wölfflin, *Das Erklären von Kunstwerken*, Bibliothek der Kunstgeschichte, vol. 1 (Leipzig, 1921), p. 26.

33. Colin Simpson, *The Partnership: The Secret Association of Bernard Berenson and Joseph Duveen* (London, 1987).

34. Justi, memoirs, vol. 2, p. 133 The uncle whom he refers to was the historian Carl Justi, mentioned above.

35. For a preliminary attempt to account for the history of museum installations in Germany at this time, see Alexis Joachimides, *Die Museumsreformbewegung in Deutschland und die Entstehung des modernen Museums 1880–1940* (forthcoming); a short summary in English will be available as "In Search of the 'White Cube': Institutional Reform and Display Strategies in Early-Twentieth-Century German Mu-

seums," in *Modern Art Museums and Their Spectators*, edited by Charlotte Klonk and Andrew Brighton (forthcoming).

36. The sociological as well as numerical expansion of museum audiences in Germany around 1900 has not yet received a systematic treatment, although there is plenty of evidence concerning individual institutions, and the trend was generally acknowledged by contemporary authors. See Hans W. Singer, "Unsere Museen und ihre Besucher," *Die Woche* 5 (1903): 1593–96, 1641–42; Irene Geismeier, "Besucher-analyse in der Frühzeit der Museen," in *Kunstwissenschaftliche Beiträge*, vol. 9 (supplement to *Zeitschrift für Bildende Kunst* 5 [1981]), pp. 4–5; Jenns Eric Howoldt, *Der Freie Bund zur Einbürgerung der bildenden Kunst in Mannheim: Kommunale Kunstpolitik einer Industriestadt am Beispiel der "Mannheimer Bewegung,"* Europäische Hochschulschriften, ser. 28, vol. 18 (Frankfurt/Main, 1982), pp. 69, 304–6.

Index

Adorno, Theodor, 45
Aldrovandi, Ulisse, 162–63, 166–68, 173–74
Alexander, Edward, 230
Alexander the Great, 165–66
Alpers, Svetlana, 229
Alvitre, Cindi, 120, 127
Ampo Fumiko, 102
antiquarians, 72
art history, 19–20, 57, 200–219
art museums, 11, 19, 208–90; in Berlin, 80,
    182–89, 200–219; Centre Georges Pompi-
    dou, 30; Hara Museum, 106; Karl Ernst
    Osthaus–Museum, 7, 35–59, 50; Meguro
    Museum of Art, 106; Museo Gregoriano
    Profano, 26, 27; Museo Pio–Clementino,
    21–23, 22; Museum Folkwang, 49, 56;
    Museum für Gestaltung, Zürich, 47;
    National Museum of Modern Art, Tokyo,
    105; Palace Museum, Beijing, 137–58,
    143–44; Städtische Galerie, Frankfurt,
    198; Vatican Museums, 21, 26–27
art of memory, 19, 21, 172
art preservation, 177
Ashmolean Museum, 70
authenticity, 70, 72
Autry Museum of Western History, 124–26

Badura, Michael, 52
Bakhtin, Mikhail, 136
Bal, Mieke, 2
Bann, Stephen, 35
Beccadelli, Ludovico, 169
Benjamin, Walter, 21, 26, 70
Berenson, Bernard, 215
Berger, John, 108

Berlin museums, 80, 182–89, 200–219
Bloch, Ernst, 41, 54
Bode, Wilhelm von, 188–89, 202–4, 203,
    214; debate with Grimm, 207–9
Bonanni, Filippo, 165
Bondini, Teodoro, 164
Borensztein, Leon, 100
Borges, Jorge Luis, 46, 60
Borromeo, Federico, 169, 172, 173, 176
Browne, Thomas, 161

Cage, John, 42–43
Calov, Gudrun, 76
Calzolari, Francesco, 170
Camillo, Giulio, 162–64, 178
Campanella, Tommaso, 164
Canonization, of art, 105–6
Carruthers, Mary, 236
casts. See plaster casts
Catel, Ludwig, 19–20
Centre Georges Pompidou, 30
Cesi, Federico, 175
Chartier, Roger, 67
classical scholarship, 180–81, 191–92
Clifford, James, 235
collective memory, 5–6, 55, 139, 149
collectors: of curiosities, 68–69; opposed to
    connoisseurs, 69; in the Renaissance, 10,
    161–78
connoisseurship, 202–6
Conze, Alexander, 197
Cospi, Ferdinando, 164, 170
Crate House, 51, 52
Crowther, David, 28
Curator's Cabinet, 52, 53

Index

curiosity: defined, 68
curiosity cabinets, 17–18, 65, 67–74
Cvjetanović, Boris, 99–100

de Beauvoir, Simone, 137
de Certeau, Michael, 135
della Porta, Giovan Battista, 171
d'Este, Leonello, 169
de vries, herman, 51
digital archiving, 29
Doni, Anton Francesco, 169
Donnino, Alfonso, 172
Dorn, Frank, 140
Dorow, Wilhelm, 183
Durham, Jimmy, 123

Ebisu Garden Place, 94
ecological art, 52
empathy (*Einfühlung*), 211
Erman, Adolf, 185
ethnology in Germany, 193–99
excavations in Asia Minor, 186–187, 192
exhibitions, art: *Crate House*, 51, 52; *Curator's Cabinet*, 52, 53; *Imitations — The Museum as the Location of the As-If*, 47; *In the Face of Silence*, 53–55, 54; *Modern Art from the Museum Folkwang*, 56, 57–58; *natural relations*, 51; *Open Box — An Exhibition to Extend the Idea of a Museum*, 52; *Revision*, 43–46, 44–45; *Rising from the Rubble*, 46; *Silence*, 42, 43
exhibitions, ethnographic: "feeding" exhibits, 128; *The People of California*, 119–20; *Spirit of Conquest*, 123–25
exhibitions, photography, 93–114; *The Founding and Development of Modern Photography in Japan*, 109–12; *-ism 95: The 1ˢᵗ Tokyo International Photo-Biennale*, 96–103; *Objects, Faces, and Anti-Narratives: Rethinking Modernism*, 103–4; *Photography and the National Museum of Modern Art, Tokyo, 1953–1995*, 105, 111; *Pictures of the Real World (in Real Time)*, 106; *Tokyo/City of Photos*, 109; *Tokyo–Tokyo*, 106–8

fakes in exhibitions, 47
Fehr, Michael, 81
Findlen, Paula, 69
Forbidden City (Beijing), 145–47
Foucault, Michel, 73, 230
The Founding and Development of Modern Photography in Japan, 109–12
Friedlander, Max J., 200, 203, 213–16,
Frobenius, Leo, 197–99

German–Greek relations, and art collecting, 186
German Historical Museum, 33
Germanisches Nationalmuseum, 24
German school reforms, 189–91
Giovio, Paolo, 67, 169
Goethe, Johann Wolfgang von, 76–77, 78–79
Greek sculpture, 182, 186
Grimm, Herman, 204–10, 205; debate with Bode, 207–9

Halbwachs, Maurice, 5
Hara Museum, 106
Hauser, Anton, 203
Hegel, Georg Wilhelm Friedrich, 20–21
Herrera, Helen, 119, 123–26
Hirt, Alois, 182
historic preservation, 9
history, relation of past to present, 93–114. See also time
history museums, 29, 75; German Historical Museum, 33; Germanisches Nationalmuseum, 24; and the Holocaust, 24–25; Palace Museum, Beijing 137–58, 143–44; Southwest Museum, 118–22
Hoernes, Moriz, 196
Horne, David, 148–49
Humboldt, Wilhelm von, 182, 189–90
Hüpsch, Baron Johann von, 76

Iizawa Kohtaro, 104
Imitations — The Museum as the Location of the As-If, 47
Imperato, Ferrante, 174

Ina Nobuo, 110
Indians (Native American), representation
    of in museums, 115–36
In the Face of Silence, 53–55, *54*
*-ism 95: The 1ˢᵗ Tokyo International Photo-
    Biennale*, 96–103

Jakobson, Roman, 120–21
Johnson, Samuel, 64
Justi, Ludwig, 212–13, 216

Karl Ernst Osthaus–Museum, 7, 35–59, *50*
Kasahara Michiko, 104
Kawada Kikuji, 103
Kim Seung-Kon, 100
Kircher, Athanasius, 172, 175, 177
Klemm, Gustav, 73, 74–75
Koshar, Rudy, 9
Kracauer, Siegfried, 112
Kulturgeschichte, 204–6, 209–10
Kuwabara Kineo, 106–10

Lacan, Jacques, 115
Ledebur, Leopold von, 81
Lepsius, Karl Richard, 184–85
linguistic analysis, 120–23; and Hopi lan-
    guage, 235; and the middle voice, 128, 131
Liu Yiran, 155–56
Locke, John, 3
Lotah, A–lul'Koy, 130–32
Luhmann, Niklas, 18

MacGregor, Arthur, 71
"magical thinking," 121
Major, Johann Daniel, 30
Marcuse, Herbert, 35
Maruyama Tomiichi, 105
Masuda Rei, 105–6
materials memory, 117–18, 122, 127–30, 237;
    dialogic, 136
Matz, Reinhardt, 98
media archaeology, 31–32
Meguro Museum of Art, 106
memory, 1–2; defined, 116; defined in Ger-
    man, 21, 75; embodied, 117, 133–34; and

forgetting, 8, 47, 81–90; as metaphor,
    3–4; and Native American Indians, 116,
    131–32; in the Renaissance, 163; and tech-
    nology, 12, 29, 31; of World War II, 93–
    114, 233. *See also* art of memory; collec-
    tive memory; materials memory
Mengs, Anton Raphael, 21, 22
Meyer, Jeffrey, 140
Modern Art from the Museum Folkwang, 56,
    57–58
Modernity, in Japan, 110
Modernism, in Japan, 103–4
modernization of aesthetics, 180
Mommsen, Theodor, 185
Montefeltro, Federigo da, 169
Morelli, Giovanni, 196–97, 213
Mullaney, Steven, 18
Murray, David, 70, 229
Museo Gregoriano Profano, 26, 27
museology, 17–18
Museo Pio-Clementino, 21, 22
museum administrators in Berlin, 185, 200–
    19
museum architecture, 43, 49–51; in Japan,
    93–94
museum exhibition practice, 35–59
Museum Folkwang, 49
Museum für Gestaltung, Zürich, 47
Museum für Rheinisch-Westfälische Alter-
    tümer, Bonn, 183, 185
Museum of Alexandria, 164–68
Museum of Jurassic Technology, 8, 47, 60–
    67, *66*
museums: defined, 67; defined in Renais-
    sance, 164–65; ironic, 35, 59; history of,
    74; in Internet era, 30; as metaphor, 5, 18,
    25; Museum of Alexandria, 164–68; Mu-
    seum of Jurassic Technology, 8, 47, 60–
    67, *66*; Roman College museum, 165,
    172; semiotics of, 23, 28, 32; Studio Aldro-
    vandi, 168. *See also* art museums; history
    museums; photography museums
museum visitors, 12, 45; responses of, 115–41;
    visitor's books, 54
Museum Wormianum, 73, *74*

Index

Nakamura Hiromi, 97, 100
National Museum of Modern Art (Tokyo), 105
Native American Grave Protection and Repatriation Act (NAGPRA), 134
natural relations, 51
Neumann, Enno, 46
Nickas, Robert, 106
Nora, Pierre, 6

Objects, Faces and Anti-Narratives: Rethinking Modernism, 103–4
obliscence, 8, 48, 81–90
obliviscence, 64
Okatsuka Akiko, 109–12
Ong, Walter, 162
Open Box—An Exhibition to Extend the Idea of a Museum, 52
Osamu James Nakagawa, 98
Ossian controversy, 73
Osthaus, Karl Ernst, 36–41
Otlet, Paul, 30

Palace Museum (Beijing), 137–58, 143–44; history of Chinese imperial collections in, 150–53
Penck, Albrecht, 194
The People of California, 119–20
Petrarch, 169
Photography and the National Museum of Modern Art, Tokyo 1953–1995, 105, 111
photography museums, 10; in Tokyo, 93–137
Pick, Franz, 77–79, 79
Pictures of the Real World (in Real Time), 106
Piero Project, 31
Pinelli, Giovan Vincenzo, 170–71
plaster casts in museum collections, 182, 183, 207
Pomian, Kryzstof, 10, 68–69, 229
portraits: in Renaissance collections, 168–72; Medici, 170

quarrel of the ancients and moderns, 179, 189–97
Quiccheberg, Samuel, 163

Ratzel, Friedrich, 193–94
repatriation, 9. *See also* Native American Grave Protection and Repatriation Act (NAGPRA)
Revision, 43–46, 44–45
Richthofen, Ferdinand Freiherr von, 194
Riegl, Alois, 215
Rising from the Rubble, 46
Roman College museum, 165, 172
Rothstein, Marion, 165
rubbish theory, 20
Rugoff, Ralph, 7, 47
Rycksman, Pierre, 151

Salon de Fleurus, 56, 57–59, 58
Samuel, Raphael, 93, 106, 231
Schäfer, Heinrich, 198
Scheffler, Karl, 188
Schinkel, Karl Friedrich, 21, 182
Schlegel, Friedrich, 79
Schliemann, Heinrich, 196
Schmidt, Wilhelm, 193
Schnapp, Alain, 247
Schöne, Richard von, 185–88, 192
Sebeok, Thomas A., 28
Sedlmayer, Hans, 41
Settala, Manfredo, 173
Shiihara Osamu, 111, 112
Sigurdsson, Sigrid, 53–55
Silence, 42, 43
Solomon-Godeau, Abigail, 231
Sonnabend, Geoffrey, 8, 47–48, 62–64, 81–90
Southwest Museum, 119–20
Spirit of Conquest, 123–25
Städtische Galerie, Frankfurt, 198
Stahr, Wolfgang, 101
Strzygowski, Josef, 195
Studio Aldrovandi, 168
Swarzenski, George, 198

Takeshita Koshi, 101–2
Tedlock, Dennis, 133
Terdiman, Richard, 117–18, 127–29
Terzago, Paolo, 173

"theaters of memory," 93; in the Renaissance, 162–64
Thompson, Michael, 20
time, Native American Indian conceptions of, 120
timelessness, 3, 145, 221
Timon of Philus, 164
Tokyo Metropolitan Museum of Photography, 93–104, 109
Tokyo/City of Photos, 109
Tokyo–Tokyo, 106–8
transitivity, 127
Truchses, Eusebius, 178
Tse Ming Chong, 98, 99
Tucker, Anne Wilkes, 100
Turing, Alan M., 30

UNESCO World Heritage List, 156–57
Urbain, Thierry, 98

Vaihinger, Hans, 48
van de Velde, Henry, 49
van Geluwe, Johan, 52

Vatican Museums, 21, 26–27
Vischer, Robert, 211
visitors. *See* museum visitors

Wallraf, Ferdinand Franz, 76–77
Wandering Jew series, 111
Warburg, Aby, 20, 23, 182
Warnock, Mary, 2
Watson, Rubie, 149, 238
Wexler, Allan, 51
Wilamowitz-Moellendorff, Ulrich von, 191
Wilson, David, 8, 60, 63–64
Wölfflin, Heinrich, 210–16, 211
Worm, Olaus, 73
Wunderkammer. See curiosity cabinets

Yamamoto Masao, 101–2
Yates, Frances, 21
Yoshimoto Banana, 102
Young, James, 8

Zhang Langlang, 154
Zuichemus, Viglius, 162

Library of Congress Cataloging-in-Publication Data

Museums and memory / edited by Susan A. Crane.
    p.   cm. — (Cultural sitings)
   Includes bibliographical references (p.) and index.
   ISBN 0-8047-3564-6 (cloth : alk. paper) — ISBN 0-8047-3565-4 (pbk. : alk. paper)
   1. Museums—Philosophy.   2. Museums—Historiography.   3. Museum
exhibits—Historiography.   4. Memory (Philosophy)   5. Culture—Historiography.
6. History—Philosophy.   I. Crane, Susan A.   II. Series.
AM7.M8815   2000
069—dc21   99-089384

Original printing 2000

Last figure below indicates the year of this printing:
09 08 07 06 05 04 03 02 01 00

Typeset by G & S Typesetters, Inc. in 10/13 Electra